Falling Slowly

ENNI AMANDA

1st Edition, August 2024

Lumi Publishing

ISBN 978-1-0670235-3-9 (paperback)

ISBN 978-1-0670235-2-2 (ebook)

Editing by Roxana Coumans

Cover by Yummy Book Covers

Designed by Yummy Book Covers
Typeset in PT Serif, 10pt

To my American friends,
who all deserve a break

Falling Slowly

The book playlist (Spotify):

tinyurl.com/fallingslowlybook

CHAPTER 1

Charlie

Dad burst into my office like a stress hormone on two legs. "We need to talk."

I'd sensed his state of mind at the client meeting and contemplated locking my door. But doors didn't significantly slow down my father, especially in the building he owned.

"Dad, it's under control. I'll get together with Trevor and Lee. We'll brainstorm—"

"With a crate of beers? I don't think so. Time to try something else." He brandished a stack of printouts.

"Like what?" Dread prickled through me.

"I'm sending you away."

"What? Where?"

A brochure landed on my desk and a mountain range caught

my eye.

"It's an art retreat in the Rockies. They specialize in getting you out of your creative rut or whatever it is." He flicked his wrist, signaling his indifference. "Fresh air, re-wiring the brain, that sort of thing. I've been up there for a conference. Food was decent."

"But—"

"The party is over, son. If you don't nail this one, we're losing more than a couple of mac ops."

"We're losing production staff?" My heart leapt into my throat. "Which... ones...?"

Dad sighed, finally taking a seat across my desk. He leaned forward, lowering his voice. "Look, I know you care about these people, but some of them are not adding value. We need creative input, not just print production. There's a new AI solution I'm looking into, and it'll replace—"

"You're not talking about Bess?"

Dad frowned, searching his memory. "Is that the redhead who cleans up after you?"

Bess cleans my mess. I'd used the stupid mnemonic device to learn her name. I had needed no tricks beyond the first week, though. Turned out Bess was very memorable.

"She does more than that! I've seen her notebooks, drawings... I think she has ideas." I was making shit up and I didn't care.

Dad harrumphed. "Well, unless she's willing to share those ideas, we can't afford to keep her. Not after we implement the new, automated system. I'm meeting with the suppliers this week."

"I'll get her to share those ideas. You'll see."

For all I knew, the notebook on Bess's desk was a dream journal. Either way, I owed her. She'd saved my ass more than once, catching mistakes that could have ended up in print, or on giant billboards. I wasn't known for my attention to detail.

Besides, I firmly believed every person on earth possessed creativity, and could contribute original ideas. The value of mine varied, but I knew how to sell them, which often mattered more than the actual idea. And that's where I could help. I'd show Bess how to play the game. I'd make her irreplaceable.

I stared at my father's imposing figure, anger brewing in my chest. I knew I had a sweet deal, including a great paycheck, but I was tired of being his puppet, charming the clients and winning the awards, yet having no control over what happened in the company.

Dad's voice turned into a hiss and his silver-grey eyes narrowed. "Do not waste your time on production staff. You hear me? We have to go lean and mean to ride out this recession. And you need to bring home the Thriver campaign, otherwise we'll start cutting the creative team. Trevor. Lee..."

I groaned. It was the shit storm of all shit storms. Economic downturn, coupled with a campaign that had failed miserably with the focus group. It was all my fault. People would get fired because of me.

I sagged back into my chair. "This target group Thriver is going for... it's not our usual bread and butter, so it makes sense we might have to try a few different angles."

Dad shook his head. "There's no time for that. If the next concept doesn't land, they're moving on. With all their money." He raked his fingers through his thick silver hair. His pride and joy, reinforced with implants. "They have a lot in the pipeline, and we need this. Can you put together our own focus group? I'd rather test in-house before we even present anything."

My gaze flicked at the brochure. "You're sending me to the mountains. What do you want, a focus group of bears?"

Dad stared back, unfazed. "There's a small town nearby. Tourism. Lots of people on minimum wage. Take your pick. It'll be good for you to get your hands dirty and connect with this... target group." I could see the disgust on his face. God forbid he connected with *those* people. "Once we fire the production people, you'll need to be a bit more hands-on anyway, making sure the AI apps do their thing."

I already hated those apps. I wanted Bess. She worked harder than anyone I knew. She didn't deserve this. But if I argued back, Dad would only dig in his heels. I needed evidence. Ideas. Something to wow everyone.

Dad tapped on the brochure. "I asked Rhonda to make a reservation so check the details with her. It kicks off Monday morning."

The chair screeched as he stood up and kicked it back in its place. As the glass door rattled behind him, I picked up the brochure, mindlessly browsing its content.

...the latest brainstorming techniques...

...varied art practice...
...rest and recuperation...
...brain-boosting superfoods...

At that moment, I looked up and saw Bess walking past my glass door. She looked rosy-cheeked, like she'd been outdoors, probably running an errand with the printers, judging by the large folder she carried. Flaming red hair brushed her shoulders as she marched ahead with determination.

I didn't know that much about her but I couldn't help staring. There was something about her... I was already on my feet, thinking of something I could ask her, when my door swung open.

"What's up, Buttercup?" Trevor bellowed, barging in. "George looks pissed off."

My Scottish copywriter folded his tall, burly frame into one of my chairs and sighed heavily.

"Yeah. The Thriver campaign was a total bust. He's sending me away to get better ideas. Talking about lay-offs."

Trevor's usually relaxed spine snapped half-way to attention.

"Not you," I amended. "Production staff."

"Bess?"

I nodded, mindlessly moving about the pile of printouts covering my desk.

"Dang. If she's fired, how will you maintain your one-sided crush?"

I threw an empty Amazon box at him. He caught it in mid-air. "Shut up. She's better than the whole production team put together. I don't want to lose her."

It was purely professional. I only stared at her ass because it was there, and perfect. Anyone would.

"Sure." Trevor snickered, stroking his dark beard. "So, what are you going to do?"

I picked up the art retreat brochure again.

'Rubie Ridge—Reach new heights of creativity!' it shouted.

"I'll think of something."

And then, just like that, the answer landed in my lap. I recognized the sensation—the thrilling calm that washed over me when an idea started to form.

CHAPTER 2

Bess

When I spotted the white envelope on my keyboard, my stomach plummeted. A blank envelope holding a severance pay was George's way of firing people. Hands-off and impersonal. But to me, this was personal. I couldn't lose this job. I simply couldn't.

I picked up the envelope without sitting down, steadying myself against the back of the office chair, which tried to traitorously roll away. I'd received no warning. I hadn't received any feedback in weeks, other than the odd thumbs-up online. But I'd noticed the frowns, hushed conversation and muffled yells that carried across soundproof doors. Something was up, which was probably why a single envelope could induce such a chilling layer of cold sweat.

With shaking hands, I pried open the glue and pulled out a

printout. When my gaze landed on a weekly schedule, relief flooded my veins.

An all-expenses-paid, 6-day retreat at Rubie Ridge.

I blinked, confused. Judging by their cutesy logo, Rubie Ridge Art Retreat was set in the mountains and, according to their by-line, all about supercharging your creativity. It made no sense. I wasn't the star of the agency, by any stretch. Not like Charlie, the Creative Director. Or even Teresa, our Art Director and my only office friend. But there it was—my name printed at the top of the welcome letter.

I glanced around the production floor. If I was getting this, everyone else must have been gifted a new car. But I saw no other envelopes or anything out of the ordinary. Only neat rows of silver iMacs and the expressionless faces staring at them, filling the room with the ever-present sound of faint clicking. George didn't believe in playing music. "This isn't a bar!" he'd shout from the top of the stairs, causing the brave soul who'd thought to cheer us with a song to quickly turn off their speakers. If workers seemed too relaxed, they obviously weren't productive.

"Anyone else got this? It's about an art retreat or something." I raised the envelope. The three people currently sharing the room with me shook their heads and raised their eyebrows.

"Is it like a flyer or something?"

"I guess so." I slipped the envelope into the pocket of my bulky cardigan—a fashion choice I hoped came across as hipster rather than homeless. A style icon I was not.

I was about to sit and continue Photoshopping another realtor with brilliant veneers for a client website when I noticed Charlie in the doorway.

Tall, blond, and so stupidly good-looking, it always seemed like he was modeling the clothes he wore, making sales on every step. I ordered my eyes to focus on the screen before he noticed the half-witted expression on my face. But I was too slow. His gaze flicked to me, and to my shock, it lingered. Those ocean blue eyes held mine and his lips parted as if words were forming on them, but nothing came out.

Two things were off. Charlie wasn't usually around on Fridays, and he never looked at me like this. He usually approached me like a smiling hurricane, launching into his first request before he'd even reached my desk, quickly offloading everything that was momentarily taking up space in his uncanny brain. I hadn't fully figured out why he chose to do that in person when we had online job tracking tools and email, but it probably had something to do with how Charlie operated. Verbally. Enigmatically. With showmanship.

It was hard to say no to him in person. Via email, I could have questioned some of his craziest ideas, but when he stormed my desk and asked, I caved every time. I found the mystery font he thought was called 'raindrops something' (it wasn't). I recreated his corrupted file. I figured out how to roll out his campaign in twenty different formats.

Charlie had free rein. Largely because he was the boss's son, but also because the clients loved him. I could see why. His work was ambitious and visually striking, albeit a little half-cooked. When it came to the realities of this world, like the pixel ratios or the awkward grills on the back of a bus... well, Charlie didn't think that far. It was up to me, his trusted production assistant, to make it all work without compromising his amazing idea.

Despite his chaotic ways, he was charming. So charming that every woman under fifty, even Teresa, turned into an eyelash-batting vixen around him. Everyone but me.

When I saw him approaching, I took a deep breath and repeated my mantra: *Oh, Charlie!*

It was all about the tone.

Instead of openly resenting his disorderly ways, obscene paycheck, and life of luxury, I chose to think of him as an adorable Labrador puppy who also happened to be a creative genius.

When I had to delete 357 items off his paste boards to see the actual design, I sighed *'Oh, Charlie! He finds inspiration within chaos'.*

When I saw he'd been linking from his downloads folder again, I took a deep breath and said *'Oh, Charlie! His ideas flow too fast for file management'.*

The most confusing part of working with Charlie, however, was the way he showered me with exaggerated praise: I was a lifesaver. He didn't know what he'd do without me... He always smiled, staring at me like no one else existed.

To a casual onlooker, it may have seemed like Charlie worshipped the ground under my feet.

But Charlie wasn't smiling now. He wasn't walking towards

my desk with that 'I just emailed you…' face. After a moment's intense staring that transferred a fresh chill into my spine, he swiveled on his white sneakers and headed towards the staff kitchen.

My fingers slid into my pocket, grasping the odd letter. Did Charlie know something about it? I gathered my courage and followed him, my heart pounding somewhere behind my forehead.

"Charlie, hey…" I waved my hand at his back, waiting for him to turn. "Do you know what this is?"

He leaned on the fridge, running his fingers through his perfectly, purposefully messy hair. "Looks like an envelope."

I resisted the urge to roll my eyes. "I'm talking about what's inside. Some sort of art retreat program. Nobody else got one so I assume it's a mistake, or a clever ad. Maybe they expect me to call and then try to sign me up for a timeshare."

His brief smile was chased by an uncertain look as he studied me. What was this new intensity in him? What was going on?

My chest and cheeks felt warm, and I fixed my gaze on the fridge door. Someone had written an ode to beer or urine using poetry magnets.

The golden liquid glistens…

"Relax, Bess." Charlie grabbed the envelope, forcing me to look at him. "George wanted to reward people who worked on the Biased beer campaign."

I always cringed when he called his dad George but kept my face neutral.

"Teresa was in the Biased team and she didn't get one. Nobody else in Production did." I folded my arms, meeting his gaze. We stared at each other for a brief moment and shiver ran down my spine.

Charlie finally broke eye contact, pulling a bottle of organic cola from the fridge. "I think she's getting a bonus," he said evasively, taking a swig. "Personalized gifts and all."

I fiddled with the envelope he'd placed back in my hands. Why, oh why couldn't it be a bonus? Instead, I got a week's getaway I couldn't possibly make use of. I opened the envelope again, browsing the details.

"I appreciate this, but it's next week. I have work lined up. I can't just go." I hoped my expression said I was grateful, yet conflicted.

My phone buzzed in my pocket. There it was. The true reason I couldn't 'just go' anywhere.

"Sorry, it's the school." I gave Charlie an apologetic smile and backtracked into the hallway, searching for a quiet corner.

He followed me, halting a few steps away. My stomach tightened as I listened to the teacher's disapproving voice, telling me that my child had thrown up in class. Again.

"Was she coughing?" I asked. "If she coughs a lot she will easily throw up. It doesn't mean she's sick. It might just be a one-off." I was grasping at straws.

"She coughed for a bit, but we can't risk it. I'm going to need you to pick her up right now."

"Okay. Okay."

I finished the call, mortified to find Charlie still standing behind me.

"Is Celia okay?" His thumbnail scraped at the cola bottle label, peeling it off at the corner.

"Yeah, she'll be fine. But I have to pick her up. I'll call my mom. Maybe she can get her so I can finish work."

I had to clearcut those pictures. They were due today. If I left, I'd lose my extra hours.

"Bring her here. She can hang out with Rhonda." He gestured at the hallway leading to the private offices, including the one belonging to our elderly accountant. "And me. I have a new robot she can play with. It just arrived."

I huffed at the ludicrous idea. "You don't have time to babysit. You're working on the credit union campaign, right?"

Charlie's eyebrows drew together as he stared at his cola bottle, his thumb scratching nervously at the corner of the label. "You mean Thriver? Yeah. But you should talk to Rhonda. I think she organized the art retreat, too."

"Oh? Okay. I'll see her after work."

"You should go now. I heard she might be leaving early." His voice rang with urgency as he took me by the shoulders and pointed me in the right direction.

A strange vibration hummed through me at his sudden touch, leaving its warm, confusing glow as I walked towards Rhonda's office.

Once I made it past the production desks, I called Mom.

"Yes?" She chirped, then quickly followed up with a 'no' as I stated my case. "I'd love to help but I'm seeing my gynecologist in one hour. I've been waiting for this appointment."

Mom worked from home and had more flexible hours than I did.

"Can you please just pick her up and bring her here?"

"Is Rhonda there?"

The last time she'd visited the office, she and Rhonda had bonded over their mutual love of Bridgerton.

I glanced through the small window into Rhonda's office. "Yep."

"Great! I'll pick up Celia on the way. See you soon."

I thanked her, slid the phone in my pocket and rapped on Rhonda's door. An absent-minded 'come in' sounded behind it. As I stepped into her potted plant adorned lair, my stress levels dropped. Rhonda was the polar opposite of every other person at Wilde Creative—in her seventies with zero interest in fashion and defiantly unhurried manner. Her office even had a couch, making it my favorite spot in the whole building. As a bonus, she loved my daughter and kept lollipops in her desk drawer.

"Bess!" She beamed at me from behind her laptop. I heard the faint sound of Bridgerton playing on her screen, all proper and English. "Come, sit. Have a cookie."

She gestured at a packet on the table. I wasn't sure how she kept her job, going about it the way she did. Maybe she had leverage, like compromising photos of George.

I sank into her couch, blowing out a breath. "Thank you."

Rhonda closed her laptop, turning her attention to me. Noticing the envelope sticking out of my pocket, her mouth curved into a smile. "I see you found the gift."

I took a cookie she offered, eating it over the envelope. "Yeah. What is this? Why me? I did nothing special. Charlie said they're rewarding people who worked on the Biased beer campaign but that makes no sense."

"But you do wonderful work. If everyone's getting something, why not you? They love doing this sort of thing for tax deductions."

"What is Charlie getting? A new Porsche?" I bit my lip.

She smirked. "Don't be too harsh on Charlie. He's a good boy. Even if he needs someone to confiscate his credit cards." She laughed, and I joined in, feeling a little lighter. This was the safe zone where I didn't have to filter myself. Rhonda knew my struggle. She knew Charlie's lack of struggle.

"But... you know I have Celia. I'm actually waiting for Mom to pick her up right now. She threw up in class."

Rhonda's eyes filled with sympathy. "Oh, poor child. Is she okay?"

"I think so. She was coughing and when she coughs, she vomits. Probably because she can't burp."

"That's fascinating."

I finished the cookie, catching the crumbs on my thumb. "Yeah... as well as disgusting. And a huge waste of food."

"Well, she can stay here with me if that helps you get through the day. But you don't have to worry about next week. I've already reallocated your work so you can attend the retreat. I called your mom. She took the week off to look after Celia. She thinks this is a great idea."

My jaw more or less dropped off and landed at my feet. "What?"

Rhonda's smile turned cheeky. "We think you really need a break and we wanted to make sure you had no excuses."

"But... but..."

"No ifs, no buts, no coconuts." She picked up a cookie and took a big, crunchy bite, shaking the front of her tunic to help the crumbs over her sizable chest.

The whole thing was coconuts. Rhonda had met my mom a couple of times during childcare emergencies, but the two weren't exactly besties. How had they cooked up a plan like this behind my back?

Rhonda shrugged, propelling more crumbs down her shirt. "Talk to your mom. You'll see it's all sorted. I hope you have a wonderful time. I've heard great things about this place." She pointed at the envelope. "It's right outside Cozy Creek, which is this divine mountain town with incredible views. I checked and next week is the Fall Festival. The autumn colors are exquisite up there." She sounded like a Bridgerton character come to life.

I sighed, allowing myself to imagine it. After working non-stop for weeks, every cell in my body cried for a break. I managed, by sticking to healthy eating and daily exercise. No vices of any kind, other than too much sitting. But I still felt the little cracks—my temper getting shorter and the occasional meltdowns over minor things.

"I've never actually been away from Celia for more than one night."

Rhonda's eyebrows lifted in shock as she leaned back in her seat. "Really? She's five years old. It's okay."

"I know. I just haven't had any reason."

Where the hell would I go? I couldn't afford a vacation. I wasn't in a relationship. I didn't travel for work.

Rhonda watched me for a moment, silent. She was one of the few people who could do that without making you uncomfortable. Watching and waiting with no judgment.

Her voice was soft and warm like a hug. "Bess. This is a good thing. Don't question it. Just enjoy, okay?" She stood up and ushered me out the door. "Now go. Finish your work. I'll grab your daughter when she arrives, and I'll give you a buzz. Then you can go home and get ready." She gestured at the little window on her door, which had a view of the elevators.

With a receptionist who spent half her time vaping on the balcony, Rhonda was the true ears and eyes of Wilde Creative. The one who saw everything and knew everything.

I left her office on wobbly legs. She was right—I needed to finish those agent headshots. But on the way back to my desk, I allowed myself a quick detour.

CHAPTER 3

Bess

Teresa stared at the screen, her forehead pinched in concentration. She had an elegant posture, a killer wardrobe and a mouth that always spoke her mind. I found her slightly intimidating, but she'd been on my side from the start, defending me with such ferocity I felt equal parts grateful and uncomfortable. It was still better than the whispers and sideways looks I received as the odd one out.

I knew I wasn't fun. I never had money for after-work drinks. I couldn't discuss the best designer outlets, restaurants, dating apps or whatever else they found interesting. Instead, I hung back, finishing mine and other people's jobs. Not because I wanted to show off. I simply couldn't sit idle. And the last thing I needed was for anyone to question my output.

A scattering of money-related icons filled Teresa's screen as she scratched her head, making her short, black hair stick out in every direction. She could pull it off, though. She was born fabulous.

"What do you think?" she asked. "Notes, coins or dollar signs? Or something vague? I'm losing my mind here. Money is the most visually uninspiring subject in the world! Everything looks... tacky. Ick." She shuddered, which her bedazzled top turned into a mini stage performance.

I sighed. "Uhh... don't ask me. I'm dreading working on that campaign again. It's so... I don't know." I hadn't yet figured out why that job bothered me so much. "Anyway, I thought Charlie was working on it."

Teresa lowered her voice. "He is. But, apparently the focus group hated it. I'm putting together some new visuals for Charlie to play with."

"Really?" I cocked my head, surprised. Charlie rarely missed the mark. "Why are they bringing in a focus group this late?"

"How the hell do I know? Mr. Broken Arrow probably did the first concepts drunk or something." Teresa huffed. "Who has a crate of beers in the middle of a workday? Trevor came out of that meeting hugging the walls."

Teresa felt left out every time there was a party in Charlie's office and she wasn't invited. She hated the boys' club, yet tried so hard to break in. I admired her determination, even if I couldn't understand the appeal.

I glanced at my hands, and Teresa's sharp gaze landed on the envelope. "Oh, my God! Don't tell me you got fired! Oh, my God!"

"Shh. No, it's not that." I showed her the invitation, fighting the instant bout of panic her first guess induced. "But there's something weird going on. I don't know what to think of this, to be honest."

Teresa perused the itinerary, her eyebrows drawing together. "Wow. This is... wow."

"It's got to be a mistake, right? Charlie said everyone on the Biased beer team is getting rewarded, but—"

"I was on the Biased team! I created that swirly pattern. Where's my reward?"

I was too nervous to mention the bonus Charlie had alluded to. What if he was misinformed? Teresa would be crushed, and she'd hate him even more.

"I know! It must be a mistake. "

Teresa took a moment, her gaze bouncing between me and the envelope, red lips pursed. "You should go. Even if it's a mistake. Maybe a client or supplier sent it as a gift, and they drew your name out of a hat. Does it matter? Your name is printed on it and you should go. If you can arrange it, I mean. I know you have a kid."

"Rhonda's already cleared my work schedule and organized my mom to look after Celia. I don't understand why they'd go behind my back."

Teresa handed back the envelope, picked up her Wacom pen and mindlessly tapped on the tablet. "Don't question it. Life is full of shit. If something good happens, grab it with both hands.

You deserve a break."

"So do you!"

"Yup." She stared at her screen, mouth a straight line. "I'm actively manifesting a vacation in Bali. Any day now…"

I laughed a little, out of courtesy, but my insides wobbled. As I got back to my desk, my hands continued to work on autopilot as my mind wandered to the Rockies, recreating the picture Rhonda had painted. The idea of taking a break seemed unreal, yet I felt a spark of excitement. What if the universe had decided to throw me a bone?

A while later, Rhonda's chat message popped up on my screen, informing me that Celia was in the building. Photoshop took that opportunity to inform me that the scratch disk was full. Praying upon the spinning beach ball of death, I employed every trick in my book to free up enough memory to save my file. By the time I made it to Rhonda's office, Mom had already left.

"Where's Celia?" I asked, peering in.

Rhonda sat by herself behind the laptop screen, Bridgerton now blasting at full volume.

"Charlie's office." She waved her hand, eyes on the screen.

I headed down the corridor to find Charlie's corner office. It was nearly as large as the entire production studio that accommodated seven people, including me. Floor-to-ceiling windows framed a panorama of downtown Denver. It would have looked impressive if it weren't for all the printouts, boxes and gadgets covering every available surface. Empty delivery boxes had begun piling up against the wall, partially reaching the high ceiling. Maybe Charlie was on a mission to turn his executive office into an Amazon warehouse.

In the middle of the room, a shiny white robot the size of my 5-year-old daughter shook its hips, dancing to a Japanese pop song that blasted from the speakers in its chest. Like a Manga character come to life, wearing an apron over a conservative black dress, it blinked its giant, glowing eyes and tossed its luminous white hair. Celia danced with it, blond curls bouncing against her purple sweater, winter boots stomping against the polished floor.

I paused at the doorway, observing the strange scene. At least my daughter didn't seem sick. Quite the opposite. I couldn't remember the last time I'd seen her this full of life.

Was her shirt backwards?

The song ended and the robot bowed, saying something in Japanese. Celia bowed back, clapping her hands. "Good job, Yuki!" She turned to Charlie, eyes sparkling. "She's so smart. I love her!"

Charlie looked up from his phone, startled to find me watching them. "Oh, hi." He covered his befuddlement with a smile. "I was just looking for a way to change the language."

"Mom!" Celia ran to hug me. "I threw up at school, but the teacher said it's okay."

"It's fine, CeCe." I stroked her back, but she wriggled away from my arms, back to Charlie and his toy.

"What is that?" I circled the robot, keeping a wary distance. It seemed to detect my presence, turning to face me with those unsettling, bright eyes.

"A Japanese robot maid."

"And you need it because... you have so much dusting to do, and our regular cleaners don't know the right dance moves?"

Charlie's smile took on a guilty edge. "Well, they just clean and leave the building. Where's the fun in that? Besides, Yuki can entertain our child visitors. She knows a lot of games. Most of them are Japanese so I haven't quite figured them out yet, but I'm working on it."

"Sounds... great." Celia was the only child visitor I'd ever seen in the building, but I had to admit she looked thoroughly entertained.

"She's so cool!" My daughter turned to me with pleading eyes that rivaled the robot's anime ones. "Can we get one, Mom? I want it more than I want a sister."

"Oh, sweetie." I sighed, searching for words to let her down easy.

Celia opened her arms at the robot. "Can I hug you, Yuki?"

The robot copied her moves, returning the awkward hug. Damn you, Charlie. My chest squeezed at the sheer adorableness of the scene.

Celia let go of the robot, turning her anime eyes to Charlie. "Is she expensive?"

"No—"

"Yes, very expensive," I cut in, flashing Charlie an alarmed look.

What the hell was he doing, fueling the fire?

"Yeah, I suppose," Charlie corrected, taken aback.

"It's all relative," I amended quickly, offering him a polite smile.

Do not offend the boss's son, Bess. You can't afford that sort of sass.

"Okay, CeCe. Time to go." I took my mutinous child by the hand and dragged her out of the room, thanking Charlie for his childcare efforts.

Why was he babysitting my 5-year-old in the first place? At his astronomical hourly rate (according to Teresa), it made as much sense as a surgeon cleaning the bathrooms.

"But I want to play with Yuki!" my child wailed.

"You can watch *My Little Pony* on my phone," I promised, coaxing her back to Rhonda's couch. "Mommy will go finish one job and then I'll take you home, okay?"

Rhonda lowered the volume on her laptop, reaching into her desk drawer. "Lollipop?"

"Yes, please," Celia said, accepting the treat before she gave me a resigned look, plonking her tiny frame on the couch and sighing like she was a hundred years old.

They didn't call me Buzzkill for nothing.

CHAPTER 4

Charlie

"Are you... cleaning?" Trevor's suspicious voice interrupted my thoughts as I was gathering potential mountain gear into a box.

I'd gone through the selection of recent online orders in my office, discovering several unopened boxes. Finally, I'd have some use for the gadgets.

"I'm packing," I said, ripping open another box.

The flashlight! That would be handy.

Trevor threw himself into an armchair, groaning. "So... excrement is hitting the fan next week and you're galloping off into the sunset?"

I blew a sigh. "I'm sorry. I'm fighting George on quite a few things right now, I thought I'd give him this one."

"So, you're going to spend a week alone in a hot tub, drinking smoothies and get a new idea that'll save all of our asses?"

I'd done my best to sell the plan to him and Lee, but Trevor could see through my bullshit. He didn't know the half of it, though. I wasn't going to tell him I'd bought two tickets and Bess would be there. This plan was already on wafer-thin ice.

"*Alone*, in the hot tub?" Trevor repeated, watching me intensely.

"What?" I fought a swell of nausea.

"So it's just a coincidence that Bess from production was gifted an all-expenses-paid week at an art retreat in the Rockies? A crazy coincidence."

"Where did you hear that?"

"Teresa."

"She talks to you?"

I knew Bess was friends with the tall, dark and scary designer, but I'd never expected Teresa to tell Trevor. She didn't really hang out with us, only glared at us disapprovingly.

Trevor shifted in his seat. "Well, I know how to make her open up." He coughed into his fist.

Something about his manner gave me pause. "Wait. Did you two..."

"A little bit, on 4th of July." He coughed again, this time all chesty and disgusting, like a dying man.

"Seriously? She's a colleague. You know better than that."

Trevor looked hurt. "Are you saying you'd never slip your USB in a company laptop?"

"Our laptops have no USB ports," I said, buying time. It

shouldn't have been a hard question. I looked him in the eye. "But no, I don't think it's a good idea."

"Fair enough." Trevor shrugged, launching into another coughing fit.

"And you need to quit smoking. Right now."

"Tomorrow," he said, handing me his lighter.

I pocketed it.

Trevor finally caught his breath. "You're going to the mountains with this woman you've been crushing on for two years, but you're not going to make a move? You're a better man than I, Charlie."

"She doesn't even like me," I said defensively.

"But if she did…" He raised his brow. "I bet you'd be willing to lower yourself from that high horse. Onto a medium-sized pony, maybe. And refrain from judging me."

"I'm *not* judging you," I insisted. Because he was right. If Bess liked me, I'd probably break all my rules.

"Whatever." He stood up. "Go to the mountains and save the company, Charlie. We're all counting on you."

Fuck, I thought as he left. Everything was hinging on this crazy plan. I already knew no amount of fresh mountain air and hot tubs would unlock my brain. I'd used every trick in my book and was drawing blank after blank, but I couldn't admit that to anyone. I'd pinned my hopes on Bess. She was the best problem-solver I knew. The solution was hiding somewhere in that beautiful head of hers. I just had to keep my stupid crush under control and focus on the job.

CHAPTER 5

Bess

Celia had just finished her dinner when Mom appeared at my door.

"I've been looking at pictures of that retreat and the little town. I'm so excited for you!" She removed her floral scarf and leather gloves to show me a picture on her phone: A mountain range bathing in bright red autumn colors.

"Photoshopped."

"You and your Photoshop. This is real. Look at the catering!" She swiped to a picture of a long buffet featuring the entire color wheel of fruit and vegetables. "And the bed. Oh... I'd give my kidney for this bedroom."

I stared at the enormous bed, laden with cushions, with the pine-covered hill rising behind the window.

"Okay. That is a beautiful room," I admitted.

"I know! Take some photos for your dream board."

I hadn't looked at my old Pinterest boards in years, but I found myself smiling at her enthusiasm. After everything she'd gone through in life, Mom was still a dreamer. She continued 'ooh'ing and 'aah'ing her way into our tiny apartment.

"And here's the building." Mom swiped to a photo of a huge, Victorian-style mansion nestled in the mountains. "Can you believe you get to stay in this place?"

Celia pushed closer to see the screen. "Can I come, Mom? I won't make any noise, I promise." She was already in her bunny pajamas, blond curly hair somewhat tamed into two sloppy braids.

"I'm sorry, babe." I crouched down to give her a hug. "I was only given one ticket. But I promise we'll take a vacation as soon as I can afford it."

After we put Celia to bed, Mom gathered our dinner plates and ate Celia's leftover vegetables. "I'll come over on Sunday after church. That way you have plenty of time to drive there before it gets dark. Do you need gas money?"

I tried to shake off my discomfort. She was on a tight budget, working as a virtual assistant, yet paid to keep my car on the road. Without her support, I would have been forced to sell it. "I should be okay."

Her eyes sharpened with concern. "Why aren't you more excited? What's wrong?"

"Nothing. It's just very sudden. I haven't wrapped my head

around—"

"Well, start wrapping that head. Look!" She showed me another photo of a ridiculously cute mountain town.

"That can't be real." I sighed.

"It's like a screensaver, isn't it?" She scooped the rest of the grated carrot into her mouth and began washing the dishes. "Your dad took me to the mountains once, in Northern California," she said after swallowing. "We were both quite clueless. It got so cold at night we packed up the tent and drove down at 3.a.m." She tucked a strand of blond hair behind her ear, blue veins popping on her delicate hand. Translucent skin, always cold. Thank goodness I'd inherited a slightly thicker skin from my father, despite him being Irish.

"Did dad have Italian blood? He once said."

Mom huffed. "He said a lot of things. I don't know if I'd believe it all. He loved a good story."

"You talk about him like he's dead."

"When you move to another continent and make no effort to stay in touch, you might as well be."

Technically, Mom had moved back to the States and Dad had stayed in his home country. But I didn't feel like correcting her, seeing she was still washing my dishes.

"He sent me an email on my birthday." It had been six months since that birthday and that email had contained one poem— one he'd written about the 5-year-old me, a child he believed was destined for greatness. That was his excuse for the hands-off parenting. I was so self-sufficient. Terrifyingly capable. Basically a 'wunderkind' who didn't need parents at all.

Mom scoffed. "Knowing your situation, I told him to send money or shut up, but he would have left every penny on the racetrack or self-published another poetry book no one's ever going to buy." Mom shelved the last cup and hung the dish towel. "There, all done. I'll see you on Sunday."

I saw her to the door, feeling grateful and exhausted. "Thank you."

Two nights ago, I'd dreamed about having a dishwasher. How lame was that?

When Mom left and silence fell, I looked around my cramped apartment. My world had become so small. I spent my days in concrete buildings surrounded by other concrete buildings, mostly staring at a screen. Maybe everyone was right. Maybe I needed this trip. And maybe it didn't matter how I'd come across this opportunity. I had to take it. Besides, declining could offend George, which was a much bigger risk.

I took a deep breath, picking up toys as I walked across the floor into the bedroom. Celia had graduated from the toddler bed and moved into mine—an old memory foam mattress that still remembered the weight of Jack, gently sloping to his side.

The room didn't fit another bed. Every inch of the apartment was filled with things from our old life, worthless things I couldn't part with, yet, even if they sometimes made me feel like the walls were caving in. That's when I took Celia to the nearby park—a little square of grass and a rusty swing set.

But if I donated the last of Jack's prototypes and materials, I'd be admitting defeat. I'd be giving up the story I told Celia about how this was all temporary and how we'd one day move into a nice apartment, and she'd get her own room and our memories would either be stored appropriately or displayed nicely, not in teetering boxes by the bedroom wall.

What would it be like to take her to the mountains? She got so excited about the swings that she squealed. It didn't feel right to go away without her. And what was I supposed to pack? I hadn't travelled in years. Did I even have a suitcase? Questions circled my brain as I brushed, flossed, and got ready for bed.

Thankfully, I still had a whole day and a half to stress about this before I had to leave. I curled up next to Celia, nuzzling her to the sloping side of the bed to make room for myself. What would it be like to have a entire cabin to myself?

I had to make the most of this. Not just for my sake, but for my daughter's. If I eventually snapped under pressure, she'd suffer for it. God had decided to give me a break and I'd use it to recharge. I'd eat all that amazing food and breathe the healing mountain air. And I'd spread-eagle in that luxurious bed, enjoying the space and privacy. Me, the pine trees, and the mountain tops.

It didn't sound too bad at all.

CHAPTER 6

Bess

"Oohhh!"

My spontaneous reaction sounded so much like Mom's that I had to smile. After a long, arduous climb that seriously tested the engine of my little Toyota, I was finally in Cozy Creek. The town center spread before my eyes like a breathtaking postcard, no Photoshopping required.

The majestic mountain range burned fire-red behind the decorative Victorian-era buildings. They looked like iced sugar cookies lining Main Street—too pretty to be real.

I felt a stab of guilt for not sharing the view with Celia or Mom, so I parked on the side of the road, got out of my car and sent them a photo. I briefly considered a video call, but it would have eaten up my data.

Wriggling my phone back to its hands-free stand, I got back on the road and followed the map instructions up a steep and winding road, shaded by evergreens. After a while, I emerged from the forest and spotted the giant building from a hundred yards away, perched on a gentle slope of windswept grass, with majestic rock formations rising behind it. Architecturally, the place looked like a modernized Victorian castle, complete with a pointy tower.

I felt underdressed in my black jeans and T-shirt, my shoulder-length bob hanging straight and limp. It was a style born out of budget concerns rather than preference. Mrs. Banshee, my downstairs neighbor, knew how to cut a straight line, and I applied the box color to hide my mousy brown.

The heavy oak door creaked as I pushed my way into an impressive reception area. Inside the building, the historical exterior gave way to fresh remodeling. Stark white walls showcased a variety of art, from traditional landscapes to modern ink blot tests and geometrical shapes. The receptionist, a young woman with high-maintenance rainbow hair, stood behind a desk adorned with bowls of giant pinecones.

She removed a piece of chewing gum from her mouth and smiled. "Welcome to Rubie Ridge. How can I help you?"

My gaze narrowed in on the name tag dangling on her shirt and I tried to memorize the name: Harleu. Was there a typo? No way was I risking the pronunciation of that one.

"I'm here for the... retreat?" I dug up the welcome letter from my backpack.

Harleu studied the paper. "You're from Wilde Creative?" Her

eyebrows drew together in confusion. "So, you're Charlie Wilde?"

"What? No!" Panic flashed through me. Was I not booked in after all?

"I'm Charlie Wilde." A familiar voice boomed across the reception, giving me a start.

I turned around, trying to hide my immediate unease. Why was he here?

Miss Rainbow Hair reacted like females always did. Sure, Charlie was six-foot-two of blue-eyed, annoying perfection that begged to be stared at. But I found it fascinating how his sheer presence could transform every woman into the sparkliest version of themselves. There were no resting faces around Charlie Wilde, bitchy or otherwise.

I'd seen this so many times I'd developed a habit of watching the gawkers rather than Charlie himself. I found it more interesting, and ultimately safer.

Charlie's footsteps echoed off the high ceiling as he crossed the floor and appeared by my side. "Hi, Bess."

"Hi, Charlie. Why are you here?" I tried to keep my voice friendly, just like at the office, but I couldn't hide the undertone of alarm. This week was supposed to be relaxing. Six days with no reminders of work. Only art classes, round-the-clock catering, and a hot tub under the stars. As much as I'd rolled my eyes at Mom's commentary, I was already invested. I'd let myself picture the absolute peace and relaxation advertised on the Rubie Ridge website.

"It sounded so good that I decided to hop onboard." Charlie

stretched his arms overhead and yawned. "Rest. Relaxation. New ideas."

He offered me a smile. A lazy, lingering smile that both heated my chest and woke up nerves in my core, just like at the office. That's what Charlie did to me. It was my dirty little secret, and the number one reason I preferred not to look directly at him.

"So, you're Charlie Wilde," the receptionist concluded, before turning to me. "And you are..."

I reached across the desk, pointing at the top of the letter she was still holding. "Bess Killian. It's printed right there."

I braced myself as she turned to her computer, clicking her mouse painfully slowly. "Right. Ms. Killian. I think we have a reservation for you."

Charlie leaned over the desk. "Of course you have. And you also have a last-minute reservation for me."

The receptionist fluttered her eyelashes. "Are you... an actor?"

"No. Do you get a lot of actors?"

"During the film festival and sometimes outside of it. They visit, fall in love and later return. Then of course we have Grayson Ames, born and bred in Cozy Creek. He always comes back for the Fall Festival."

I recognized the name while Charlie blinked. "Who?"

The receptionist turned back to her computer screen, so flustered that she placed her hand on a stack of sticky notes instead of the mouse. "Yes, I can see both reservations. You're both at the Cerulean. All chalets are named after colors."

"We're not... sharing, are we?" I squeaked.

Her eyes flashed with uncertainty, and my throat tightened. I'd have to drive back home, navigating those steep hills and tight curves in the pitch dark.

I nudged closer, trying to establish a pleading eye contact. "Listen. I'll take any other color. Puce. Chartreuse. Burlywood. Gamboge."

"Impressive." Charlie raised his brow at me, then turned to the receptionist. "I did request separate lodging."

The receptionist's face took on a deeper shade of puce. "There must have been a misunderstanding. Cerulean is the only chalet we have left."

"Is it a two-bedroom one?" Charlie asked, and I swallowed hard.

Maybe that could work, for one night.

Miss Rainbow looked so torn that I almost felt sorry for her. "It's a... um... open plan. But there's a loft." She dangled a key attached to a giant key ring—a piece of plank that had been painted blue. Cerulean, obviously. I'd had fun learning the more obscure colors when I'd helped Teresa prepare for the designer pub quiz. Apparently, she'd wiped the floor with the guys, which incidentally hadn't helped her break into the bro club.

I looked out the window. The sun had dipped behind a line of tall spruce trees. It was getting darker by the minute.

Charlie took the key, his eyes on me. "Can't hurt to look?"

Looking could definitely hurt. Like the way he looked at me with that unnerving intensity, eyes sparkling like we shared a secret.

It was his way, I reminded myself. That's how he got everyone on his side and could sell any idea to any client. I simply hadn't been the recipient of that look before. It was easier to avoid that sort of thing at the office—keep your eyes on the screen, or the printout. Always stay busy and focused on the job. I fixed my gaze on the bowl of pinecones, trying to calm my nerves.

"Turn left and follow the path along the house, it's the third cabin with a blue door." Harleu, if that really was her name, gestured at the door.

I followed Charlie outside and down the winding path, fingers wrapped around the shoulder straps of my backpack. The rest of my clothes sat in the trunk of my car, packed in two reusable shopping bags I wasn't planning on letting anyone else see. Maybe I could sneak back to my car and repack what I needed into my backpack. Toiletries, a change of underwear—enough to get me through the night. Charlie would never have to see my sorry travel gear.

We passed two cabins, one with an orangey red, another with a greenish door. Probably vermilion and sage or something. Our blue door came with a matching blue welcome mat, framed by pot plants that had long ago finished flowering.

Charlie held the door open, and I snuck past him, feeling awkward like a schoolgirl with my backpack. He didn't seem to have any luggage. Maybe someone would bring them in.

The cabin was decorated in shades of blue and white, giving Greek island vibes. It was obviously a new build, but featured so much weathered and distressed material you could have almost been fooled. A gorgeous wood carving sat on the hall table, as if formed by nature itself. Art around here was high caliber.

The receptionist hadn't been kidding about the open plan. Everything was visible at a glance—the sitting area featuring designer chairs, kitchenette and the enormous bed. Even the bathroom had one partially frosted glass wall. Whoever had designed this didn't believe in walls or privacy.

What would it be like to live with this much room height, I wondered. There was easily space for two stacked apartments, but the second level had only been utilized by a small, open loft.

"There's a couch up here," I reported as I rushed up the floating staircase. "I'll take this."

Charlie followed at my heels, observing me as I set down my backpack and sunk into the low 2-seater, patting it with conviction. "I mean, just for tonight. I'll drive home tomorrow. I'd go right away, but it's getting dark and I'm not that confident driving at night, especially on these windy roads."

He frowned at me, or maybe at the couch. "That's not big enough for you."

"Oh, it is. Absolutely. I always sleep curled up like this." I lay down on the navy velvet, propping my head on the armrest and folding my legs so tightly that there was enough room for another person at the end.

"Nobody can sleep like that. You'll mess up your neck and won't be able to drive anywhere. I'll get my camping hammock and set it up somewhere downstairs. I've been wanting to test it."

"You brought a camping hammock?"

He grinned. "It's called Happy Glamper. They had a cool Kickstarter campaign."

Charlie was a Kickstarter junkie. The cleaners refused to deal with all the delivery boxes in his office, so Rhonda sometimes snuck in late at night and cleared away the recycling. I'd helped her once, ripping and flattening the countless packages, wondering what might have been in them.

At the end of the year, Charlie donated random items to the agency Christmas present pool, where everyone got to choose something to take home. I wondered if he noticed the gasps at the sight of his fancy gadgets among the low-value sample products and corporate gifts from clients and suppliers. I never got the first or even the second pick. Charlie's buddies Trevor and Lee scraped the cream off the top, pulling out Apple Watches and drones. After that, the other designers grabbed the champagne bottles and food samples. By the time the production people were dipping in, the selection had been thinned down to mugs, calendars, and stress balls. Thankfully, Celia loved stress balls—a fact I didn't want to dwell on.

"I don't mind," I insisted, closing my eyes and getting as comfortable as I could. If I pretended to fall asleep, Charlie would have to give up and take the bed.

"Is that all you packed for the week?" he asked, picking up my small backpack. "How did you fit everything in this?"

"Magic," I mumbled, eyes still closed.

But he had a point. My toiletries were still in the car, and I couldn't go to bed without brushing my teeth or flossing. My job didn't come with a dental plan, which had made me a vigilant flosser. Maybe a teensy bit obsessed. But I figured it was fine, like being addicted to salad greens.

I waited, feigning sleep, but Charlie didn't leave. Instead, he sat at the end of the couch I'd ostentatiously left vacant, man-splaying his legs so wide that my curled up sleeping position began to feel fetal.

"It's not very comfortable." He bounced against the couch.

I pushed myself back up to sitting. "What do you mean? It's a couch. It's got cushions."

"This feels like basic polyester foam."

"And that's bad because…"

He shrugged. "I prefer feather down."

I picked a spot on the floor and stared at it, to keep my eyes from rolling.

He's the boss's son. You need this job.

"Also, couches can have flame retardants and those give out toxic fumes, so you're not meant to sleep on them."

I turned to face him. "Okay. How do you know so much about couches?"

He beamed at me, pleased with himself. "We pitched for a campaign for EcoSoft last year. Didn't get it."

I thought back to all the campaigns and pitches that had gone through the studio. "I don't remember seeing that."

"That's probably why we didn't get it." His mouth twisted, those perfectly sculpted lips puckering. "I did the final art and printed it myself late at night, last minute. It wasn't polished, but I figured it was worth the shot."

"Oh." I could imagine the level of 'not polished' he'd produced, but I couldn't imagine him working late, finishing anything by himself. I'd heard stories of this happening, mostly from Rhonda, but I'd always doubted them. In my experience, Charlie left early, often with an entourage.

He gave me a rueful smile. "I do sometimes go the extra mile."

My cheeks flushed with heat. "No, I didn't mean... I don't think that—"

"Relax. I know I'm not the most organized person in the office. I don't even try to be. That's not my goal. And I do value people who can polish the turds I produce. Like you."

I tried to push away the mental image of me polishing his bowel movement, focusing on his wide grin.

This was the first time we were alone. I couldn't remember ever sharing a room with him, with no one else around. The magnitude of his undivided attention made every hair follicle on my body take notice.

Charlie was best enjoyed in small, diluted doses. I listened to his wild stories and laughed at his jokes, which were often funny, as part of the group. The invisible one, at the back, standing behind Trevor or someone else who took up a lot of room.

Aware that I could no longer hide my fluster, I got up and rushed down the stairs. By the time I got to the door, I remembered my backpack, still lying on the floor by the couch. Oh, well.

"I'll go get my things from the car," I called from the door and skipped outside.

The darkness had fallen, and it wasn't the kind we had in the city. It was like someone had thrown a blanket over my head and told me to cross the road safely. The only light burning in the pitch black was the floodlight outside the main house, at least a hundred yards away. The parking lot must have been somewhere to its left, I thought, turning on my phone flashlight. It illuminated my feet just enough that I could navigate the stairs without tripping.

When I'd advanced halfway down the path, a blindingly bright spotlight suddenly lit up the ground, giving me a start. I heard Charlie's voice behind me. "Watch your step."

"What is that? A streetlamp?"

As he got closer, I saw he was holding a small yet extremely powerful flashlight. "This is a… Pocket Lightsaber." I heard the cheeky smile in his voice.

"Kickstarter?"

"Yeah. They reimagined the flashlight. What do you think?"

I shielded my eyes. "Well, I never imagined I'd lose my eyesight from directly looking at one, so I guess they have."

"Look how powerful it is. I can see the whole parking lot."

The door of the nearby cabin creaked open. "Hey! Cut it out! We're watching a movie here."

"Sorry," Charlie called back, dimming the light. It didn't only dim but turned purple. "Oh, crap. I'm not sure how this works. Hang on."

He kept pushing buttons and turning dials on the device

which, now that I could look directly at it, resembled a cut-off light saber. It was like someone had concluded that the original didn't look enough like the male organ and decided to remedy the situation. Penises didn't blink in rainbow colors though, so this one was an upgrade.

"Oh, man. I didn't even know it could do that," Charlie said, pushing another button. The rainbow blinking turned into a steady, pink glow. "That'll do."

I clamped my mouth shut to hold back any comments on the way he held the pink wand against his crotch.

Don't be stupid, Bess. Do. Not. Be. Stupid.

We walked down the path and crossed the parking lot. My battered silver Toyota glowed faintly in the corner, dwarfed by Charlie's red, electric Porsche. I popped the trunk and reviewed my two canvas bags, trying to remember which one held my toiletries. I didn't use pajamas but slept in whatever slacks and T-shirts I could find. Clothes needed to be multi-functional to earn their place in my wardrobe—or in my sad canvas bag.

I ended up dumping the contents of both bags inside the trunk and quickly folded the necessary items into the bag that wasn't ripped. The rest went into the other bag, as quickly as possible. Charlie moved closer, carrying a huge leather bag, and lifted the pink light above my shoulder to expose the mess.

"You know, I once threw my stuff in plastic crates when I couldn't find my suitcase. Doesn't work if you're catching a plane, but I was going fishing and it ended up being quite handy."

"Yeah, I was running late and just grabbed the first thing I could find." He didn't need to know it was the only thing.

"Let me." He tried to take the bag as I was reaching for it, but I was faster.

"No need."

Charlie took a step back. "Okay, then."

He sounded hurt. I didn't know what to do with that. Did he expect me to turn into a damsel in distress so he could feel important? I'd been too busy channeling competence and efficiency, my office staples, to even consider that approach. Besides, this was Charlie. He was as self-involved as anyone living in the rich-and-handsome bubble, but as far as I knew, his ego wasn't that fragile.

I secured the bag onto my shoulder and closed the trunk. "Ready!"

"What about the other bag?"

"I'm staying for one night. No point bringing everything."

He huffed a sad, little laugh. "We're still on that?"

"Still on what?"

"The whole 'I'd rather drive home than share a cabin with Charlie.'"

"There's only one bed!"

"I told you; I have a solution." He lifted his left hand, and I noticed a boat-shaped bag. He must have grabbed it from his car along with his bag.

"Is that the hammock?"

"Happy Glamper!" Lit from below and glowing pink, his smile looked borderline creepy.

"Where are you even going to attach it? I didn't see any trees growing inside."

"I'll figure out something."

Fifteen minutes later, I heard the crash. I stood in the bathroom, shower fresh and in my most presentable slacks and tank top, cleaning my teeth, when the entire cabin shook. I rushed out and found Charlie sitting on a pile of fabric that must have been the hammock, staring at pieces of crumbled drywall scattered across the floor.

He looked up and smiled. "Turns out the hook on the wall was... decorative."

"Oh, my God!" I located the wrought iron hook that had been holding a potted vine in a macramé hanger. The hanging plant lay awkwardly across the floor. I lifted it to safety and started going through the cupboards in search of cleaning equipment.

Charlie stood up, brushing flakes of paint and plaster off his jeans. "I guess we're not hanging the hammock there. What are you doing?"

"Looking for a vacuum cleaner. Or a dustpan. Anything." The only thing I found was a small microfiber cloth under the sink.

I returned to the living room, examining the hole in the wall. Too deep. "We can't paint over that. But if we find some putty, it might work. Maybe there's a hardware store in that little town... Cozy Creek?"

Charlie blinked at me. "Why would we try to fix that?"

"So they don't charge us." I got a small trash bag and started collecting the larger bits off the floor. "I'm sure their room rates don't cover renovations."

"They'll just add it to the bill. It's fine."

He detached the other end of the hammock, tied up to the loft baluster, and joined me in cleaning the floor. Well, sort of. After moving some drywall bits with his sock, Charlie started picking them up and flinging them across the room, deep in thought. I wanted to whack him in the face with the cloth.

"Please, Charlie. That makes it harder to clean," I begged.

"The cleaners will come tomorrow. They'll take care of it."

"Why make it harder for them?"

He snatched the cloth from my hand, forcing me to stop. "Come on, Bess. It's not your mess." A grin spread across his face. "Hey, that rhymes."

Your mess is always my mess.

The thought was instant, like a reflex. I'd been living it true for two years, cleaning after him at work like he was some sort of oversized toddler.

I sighed, letting my shoulders sag. "Fine. Are you done with the hammock, now? Will you let me sleep on the couch?"

"I'll take the couch. You take the bed. That's my final offer."

"That's stupid. You're a foot taller than me."

"Which makes my sacrifice greater. One night and I'll reach martyrdom. There's a lot of value in that. Undying fame." He gazed at the ceiling, regally, as if posing for an oil painting.

"I thought you had to die to become a martyr."

"I told you about the toxic fumes, right?" He winked at me, and my insides wobbled.

It was getting harder and harder to remember who I was dealing with. This wasn't a random guy I could joke with and make fun of. This was Charlie. I had to return to the office and work with this man—cleaning his messy files and doing his bidding. I'd only spent an hour in his company and my carefully curated act was starting to crack. I needed to get away. I needed a door between us and since that wasn't possible in this open plan nightmare, I needed that loft all to myself. Why even build a loft if you were not going to put a bed up there?

Something occurred to me. "Wait a minute. We asked the receptionist if this cabin had two rooms, and she mentioned the loft."

"So?"

"She offered that as an alternative, so maybe it means there *is* a bed up there. A sofa bed."

"It didn't look like one," Charlie said, but followed me upstairs.

I opened cupboards along the wall and discovered pillows, blankets and sheets. "Bingo! It must be a sofa bed. Why else would they keep these here?"

It took us a few minutes to confirm that the couch was indeed hiding a bed, and a further ten minutes to figure out the mechanism. When the seat finally transformed into a full-sized bed, we both cheered.

I threw myself across it diagonally, spreading out. "So much space!" I moved my arms like angel wings and suddenly felt cool air brush against my stomach. My cropped tank top had ridden up to reveal a lot of skin. Oops. I should have covered up, but I didn't want to back down.

"I can take this; you take the bed." Charlie's voice sounded a little thick, and it sent an unexpected tremor through my core.

I sat up, feeling the adrenaline mixing with exhaustion. "Nope. You had a problem with the couch being too small. Now there's no problem." I stared at him, not blinking, my heart thumping away like it was trying to win a prize. I wasn't sure why I felt so strongly about this. I was fighting for my own discomfort, but I couldn't let it go. I couldn't let go of this bullish feeling. This connection.

Charlie folded his arms, slight surprise and amusement playing on his lips as he tilted his head, staring back. There was something new between us, something almost equal. Exhilarating.

I'd never had the nerve to spar with Charlie. I laughed at his jokes for an appropriate amount of time, asked any question I had to ask, and scurried back to my desk before the burgeoning blush showed up on my face.

"The bed is still way more comfortable and it's my duty to make sure you're comfortable."

"Or, what? You lose your membership to the 18th century gentlemen's club?"

"Is that a real thing? I want to join." His eyes sparkled, and I felt my nipples harden against the tank top, far too noticeable.

I tried to keep a straight face. "Look it up on Kickstarter.

Someone may be selling a related gadget."

"Like a shiny armor?"

"Exactly."

"If it comes with a touchscreen or converts into something else or... folds inside a travel mug, I'll probably buy it."

"That's a powerful addiction you have there."

He shook his head, eyes comically wide. "You have no idea."

I laughed, and a warm buzz brewed in the pit of my stomach. Charlie was staring at me with such focus, I felt like I was being recorded. Every feature on my face and body cataloged, every detail memorized for posterity. This sleepover was slipping into a dangerous territory.

CHAPTER 7

Charlie

I didn't mind losing the sofa bed battle. Witnessing Bess drop the polite, distant act and bring out the sass, I knew I was, in fact, winning. She'd never been like this at the office, yet I'd always sensed she'd been hiding something. An edge. A wit. Like someone had painted over vibrant colors with beige, but hadn't done a very thorough job.

I'd been right about her. If she had this much spunk, she'd have thoughts and ideas to share. She just needed to ditch that office persona and be herself.

I insisted on helping her make the bed with extra pillows and blankets to make sure she was comfortable and warm. When the bed was done, she picked up her phone. "I need to call my daughter before she goes to bed."

"Sure."

As I descended the stairs, I heard her on the phone, asking to hear every detail of Celia's day. I held still, listening to her voice turn higher and softer. When I realized she'd dropped her volume to almost a whisper, I went to brush my teeth to give her privacy. I ran the tap deliberately loud, hoping she'd feel comfortable to say whatever she wanted to say.

The annoying guy from the office is here and I have to share.

The annoying guy broke the wall in my cabin. I wish I could send him home but I'm a nice person, so I choose to sleep on the couch.

I was pretty sure she didn't approve of me. She hid it well and never said anything to that effect, but I could see it in her eyes, along with the desire. She never flirted with me, either. Until tonight, if you could indeed count our sofa bed argument as flirting.

I closed the tap and retreated to the downstairs bed, peeling off the covers. The cabin was quiet now. I lay awake for a good hour, browsing my phone with the sound off, wondering if she was asleep or awake and if that sofa bed was as uncomfortable as it looked.

Why couldn't I stop thinking about her? She was an employee and a single mother, which should have placed her deep into my friend zone. But Trevor was right. I'd been crushing on her for two years. She'd kept her distance, forcing me to keep mine. I'd prided myself on being professional, but it had been Bess holding us to the status quo. The moment she'd returned an ounce of my affection, my eyes had gone rogue, roaming her body. I'd noticed the curve of her breasts under that white top. I'd noticed that top hitching up as she threw herself on the bed. I'd stared for longer than was appropriate, filing away images I had no business saving. And now, the images came back, playing in a loop.

It wasn't just those curves. It was the brazen smile that appeared like a sun from behind heavy clouds, blinding me with its power. She'd been brave enough to tease me, put me in my place. I needed more of that.

I imagined that smile on her face as I lowered myself on top of her, trapping her against that sofa bed. It didn't take me long to get off and take care of myself. Thank God I had the bed to myself.

•••

The next morning, I woke up to her presence. Startled, I jerked upright, my head swimming. Bess stood by my bed, fully dressed, the little backpack on her shoulder. "I wanted to say goodbye."

"Goodbye?" I was fully awake now and standing. "Wait, what? You're not off right now, are you? There's... breakfast." The thought was triggered by the hollow feeling in my stomach, which I suspected wasn't even hunger.

"It's okay." She smiled sweetly, moving towards the door.

Back to the distant, polite bullshit, were we?

"The reservation is non-refundable, you know?" It was the only thing I could think of. "I'll tell George you wasted yours." I winced at the words. I was playing dirty now, but I couldn't let her leave.

Bess froze at the doorway. I could almost hear the gears turning in her head as she debated what to do. Finally, she turned around, her shoulders moving up and down as she took a deep breath. "What do you mean? The place is overbooked."

I adopted a friendlier tone. "I know. It's far from ideal, and I'm sorry. But you have a bed, right? Is it okay to sleep in?"

She gave a wobbly nod. "It's fine."

"And you've arranged to stay here for the whole week?"

She hung her head, staring at the scuffed ends of her sneakers. "I did. But I told my daughter I'd be back today. We spoke last night."

My stomach tightened. This is what I'd missed running the tap in the bathroom. "Okay. So, your mom's babysitting?"

"Yes."

"Let me ask you something. Was she happy with your decision to come back?"

Her gaze flicked at the door, then at me. Trapped. I closed the distance, trying to ignore the fact that I'd slept in my boxer shorts. This was too important. I couldn't let her lie to me. I stepped close enough that I could read her eyes. "Be honest."

Bess blew out a sigh, her eyes still roaming about like she was looking for a way out. "She was disappointed. She asked me to reconsider. Like you said, I have a bed and a loft to myself. But it doesn't feel right. And Celia misses me. I haven't been away from her, ever."

"How old is she? Four?"

Her blush was instant. "Five."

"That's so... great. I mean, it's great you're always there for her. But do you think she'd maybe be okay for a couple of nights? Even if you don't stay the whole week. How about three nights?" I was bargaining now and starting to sound desperate.

She finally looked me in the eye. "Why is it so important to you? If I go, you'll have the cabin to yourself."

Warmth pushed up my chest, and I wondered if I was going to blush as well. Because it was an excellent question.

"I don't want the cabin to myself. Bess... please. I need help. I'm here because I'm stuck with this campaign. And if I don't get this right, we're... um... we're in a lot of trouble. George... my dad, thought that this retreat would get me out of my rut and the ideas flowing, but I honestly don't think I can do it by myself. I'm used to spit balling with Trevor and Lee. You know that, right?"

She nodded, her face softening, until a new crease appeared between her eyes. "Why didn't you bring them?"

Now I was definitely blushing, my mind frantically organizing the facts and fiction into something palatable. Something I could tell her. "It was really last minute. The agency had bought a bunch of vouchers for this place, one of which was gifted to you. But we have a lot of other work on. We can't send away that many key people. Plus, the first concepts we did with Trevor didn't test well. So, Dad thinks we need to mix it up."

"George thinks we should team up?" Her confusion was palpable.

"No," I said. She'd never believe me on that. "But I saw you were coming here and I thought I'd join you and maybe you'd let me pick your brain."

"*My* brain?" She repeated, looking at me like I'd suggested harvesting her organs. "What campaign are you talking about?"

"The financial literacy one for Thriver Credit Union."

Finally, a glimpse of understanding. "Ah. You need someone financially illiterate to test your ideas on?"

"What? No. Did I say that?"

Her hand flew to her mouth and she blushed even harder. "I'm sorry. I didn't mean... I mean, how can I help?"

"Don't apologize. I need your unfiltered thoughts and ideas. For the campaign. Can you do that?"

For a moment, I wondered if she'd stopped breathing. I took a deep breath, to remind us both of that vital activity. When I saw her chest moving again, I relaxed a little.

"I have to call my mom."

"Please, do."

She pulled her phone out of her backpack's side pocket and stepped outside to make the call.

Guilt turned my stomach. I was blackmailing her, appealing to her sense of duty and unwavering work ethic. She'd do anything to keep her job—a job she'd already lost.

I would turn things around. I'd help her tap into her creative side. Once everyone saw her ideas, she'd become irreplaceable. My determination was underscored by a foreboding cold shiver, but I shook it off. I was used to taking bold risks and winning. Why would this be any different?

CHAPTER 8

Bess

Charlie had been right about Mom. She was relieved and happy about my decision to stay, insisting that she and Celia were doing fine. I heard my daughter's protests in the background, but she settled as soon as Mom promised her an amazing souvenir. So, now I had to find her a souvenir.

I finished the call and stepped back into the cabin. To my relief, I found Charlie fully dressed, sitting in one of the armchairs with his laptop. It had taken a lot of concentration to keep my gaze away from those boxer shorts.

He looked up, eyes full of expectation. "What did she say?"

He must have been desperate with this campaign. Could I help him with it? What if I made things worse and we lost the client? Would I lose my job?

"She's fine with it. I'll stay."

He jumped to his feet, bagging his laptop. "Hurray! Breakfast?"

"Sounds good."

I returned my backpack to the loft and we walked together to the main building. In daylight, the place looked like a palace, nestled within manicured gardens, perfectly complimented by the mountain backdrop. A touch of frost lingered on the ground and the air felt crisp in my lungs.

Neither of us knew where to go, but Charlie led the way until we spotted a sign leading to the dining hall. We found a lavish buffet of breakfast foods, and a handful of other attendees, sitting at round tables scattered across the vast space. A floor-to-ceiling panelled windows opened to the gardens, framing the postcard scenery.

Charlie found us a vacant table and plonked his laptop on it. "Reserved." He smiled, gesturing for me to tackle the buffet.

I eyed the wide selection, my mouth flooding with saliva. Could I take a little bit of everything? I didn't want to appear greedy, but I hadn't seen such a spread in a long time. "It's like a... wedding buffet."

The selection seemed geared towards healthy and premium, with an endless array of nuts and seeds, and individual bottles of 'energizing' and 'brain boosting' juices. Charlie stood behind me, waiting patiently as I mixed a spoonful of each muesli, cereal, and nut topper into the same bowl.

"That's an interesting way to enjoy cereal. You must have an impressive selection at home."

"Haha." I rolled my eyes. "I've never tried most of these, so I want to test them out."

"Wouldn't it make more sense to test them one by one? Unless you're planning on buying all seventeen and mixing them?"

Yes, that did make more sense, but my cereal-deprived body wasn't listening to reason. I'd been making oatmeal for two years, carefully steering my daughter through the grocery store without even visiting certain aisles. What I really wanted was to box everything and take it home.

"I... don't know how long I'm staying," I explained, cutting the rolls and pastries into smaller pieces so I could taste everything.

"You know what? I'm gonna do the same." Charlie picked up the leftover quarters of my pastries, loading them onto his plate. "I'm always trying to choose the best looking one and then wondering if I made the right choice, when I could have been sampling everything. This is genius."

I smiled, feeling a little lighter.

We returned to the table, our trays filled with various treats, juice bottles and cereal, as well as cups of steaming coffee.

"This is amazing." I sighed.

Charlie frowned, studying his tray. "I'll see if I can order some eggs. Do you want any? Scrambled okay? That's probably fastest."

"Eggs?"

"Yeah. Protein. But don't get your hopes up yet. They might not have the chef onsite right now."

I hadn't even considered that the breakfast buffet could be

lacking something. Not waiting for my answer, Charlie got up and traipsed across the hall, slipping through a doorway marked 'staff only'. I held my breath, stunned.

After a moment, he returned with a triumphant grin, and a few minutes later, a server brought us two plates of scrambled eggs and sausages. I was already quite full and only had a taste, but I had to admit they were delicious.

"I need protein in the morning," he explained. "Don't you?"

"No, I live exclusively on carbs and fat."

He laughed at my stupid joke. "Okay, yeah. I meant I prefer a better balance. Less sugar."

"We usually have oatmeal with jam. Celia's preferred balance would be jam with a smattering of oats."

"Oatmeal is great. More protein than cereal."

"That's what I tell myself when I can't afford anything else." I instantly wanted to swallow the words with the scrambled eggs. I was here to add value, not to have a pity party. "So, what was the feedback on that Thriver campaign?"

To my relief, Charlie switched gears. "The focus group thought it wasn't relevant to them. Basically, nobody felt like taking action. So, I guess we need to make it more direct. Although I don't know how much more direct it can get. I mean, the words 'learn money management' are right there."

"Uh-huh. And the people you're trying to reach... who are they?"

Charlie took a long sip of coffee, looking away. "The lower socio-economic quartile. Families on single income, seasonally employed—"

"The chronically broke?"

Charlie squirmed in his seat. "Yeah, I mean... no..."

"It's okay. That's how I'd describe myself." He'd asked for my unfiltered thoughts. I didn't want to complain about my situation, but if my misfortunes helped him with this campaign, maybe it was worth it.

Charlie met my gaze, swallowing but no longer looking away. Waiting for me to continue. Adrenaline rushed through my veins, but it was too late to back out. "The thing about being broke is... it brings out the worst in you. Makes it harder to plan or up-skill or make decisions that will benefit you in the long term. Because you need money now. You're in a state of stress, and that stress is narrowing your vision to what's right in front of you. Tomorrow is hazy. Next week looms there on the horizon. Next month doesn't exist. Do you understand what I'm saying?"

Charlie propped his elbow on the table and leaned on his hand, staring at me like I was giving a riveting Ted Talk. "Yeah. That makes sense. So, asking a person to sign up for a training that will help them in the next six months or a year..."

"Exactly. It doesn't make sense. It's not a solution to your immediate problem, which is what your brain is acutely trying to solve. Like the next week's rent, or the medical bills, or daycare fees... or the loan shark repayments."

His eyes widened.

"For some people," I quickly added.

He didn't need to know I was some people.

"That's something I've never understood," he confessed. "Like... why would you go to a loan shark? There are options like payday loans, cash advance..."

I nodded. "Yes, and when you're in a relaxed state of mind, with moderate stress levels, you're able to research those options and make good choices. But the thing about financial stress is that it sort of creeps up on you. Things get harder, deadlines get closer, your balance is running out... and sometimes, you're still there, half-hoping for a miracle, thinking you're okay for a week or two, when something happens. It doesn't have to be big. Like a flat tire. Or your kid's sick and you don't have any sick days left. You know they'll deduct your pay. And suddenly, it's panic city."

Charlie's voice was low. "And that's when you take the first offer, eh?"

"Maybe." I attempted to smile, focusing my energy on polishing my plate.

I couldn't help the memories from surfacing. Those months after Jack's death, when it had all been on my shoulders. The sky had fallen, and somehow, it kept falling, no matter how hard I worked. I'd ignored the red flags and accepted the first rental offer, suddenly blindsided by the maintenance fees that I couldn't afford. But beggars couldn't be choosers and somehow, we'd survived. I'd only recently managed to pay back Mom who'd come to my rescue, covering the cost of our next move. So much money down the drain.

"Must be really hard to do it on your own." Charlie's soft voice hit me in the middle, and I straightened in my chair.

We'd never talked about my old life, but Teresa knew. The office knew.

"It's okay. I've had some time to adjust now." I met his eyes and saw the question in them. "Two years. It was over two years ago."

My insides clenched, bracing for a follow-up question, but he simply nodded, turning his attention to the remaining eggs on his plate.

We finished our breakfast in silence, took our dirty plates to the conveyor belt carrying them back to the kitchen, and followed the trail of retreat attendees down a long hallway. I counted only ten of us, which upped my anxiety. I'd been hoping to hide in the back row, not drawing any attention to myself. But with such a small group, the classes would be intimate. Or worse, interactive.

It made sense, though. Everything about Rubie Ridge felt exclusive. Its understated luxury intimidated me more than any brazen displays of wealth. Subtle messages hidden within the details, only readable by those in the know. Like Charlie, and all these ladies around us. Most of them looked older than me, maybe in their forties and fifties. Judging by their all-black outfits, they worked in design, advertising, or something else commercially viable. Rubie Ridge was not a place for starving artists.

"Are you ready for the first class?" Charlie asked me.

One lady ahead of us turned around. "I heard they always do a surprise warm-up exercise. Nobody knows what it is." Her voice dropped into a stage whisper. "One time, it was interpretive dance."

My muscles clenched so hard that I could barely walk.

Please, God. No dance.

CHAPTER 9

Bess

Reaching the end of the hallway, we spilled inside a large art studio. Individual tables and easels were scattered across the space. Huge, panelled windows reached all the way to the high ceiling, framing an even more impressive mountain view than in the dining hall. Like a modern cathedral.

"It's a nice view," Charlie confirmed, and I realized I'd gasped out loud.

He led us to a table by the window wall, pulling out a seat for me.

I spied the other attendees, checking if they were going to sit or stand. There were only two other guys besides Charlie. One reminded me of George and the other one had a flamboyant vibe. His pink shirt and blue suspenders stood out against the sea of black like a clown outfit. After a moment's observing, I deduced he and the George lookalike were a couple, which led me to the frightening realization that Charlie was the only available, straight man in a room full of women.

It didn't seem to take much longer for the said women to realize the same. They bombarded him with sideways looks and smiles, casting silent questions at me. I took a step away from him, hoping to signal we were just colleagues.

A voluptuous woman in bright red glasses and a matching kaftan stepped through the doorway, addressing the class with a bright smile. "Hello everyone! My name is Leonie Miller. I will be your facilitator this week. I'm here to make sure everything goes smoothly." She gesticulated wildly with her bracelet-adorned hands. "You're here to unlock your creativity. The first things we ask you to do when you enter the studio is to turn off that phone. Don't use it unless you absolutely must. We believe in freedom, but we don't believe reading work emails or browsing social media ever helps. You're here to journey into your own mind. It's the greatest adventure you'll ever take!"

Charlie cast me a half-terrified glance, but turned off his phone, along with the rest of the class. I felt a bit left out since I didn't have a phone to turn off. Mine had a terrible battery life and was currently charging in the cabin.

"I recommend you also try to turn off those work-related thoughts. You may have a creative problem that you're actively trying to solve. You may feel stuck. You may feel like you need to keep at it, but trust me, you don't. The only way you're going to get anything out of this week is by immersing yourself in the activities and exercises we offer. Focus on what's in front of you."

Charlie angled himself to fully face me, smiling. So, he was going to focus on me? Not sure what to do with my eyes, I turned to face the table.

Leonie's voice rose with excitement. "We have a couple of very exciting visiting teachers this week. You can check the schedule at the reception and on our website. Now, without further ado, let's get onto the first exercise. Surprise!" She flicked her wrist at the door and a young man in a white apron carried in a huge stockpot, setting it on a table. He ran back and soon reappeared with a stack of paper plates and a ladle.

"Let's thank Tag, our kitchen helper for his assistance." She mimed applause, and the class clapped.

Tag cast a bewildered look at the pot and rushed off.

"Are we having soup?" Charlie raised his voice, grinning at the facilitator.

Leonie smiled back, unperturbed. "This should be mashed potato. Let's have a look." She removed the lid and peered inside. Her glasses fogged. "Oops. It's still a bit warm, but I'm sure it'll cool down soon." She took the ladle and began filling plates with huge piles of mashed potato, passing them onto two of the closest ladies, who distributed to the rest of the class.

I lowered down to sniff at my plate. It smelled and looked like actual mashed potato, but there had to be a trick.

"What do you think it really is?" I whispered to Charlie, who scooped a bit onto his finger and into his mouth. "Stop," I hissed.

"What if it has glue in it or something? She didn't tell us to eat it."

"I can't taste any glue," Charlie mused, shoving another sample into his mouth.

"No glue!" Leonie confirmed. "Only fresh mashed potato we will use for sculpting. Don't eat all of it."

I stared at the pile on my plate, trying to swallow the lump that began swelling in my throat. So much food. Someone had made enough mashed potato to feed an army, and we were supposed to play with it? No wonder the kitchen helper had looked so confused.

"What are we supposed to make?" asked one of the ladies.

"Anything you want!" Leonie declared. "Don't think too much. Let your fingers guide you. Ask the material what it wants to be and let it take you there. There is no failure. There are no limits, except you need to be done in ten minutes. Ready, set, go!"

Charlie rolled his sleeves, peering at his potato plate. "What do you want to be?"

Leonie walked around the room, passing us tools—palette knives, funny looking plastic scalpels, and larger gear I imagined masons would use. I grabbed one blunt knife and began shaping the pile of potato. Maybe if I respected the natural hill-shape on the plate, I would end up with something that was still edible after the exercise.

"What are you doing?" Charlie voice brought me back to the room.

I looked around and noticed most people had abandoned the

tools and were working with their hands, shaping and molding the potato like it was clay. I saw phallic towers, busts and one perfect sphere. Charlie's pile had turned into an abstract, gravity-defying shape I couldn't make any sense of.

"I... I don't know," I muttered, staring at the anthill on my plate. It was still a pile of mashed potato, just tidier.

"Time!" Leonie approached us. "Drop your tools and step away from the table. It's time to walk around the room and see everyone's creations."

I dropped the knife, my stomach in knots. There was no failure, yet I'd managed to fail. I hadn't thought outside the box, not even a little. I trailed behind Charlie as we wandered around the room, viewing each other's creations like we were visiting a prestigious art gallery. Nobody said anything about my boring anthill, but I could feel the judgment in the air. Leonie made appreciative noises on every out-breath, thoughtfully commenting on each potato sculpture. It was incredible how quickly we'd all fallen in line with the new dynamic—grown up professionals vying for praise for completing a ten-minute kindergarten activity.

No one received more praise than Charlie. He'd pushed his potatoes to the limit, creating a sculpture that resembled a cat-like animal in motion. "If only there was a way to preserve this," Leonie exhaled, her eyes filled with reverence.

When she got to me, she took a beat to compose herself. "It's very... tidy. Maybe don't worry so much about making a mess next time?"

She pivoted on her heels and returned to the front of the class, talking animatedly about creativity and risk-taking, mentioning Charlie by name at least three times. She must have known him since nobody was wearing a name tag. I could tell the other ladies were storing the information.

Dwelling on my failure, I missed the beginning of Leonie's next exercise. It had something to do with paint, or pain. Probably pain.

I spent the rest of the morning trying to emulate Charlie's approach to dealing with anything thrown at us—dried flowers, paper plates, Jenga blocks and glue… I didn't shine, but I blended in. As time went on, Leonie's enthused voice grew a tad wary, even if she tried to offer me some encouragement. She had her pet student in Charlie, which was fine with me. All I wanted was to hide in my corner and not be noticed for the rest of the day, or however many days I had to stay here to not anger my boss.

When Leonie announced it was lunch time, I tidied up our tools and materials, eager to get out. I could feel Charlie's eyes on me.

"Are you okay?" He cornered me, stepping so close that I instinctively shifted further away. He kept advancing until my back was against the window. "You seem… distressed. No. Anxious."

"Thanks for the psychoanalysis, but I'm hungry. Can we go to lunch?" I pasted on a smile to satisfy his concerns.

Charlie narrowed his eyes, staring at me for an unnervingly long time. "So, what did you think of the exercises?"

"They were fine. Lots of variety. You?"

"I lost the sense of time. I must have been in a state of flow."

"Sounds great." I could have sworn the morning had already lasted about 24 hours.

"It happens when you are working on something that you're skilled at but that's almost too hard. Did you feel like it was too easy or too hard, maybe?" He studied my face like I was a puzzle he couldn't solve.

"It was difficult. Especially the potato one. I have a hard time playing with food. I mean, I've been teaching my daughter the opposite for years." I attempted to smile.

His jaw dropped. "Huh."

"Can we go to lunch now?" I asked again. My stomach growled. "Otherwise, I'll eat my potato sculpture."

Charlie's laugh sounded embarrassed. "Of course."

Leaving my pile of worthless sketches on the table, I let him escort me towards the doorway. I noticed one of the ladies had also stayed back and joined us at the door.

"Hi! Charlie, is it? I was really impressed with your work this morning. I'm Miranda, from Wave Collective." She offered him her hand, tossing a strand of expertly colored honey blond hair over her shoulder.

"Great to meet you." Charlie gave her a quick handshake and gestured for her to go ahead of us. Instead, she parked herself at the doorway, blocking our way with her giant handbag.

"I'm so glad to bump into you, to be honest. We've been following Wilde Creative for a while, and I'm so impressed with your work. That cheesecake campaign... Inspired! I'd love to talk to you about it."

My stomach grumbled even louder at the mention of cheese-cake. Charlie laughed. "That's great. I appreciate it. Let's have a chat later."

She lowered her voice, a wicked smile making her eyes glint. "You know about the hot tub under the stars, right? I heard it's incredible. I'm going tonight and wouldn't mind seeing you there." She winked at him.

She was probably in her forties and looked immaculate.

Charlie turned to me with an exaggerated grin. "Did you hear that, honey? A hot tub under the stars! This is going to be the best anniversary."

I stared at him, stunned silent.

"She's so excited she can't even process it," he explained to Miranda.

Her flirty smile gradually faded into disbelief, then genuine surprise as she witnessed Charlie slipping his arm around me. "Babe, I told you this was a five-star place, didn't I?" He turned to Miranda, who was now only hanging around out of sheer politeness, her focus on the phone she'd unearthed from the giant bag. "She was so disappointed when she found out our cabin didn't have a bathtub."

"Uh-huh. I hope you enjoy!" Miranda flashed us a forced smile and stepped into the hallway, waving her hand.

As soon as she was out of earshot, I turned to Charlie, my insides flaming. "What was *that*?"

"I'm so sorry. I can't take these women. Not this week. Please, help me. Please!" He pressed his palms together, those blue eyes begging for... what, exactly?

"What do you want from me?"

"You don't have to say anything. Just, don't correct them. Let them assume we're together, and they'll leave me alone."

I drew a breath. "First of all, there are plenty of women who couldn't care less about your relationship status. They'll see it as a fun challenge. Second, they might ask questions. What do you expect me to tell them?"

Charlie blinked, confused. "Why would they ask questions? What kind of questions?"

I had to raise my voice to talk over my gurgling stomach. "Questions like 'how did you two meet?' or 'how long have you been together?'"

"That's easy. We met through work, and we've been together for two years."

"So, basically from the day I started at Wilde Creative?"

Charlie laughed. "What can I say? You caught my eye."

He'd called me Becca for the first two days, until I'd corrected him.

"Okay." I sighed. "I'll try to keep my facts straight." I was here to assist Charlie, in any way I could, and nobody could say I didn't go the extra mile.

"Don't worry. We can iron out the details in the hot tub."

That's right. I didn't have a choice. He'd introduced me as a devoted hot tub enthusiast. It didn't matter that I'd packed an awful, fraying swimsuit I'd only planned on using alone, in the dark.

"I didn't pack a swimsuit," I lied. "I didn't realize there was a hot tub."

"Really? There's a huge picture on the website."

"I must have missed it. Sorry." I bit my lip.

I had to get out of this. No other human with eyes was allowed to see that two-piece.

"That's okay. We'll go shopping in Cozy Creek!"

I'd sidestepped one horror, only to land into another. I imagined myself posing in various bikinis as Charlie voiced his opinions and shuddered.

"I didn't mean it like that." Charlie corrected, seeing my horrified expression. "I'd drive you there and hand you a credit card."

I nodded, drawing a fortifying breath. "Lunch?"

"Okay, let's go before you pass out."

He placed his hand on my lower back and guided me to the hallway. I tried to ignore the sensation, but the full body tingling only intensified, zeroing in between my legs. I couldn't control the reaction any more than I could control my rapid breathing. I'd been alone for so long that my body had its own ideas by now, completely independent from my brain. Oh, dear. This gig was getting harder by the minute.

CHAPTER 10

Charlie

I shouldn't have used Bess as a human shield. It wasn't fair to her, but I was desperate. And now that I had an excuse to touch her, my hands couldn't get enough. The curve of her waist under my palm was so deliciously distracting that for a moment, all thoughts of shame vanished.

I led her to a table by the window and pulled out a chair for her. "A bit of everything, right? Wait here."

"You don't have to serve me." She tried to get up, but I anticipated her move, resting a heavy hand on her shoulder.

"Please, let me. You're not allergic to anything, are you?"

"No."

Heads turned as the others observed our interaction. Bess swallowed her protests and settled into the chair, playing her part, and I left to fetch her lunch. I made sure to include absolutely everything—Italian pastrami and cheeses, olives, and antipasto, with various breads.

I placed my haul in front of her and was rewarded by a shocked gasp. There was something so genuine about her, glimpses of childlike enthusiasm and moments of depth and clarity that drew me closer. I wanted to watch her face like one would observe a rare phenomenon, like northern lights, trying not to miss anything.

"I'm sorry," I whispered. "If it's too much, I'll go and straighten out everything with Ms. Whatshername."

"Miranda," she amended.

"See? I was close." I grinned. I'd genuinely forgotten the woman. Name, face, everything.

"Then you better inform her entire table because she's already passing the news." She glanced over my shoulder, and I turned to follow her gaze.

Miranda and her three lunch companions turned back to their meals in such a hurry it was obvious they'd been gawking at us. Bess may have been right. If I went there to explain how I in fact was single, they'd latch on and never let go. I knew the type. They were wealthy, bored and horny. In a client meeting, I could have worked that to my advantage. Flirted enough to win them over, led them on a little but not too much... unless I was ready to get involved later. I hadn't felt like doing that for a while, though. That game exhausted me and, in this environment, it felt like an irritating distraction—another thing draining my energy when I needed to focus on breaking through this creative block. Working with Bess.

I swallowed. "They'll eat me alive."

"It's okay. I'll be your fake girlfriend," Bess said, taking a sip of orange juice. "Let them wonder why on earth you'd be with someone like me. I enjoy watching their heads explode." She gave a wry smile, her eyes flicking at the other table.

"Why?"

My question made her jerk back. Pink blotches spread across her cheeks. "We both know I'm not your type."

"How do you know my type?"

She evaded eye contact. "I... I guess I don't. Apologies."

Back to that polite bullshit? "Come on. You can say it. We're friends. And fake lovers."

Her reply was almost inaudible. "Can we change the subject?" She glanced at me, desperation glowing behind her eyes.

"No, Bess. We're not going to change the subject. I have to crack this case, and I need you to be real with me. Offend me. I don't care. But be honest."

She looked so torn that I regretted my forceful tone. This wasn't working. I was only pushing her further into her shell. The cheeky, brave woman I'd seen a glimpse of last night would forever disappear behind that veneer.

"You know we're not really friends, don't you?" She looked at me with sadness, head tilted, a cherry tomato dangling from the fork in her hand. "You're the boss's son."

"I'm not George. I didn't hire you and I can't fire you."

Her mouth dropped open as the realization took hold. Had she not understood this? "I know," she said quickly, but I'd already seen behind the curtain.

I blew a deep breath. "You have no idea how little say I have." I wanted to tell her everything, right there and then. The urge was so overwhelming I stuffed my mouth with three olives to keep quiet. To think. Because I knew she wasn't ready. She didn't really know me. She didn't trust me. If I told her she'd already been fired, she'd lose heart. All the work to unlock her creative thinking would be pointless if she was panicking about her future. She didn't know George. My father could change his mind in an instant. We only needed to give him a reason. And I knew Bess had it in her. My gut told me so, and I'd long ago stopped questioning that intuition.

"Any further thoughts on the Thriver campaign?" I asked.

"Didn't Leonie tell us to not think about the work stuff?" She winked.

Relief flooded my body when I saw her smile. "I'm not big on following rules."

"Why do you think she said that, though? They've been running these workshops for ten years. I read the online reviews— everyone says that if you commit to the program, it really works. When you focus on the exercises, your subconscious mind keeps working on those other problems and then suddenly, the answers come to you. It's all about lowering your stress levels and distracting your brain so you don't exhaust yourself hyper-focusing on the problem."

I stared at her, dumbfounded. "You read the online reviews?"

"Of course. I wanted to understand how it works, and I like how it sounds. It probably works, in theory."

"Not in practice?"

"Not for everyone. I mean, if you come here from a high-stress environment, even if you manage to relax a bit, you'll be going back to your old life and old habits, right?"

"Possibly. But if you get one great idea, it might be worth millions. It'll change your life forever."

She let out a sad laugh. "You and your million-dollar ideas."

"They're real," I insisted. "Lots of people make millions with one decent idea."

"Especially people who already have millions." The inkling of defiance in her eyes excited me more than anything.

"Fair point."

"Honestly, I don't think anyone like me has ever attended this retreat. Not because I'm unique. There are billions of us who could never afford this sort of thing."

"That doesn't mean you can't tap into your creative thinking."

"I guess not, but I can't change my reality." She smiled, but there was a sad tinge. "I live in survival mode, Charlie. That's my baseline. I'm not saying my life is horrible. It's fine. I love my kid. I find joy in little things.... but the sort of creative thinking you do isn't that important to me. Not anymore. I worry about other things, like making rent, keeping my car on the road, keeping my job..."

I tried not to visibly wince as she said that. "But, wouldn't you rather advance your career? You could move from production to design or become an account manager. Better pay, better benefits."

I didn't even know how much she earned, but it couldn't have been as much as the designers.

Bess fell quiet, staring at her half-empty plate. "It feels like a lot of responsibility. What if your ideas suck? What if everyone hates what you do?"

"Then you get sent to a retreat to get better ideas. It's not that bad." I gestured at the flaming red and yellow fall scenery outside the window.

"Well, it's not like your dad will fire you." She lifted a shoulder, a little cheeky, a little defiant. I almost cheered out loud.

"Maybe not. He prefers to keep me close so he can yell at me."

"I'd get fired. I know that." She shook her head, eyes wide.

"It's the risk you have to take, isn't it? If your job is to deliver ideas... stand-out, different, memorable ideas, you can't play it safe. And that means some ideas will be too wild. Too crazy. That's part of the deal. If you never hit it out of the park, you're not being brave enough. You're playing it safe."

"What's wrong with playing it safe?" She fixed me with a fiery gaze. "When you're responsible for another human, keeping them safe and fed and warm. And for them to be safe, you have to be safe." I saw her hands shake. She dropped her fork and hid them in her lap.

"Are you not feeling safe?" I asked. "What would happen if you lost your job? Would it be the end of the world? You're so skilled.

You'd find another job."

She bit her lip, staring out the window.

"Tell me, Bess. Help me understand. I'm aware of my privilege, and I know it's the biggest roadblock for me with this campaign. I don't get it, but you do. Your reality is different, isn't it? There's a reason you're not that chill about finding another job." I was shooting in the dark, but as her eyes flashed with pain, I knew I'd hit something.

A cold sensation engulfed my stomach before she even opened her mouth. I needed to hear this, but could I handle it?

"Listen, Charlie. I'll tell you, but you have to promise you won't make me your project... or charity case. Nothing like that, okay?"

"Okay," I managed, my windpipe tightening.

Bess finally looked me in the eye, those deep greens holding a film of tears that wouldn't spill. "I was married. My husband died, and I was left with the debt from our failed startup business. I sold everything of value, but I couldn't cover it, and now I'm dealing with the debt collection agency, compounding interest and all those fun things. I have to make the weekly payments. I have to. I'm not able to save much, so I wouldn't survive unemployment. I don't have enough to bridge the gap. Not right now. I have nothing left to sell. But I'm saving as much as I can and taking extra jobs on the side." She cast a half-horrified look at me. "Small business stuff, people who couldn't afford to work with the agency. I'd never—"

"Relax. I'm not going to report you."

Her shoulders dropped. "Anyway, I haven't had much extra work lately and it's hard to find the time. But I'm okay, I really am. If I can keep my job, I can keep making the payments and everything will be fine." Her eyes glowed with resolve, and she resumed eating, wiping her plate clean with a piece of bread.

I pushed my plate aside. I'd suddenly lost my appetite. Bess needed her job more than I'd ever needed anything. A job she'd already lost. In that moment, everything made sense. Her willingness to jump through any hoop, her fear of putting a foot wrong with me.

"Thank you for trusting me with… that," I said clumsily. I wanted to say 'her story' but it didn't feel like a proper story, only a depressing litany of facts. "The debt collection agency… how are they operating? Are we talking about threatening letters or a man with a shotgun?"

Bess tried to smile. "So far, it's just been letters. But I know if I miss any payments, they'll come to collect anything I have, starting with my laptop, which is not worth much to them, but to me…"

"It's your one chance to make more money?"

"Exactly."

"So, if you lose your job, you'll lose your laptop and can't use your skills to do any freelance work while you're looking for another one?"

She nodded. "It's not the best scenario."

My lunch tried to travel upwards. "You can't ask me to not do anything now that I know. I mean, I can get you another laptop.

I can—"

"Charlie. You promised. No charity." Her eyes were hard. "I have skills and I work for everything I have. That won't change."

"But—"

"No."

With great difficulty, I closed my mouth and nodded. She wouldn't accept any offer. Not now. But I couldn't let this nightmare play out for her or her daughter. I'd find a way.

CHAPTER 11

Bess

Why had I told him? I'd sworn I'd never burden anyone at Wilde Creative with my tragic story. If they didn't know, they didn't have to treat me differently. They thought I was boring and a bit of a workaholic, but nobody felt sorry for me. As soon as I saw the shock and pity in Charlie's eyes, I remembered my rule. This was why I didn't tell people.

Now I could never go back to how things had been. Being equal.

Had I ever been equal to Charlie, though? Definitely not. The thought gave me the surge of energy I needed to launch myself up from the chair. "I think the next session is about to start. I read on the wall that we have a visiting teacher from Estonia."

"Oh, really? What wall?"

"That giant timetable they've got up on that screen in the hallway."

"There's a timetable?" Charlie blinked, oblivious.

He seemed a million miles away, maybe still processing our conversation. Although his general lack of attention to mundane details was nothing new. The man floated through life, buoyed by his own creative brilliance, while others took care of the rest.

I couldn't help it; I felt compelled to memorize every detail I knew he wouldn't. If every woman around him had this same urge, he'd never have to do anything non-creative or remember anything at all. We were all enabling him, enjoying the gratitude and attention he showed in return. Even if I didn't believe half of his praise.

The attendees trickled back into the art studio and settled at the same tables. I noticed the gay couple and two of the ladies gathered around an iPad, and tiptoed a little closer, curious.

"Nobody knows her over here, but she's actually huge in Russia and Europe. Exhibitions all over the place. Top galleries."

"Are you talking about the Estonian teacher?" I asked.

Others made room for me and Charlie, who stopped right behind me, placing a hand on my waist. Everyone turned to him with keen interest. "We did a quick search, out of interest. Look at this!" The suspender guy angled the iPad to show it to Charlie.

I reached on my tippy toes to get a peek at the screen. It was a watercolor painting with a flower motif but primarily abstract. Gorgeous.

"Incredible skill," Charlie confirmed, adjusting the screen so I could see it. "Look, babe. I know you like this style." He pecked a little kiss on my temple, and I jumped, startled.

Charlie forced a laugh. "Sorry. Forgot to ground you with my hand." He rested his hand on my shoulder, effectively holding me in place, and kissed the side of my face again, slowly, deliberately. His warm breath lingered on my skin.

I smiled, trying to relax. I needed to question him later about the level of PDA necessary. Right after I let myself enjoy the tingles traveling down my spine and stopped inhaling his scent. Citrus and pine trees. A hint of something smoky. Intriguing and dangerous.

The suspender guy laughed. "Matthew's the same, except he'll throw you to the ground like a ninja if you try to sneak up from behind. I have to announce myself when I enter a room."

"It's my jiujitsu training. I can't help it." Matthew pursed his lips. He was starting to look less like George.

"I'm Harry," the suspender guy said. "I'm an artist. Matthew will tell you he's an art dealer, but he's an artist too and more talented than I am."

Matthew harrumphed, but couldn't help smiling. No, he definitely didn't look like George, I concluded in relief. In fact, he looked a little like Charlie, but older. Probably because Charlie resembled his dad, even if I tried hard not to notice it.

"Charlie Wilde from Wilde Creative. And this is my better half, Bess. She's a brilliant designer."

I blushed and the guys cast dubious looks at me. I could hardly blame them—they'd seen my pitiful sculptures and drawings. "I work on the production side," I quickly amended.

"Bess is multi-talented," Charlie insisted, and I subtly elbowed him in the stomach. "Uhh. I'm just telling the truth, Bessie-Boo." He chuckled, sliding his arms around me, locking my misbehaving elbows against my body.

My mind registered the stupid nickname, but I could barely focus on that part, suddenly distracted by his touch. Heat flooded me from the inside out. This was the closest I'd ever been to him, my entire backside pressed against solid muscle. Something else solid dug into my bottom. I tilted my pelvis, just enough to confirm I wasn't imagining things. No. A couple of layers of denim did nothing to disguise the situation between my butt cheeks. That was definitely Charlie's penis. My body took this as a signal to fire out every hormone related to arousal, sputtering sensations like a rusty engine that hadn't been started in a while. I couldn't move. I didn't want to. I heard sounds of humans speaking but struggled to understand words.

To my relief, Charlie carried the conversation. Something about art and Estonia. Was I imagining things, or did he deliberately grind himself against me? His fingers wrapped around my torso, mindlessly brushing the sides of my ribcage as his breath tickled my ear. Charlie was everywhere, taking over my senses.

It was unfair. This may have been easy for him. I was just another date to touch and tease. But I hadn't been touched. I had no routine, only a crater of unmet need I'd shoved so deep down I'd almost forgotten it was there. A mere hug from a male sent me into a state of overwhelm. It was part frustration, confusion, and unrelenting full-body ache.

I had to get my vibrator from the car. I'd packed it on a whim, thinking maybe I'd use it, the same way I thought I'd finally use that face mask Teresa had gifted me last Christmas. That's what a vacation was for, right? But I'd never expected to feel this level of need. All I could think of was sneaking that thing into my bed. The vibrator, not the face mask.

To my relief, the teacher arrived, and everyone returned to their respective tables. Charlie released me, grinning. But I noticed a hint of deeper color on his face as he discreetly adjusted his jeans. Had he got a little too excited?

For a moment, I allowed myself to imagine it. Imagine him. It couldn't happen, but my mind ran scenarios without my permission, and they all felt amazing. It would be perfect fodder for my imagination tonight.

"You're evil," he hissed at me as we got behind our table.

"Why?"

"That ass of yours." He took a deep, exaggerated breath. "I hope you know what you're doing, Bess."

I glanced up at him, as innocently as I could. "What am *I* doing? This is all your plan."

"You know what I mean." He winced, raking his fingers through that stylishly messy hair. "You know you're hot, and I'm just a man..." His words trailed off as he blew out a sigh.

I could hardly process his words, every nerve on my body still buzzing from our encounter. He thought I was hot?

"Everyone! Let me introduce Ilme Kuusk. She's fresh off the

plane from Estonia."

I had to drag my attention to Leonie and the Estonian artist in front of the class. Ilme was maybe in her fifties and had long, dark hair done up in a messy top knot you'd never find on Pinterest. Her long-sleeved lab coat was covered in paint—layers and layers of color. Her pitch was low and she didn't smile, but something about her immediately put me at ease.

"Thank you for inviting me. I look forward to putting on weight," she deadpanned.

Leonie stared at her, stunned silent.

"Food is very tasty here," Ilme continued, dead serious. "I store it on my hips to take away. Don't have to pay extra for the carry-on."

Was she joking? She must have been.

Leonie found her voice again. "Ilme specializes in watercolors, but she said she wants to give you freedom of expression, so this is not a watercolor class, per se."

"No. I try every material and medium I can get my hands on. Not everything is available in Estonia, but we make do. We get the best watercolor from Russia. Gorgeous color. Intense, deep color. I brought some with me for you to try. It looks like candy, but don't eat." This time, a couple of people laughed. "I also use razor blades, but I was asked not to bring, for legal reasons. They're worried someone will kill themselves in the class. So, we will use these blunt plastic knives instead. They don't work, but that's okay."

Leonie coughed, her face as red as her tunic. "Our management is very safety-conscious."

"Isn't *she* management?" Charlie whispered.

Ilme turned back to us. "This week, I have a special assignment for you. I want you to create the piece that you would charge a million dollars for. It is only an exercise. Nobody will pay you a million dollars. But this is what I want you to think. What makes art priceless? Think about it. I was given this catalog of art supplies." She lifted a hefty booklet off the table. "You can order from this and everything will be delivered tomorrow. But I ask you to think about the value of your art as separate from the material value." She brandished the booklet, eyebrows raised. "Buying expensive supplies doesn't make art more valuable. Most of this you can buy for a fraction of the price in Estonia."

"I'll let you get on." Leonie scurried away, her cheeks glowing pink.

"She's running to cancel any future classes taught by Estonians," Charlie predicted, his mouth curving in amusement. "I like the million-dollar assignment, though."

"Of course you do." I turned so he couldn't see my eye roll. Charlie had no hesitations about charging a million dollars for a day's work. Or one idea.

Ilme walked around the room, handing out order forms and catalogs. As soon as I glanced at it, I froze. Were art supplies really this expensive? I flipped through the catalog, desperately searching for something I could afford. Where was regular paper? Why did it have to be acid-free, thick, and textured? I'd be too nervous to breathe on it, let alone draw or paint.

"Are you okay?" Charlie's voice landed soft in my ear, distracting me from my panic. "Please keep breathing."

"It's so expensive—"

"Excuse me," he called out, stopping the teacher in her tracks. "Would it be okay to use found materials? I'm hugely inspired by... nature. There's a forest outside, I think. Materials, like... sticks... um... leaves? Pinecones!"

It was obvious Charlie didn't forage.

Ilme cocked her head. "What are you thinking of? An installation? A sculpture? Little animals with stick legs and googly eyes?" She mimed little pinecone animals with her fingers.

Harry laughed, along with Miranda and a couple of the other ladies. Ilme cast them a sharp look. "You think nobody will pay a million dollars for pinecone critters? You're wrong! The rich buy the stupidest things." She gestured at her forehead. "Forget the buyer. Focus on the value. When you say, 'this is worth a million dollars,' what you really mean is 'I love it so much I don't want to sell'. Some of you will say 'this costs a million dollars' because you think you're a big deal and you want to sell it to some rich sucker out there." She narrowed her eyes at Charlie. "And, some of you will think 'nothing I do could be worth a million dollars'." She looked at me.

I swallowed. Was she psychic or something?

Ilme waved her finger at us. "Either way, you're missing the point. You're focusing on yourself. Ego stands in the way of creation. You must surrender yourself and let ideas flow through you... Tap into the divine!" Her eyes burned with conviction, her posture challenging. "It is not you. You're only a medium channeling it onto paper or canvas or clay or whatever you work on. And it doesn't matter what material you use. Pinecones are fine."

"I'd like to use natural materials, too," I piped up. "Maybe some autumn leaves."

Her eyes scanned my outfit and softened with understanding. "Okay. I think they have some resin in the storage room you can use. I'll show you how."

My lungs deflated in relief. "I'll look it up online. I'd love to learn that technique." I'd google the shit out of this.

"Great. Do that." She walked back to the front of the class, addressing the whole group. "I was asked here to run a workshop for creative people who are stuck. You think, if you just breathe mountain air and sit in a bathtub and have a green drink, you find a million-dollar idea. But I tell you a secret." She leaned in, stage whispering. "Sometimes, you're stuck because you need to be stuck. Your mind is trying to tell you something but you're asking the wrong question."

Charlie raised his hand. "What's the right question? Can you tell us now and save us the time?"

Miranda laughed.

Ilme cocked her head at him, unfazed. "Sounds like your subconscious is hard at work on something. Focus on the pinecones and you'll get there."

"Thanks for the palm reading," Charlie muttered, but there was a smile on his face.

A soft murmur went across the room. It felt like a mix of fear and confusion, as well as a trickle of understanding. I couldn't decide if the Estonian teacher was totally unhinged, a genius or something in between. I was leaning towards the in-between. People were hardly ever either. In a way, her words made sense. Thinking of creativity as a force flowing through us relaxed me. Maybe I could partake in that without the burden of being an artist and having incredible ideas. Whether or not there was a current of divine creativity floating in the air we could tap into, thinking this way lessened the pressure I felt. Maybe that was the point of it.

I set the catalog on the table, relieved I didn't have to order anything. I'd collect leaves and wait for that divine intervention, as promised.

Ilme's low, resonant voice halted my thoughts. "Tomorrow, we're going on an excursion. Dress up warm. Those of you who are planning on using natural materials, bring bags for collecting. I've been told there are a lot of things up on the mountains. Pinecones, leaves, sticks, rocks... even bears." It was the first time I saw Ilme smile, and I realized she was missing one of her front teeth.

CHAPTER 12

Charlie

"Let's pop into town now," I suggested to Bess as soon as we stepped outside of the studio. "We can get you that swimsuit and make it back before dinner."

The afternoon class had just finished.

Bess smoothed her black jersey, which she'd somehow kept tidy where mine was covered in splatter after exploring acrylics. Her eyes widened with alarm, flicking to the left and right to make sure nobody could overhear us. "Maybe you can tell everyone I wasn't feeling well so I decided to go to bed early or something. Tell them I *really* wanted to come but I didn't want to get everyone else sick in case I was coming down with something." Her earnest eyes blinked at me, pleading and hopeful.

I took a deep breath, gathering my thoughts. Everything she

said made sense. It always did. But I didn't want an excuse. I wanted to take her to that hot tub under the stars. I'd seen her eyes light up at the mention of it.

"Do you really want to add fake illness to the list of things you're faking?" I asked.

She halted. "Um..."

"And do you actually want to skip the one thing in this place that doesn't involve any exercises or confusing metaphors? Just your cold body surrounded by hot water and a sky full of stars winking at you?"

Her eyes narrowed. "You sell these tubs or something?"

"You know I could." I grinned, but the thought of advertising made familiar frustrations bubble up. "I'll sell anything. Anything other than that financial literacy program."

I opened the front door for her, and we stepped into the crisp air.

"It'll come to you," she said in a soothing tone. "Just focus on the pinecones."

She masked the sarcasm so well it took me a moment.

I laughed. "I've never paid any attention to pinecones. Are there like lots of different kinds? Is this a good season for them?"

Bess smiled. "You mean, are we having a good pinecone year? No idea. Let's investigate your million-dollar material, shall we?" She led us towards the closest evergreens behind the main building.

We scanned the ground until Bess spotted the first pinecone, picking it up. "This one's pretty. It's open on one side. Great for inserting stick legs. I think they open quicker if you put them in the oven."

"I should create a giant petting zoo full of pinecone animals, for everyone's amusement."

"Why not? I don't think it really matters what we do with these exercises. As long as we focus on the task and let our minds wander or something. Tap into the divine."

"Do you believe that?" I asked. "I always thought of you as… I don't know… evidence-based?"

She crunched up her nose adorably. "Evidence-based? Can you even say that about a person? It makes me sound like a government program."

"Or like a financial literacy program?" I crouched down to pick up another pinecone. A bigger one.

"You can't get your mind off that job, can you?"

I winced, focusing my energy on the ground. "It's hard to switch off."

In all honesty, it had been easy in the past. But the stakes had never been this high.

Bess had already found a handful of cones and was using the hem of her jersey to store them. We hadn't put on our jackets, intending only to cross the path from the main building to the cabin, and the cold was starting to penetrate my thermal Henley.

Bess rubbed her hands together to warm them up. "What if the campaign isn't flawed, but rather, we need to convey the message when people feel more hopeful, relaxed, and optimistic about their future? Like, on their payday? Or when they get tax returns?"

My hand froze mid-air, a pinecone dangling from my fingers. "You might be right. Why did I not think of that?"

"Because you don't live from paycheck to paycheck?" she replied dryly, picking up another cone.

"You don't have to pick up cones for me. Focus on your own assignment. Leaves?"

She looked up at me, a little startled. "Oh. Yeah."

Was she so used to doing my bidding she didn't even consider her own creative challenge?

"What are you going to use for storing them? I know she said bags, but leaves are fragile."

She hugged herself, rubbing her arms. "I don't even have a bag. I was going to take a look at their recycling bin. If I find a good box, I'll grab that."

I stopped myself just in time. She'd already caught me flying my privilege flag. I wasn't going to do it again by throwing money at a problem. "That's a good idea. But also... I brought a pair of shoes that are still in the box. You can have the box if you want? And speaking of shopping, shall we get that bikini for you?"

"Swimsuit," she corrected.

"Worth a shot." I grinned and she relaxed, giving me a reproaching glare as she flicked a pinecone at me. It hit my leg, delivering no pain.

"Trust me, this is awkward enough."

"Why?" I threw out my arms. "We're friends. Colleagues. Designers... with eyes."

"So you're coming to give me your artistic opinion? What happened to you driving me there and handing me a credit card?"

I shrugged, slowly and exaggeratedly. "I mean… if that's what you want. But you can also think of me as a friend. A gay friend if that makes you more comfortable. I'm great at picking out clothes."

"Great. Except… are you gay?"

I sighed. "I'll stare at your boobs and ass the whole time. So… no."

She rewarded my honesty with a huff and a smile. "Okay, I'm freezing now. To the point that I'll go anywhere with you if your car has a heater."

I gestured at the parking lot, excitement building in my chest like silent laughter. I was winning. "How about a seat warmer?"

Her eye roll was undermined by a brewing smile. "Well, that's just excessive."

CHAPTER 13

Bess

Charlie parked along Cozy Creek Main Street and I gasped. It was late afternoon, like on Sunday when I'd first arrived, and the pretty postcard scene was no less magical. If anything, it had taken on new golden hues, like those final touches we'd do on Photoshop before prepping for print.

"I'm not entirely convinced this town is real," I said, my gaze brushing across the intricately decorated houses. The red brick and striped awnings glowed in the warm sunlight. "Even the lighting feels deliberate, doesn't it? This perfect glow to make the tourists look amazing in their own photos."

I caught Charlie looking at me. "Your hair looks like it's on fire."

I instinctively brushed my flaming locks behind my ears.

Cheap home colors were garish. From the heat creeping up my neck, I knew my face was starting to match my unnaturally red hair.

"I'm not criticizing you. You know that, right? The color suits you. Trust me. I'm a designer."

"Haha." I jumped out of the car before he could say anything else.

I'd told him about my financial woes and now he felt bad for me. I'd have to listen to these lame compliments for the rest of the week as Charlie grappled with the giant wealth gap between us. Why was life like this?

We walked down Main Street, browsing the shop windows, all decorated in fall and harvest themes, some with early Halloween displays. I caught a poster advertising the Fall Festival with a hay maze, live music and games for kids. Celia would have loved that.

We passed a bar called Bookers, a general store and an adorable cafe with a sign 'Cozy Creek Confectionery'. I felt like I was walking through the set of Gilmore Girls. A few steps down the road, we found the first clothing shop. The selection was geared towards mountaineering, with no swimsuits of any kind. Charlie asked for help from the young shop assistant who guided us to the only place he could think of—a thrift store around the corner.

"Oh, no. I meant new clothing." Charlie looked horrified.

The shop assistant shrugged. "Well, the closest place is... Denver, I suppose. Swimming suits aren't really in season right now."

"Why not?" Charlie demanded. "It's hot tub season."

Sensing an up-coming rant, I dabbed him on the arm. "I don't think that's a thing. And I'm happy to check out the thrift store."

I could see the battle on his face. He was disgusted by the idea but not ready to give up. "If you're sure," he finally said.

We returned to the sidewalk, rounded the corner and descended the stone steps. Reaching the end of the narrow alleyway, we landed upon the store that time had forgotten. Peeling vinyl covered the small windows. The inside was tucked full of tightly packed hangers and heaped crates of clothing categorized broadly as 'tops', 'bottoms' and 'dresses'. A white-haired woman with a permanently hunched spine appeared from the back, fitting in her dentures before she greeted us. She seemed a little startled to encounter humans and quickly retreated behind the counter, muttering something to herself.

I gestured at the small cash box she rested her bony fingers on. "I don't think your credit card is good here."

"What?" Charlie started digging through his pockets. "I don't know if I have any cash."

I smiled. "That's okay. I can afford this stuff." I'd already spotted a crate labeled 'MICS—$2 each'. Seeing no microphones, I figured they were miscellaneous items.

I took one last breath of fresh air at the doorway. As soon as I ventured in, my dust mite allergy would activate and I'd have about fifteen minutes before the first very unattractive sneeze attack.

As far as secondhand shops went, the place was a dog's breakfast, but I also had years of experience. It didn't take me too long to land on a blue swimsuit with excessive lime green ruffles that was roughly my size. It was more like a circus act than a swimming costume, but in that moment, it felt like the more palatable choice, almost like something you'd wear on a dare. My own swimsuit was plain awful but it was mine and I had no excuse.

I held it out for Charlie, grinning from ear to ear. "Score."

"Okay... How do you know it fits?" He coughed. "I mean, that's a lot of material and you're not that big." He tilted his head, scanning my body up and down, making me feel hot.

I looked around the room. "It doesn't look like they have changing rooms. I'll risk it."

"How much?" He asked and resumed searching his pockets.

I pulled out a five-dollar bill and took my find to the old lady. "This is from the two-dollar pile."

She popped the cash box and spent two minutes finding my change. When we finally made it out on the street, I sneezed twice.

Charlie groaned, looking back at the shop. "Oh, my God!"

"Hey! Don't judge thrift stores based on that. Some have changing rooms. Even ventilation." I tried to keep my face straight but failed.

He burst into laughter. "Ventilation? Well, that's fancy. I mean, to have air when you shop."

"One of those non-essentials. Like credit card readers."

"And what was up with that hundred-year-old lady? Should she still be working?"

"Maybe her pension doesn't cover the cost of dentures?" My

light tone turned heavy because it was probably true.

Charlie blew a sigh. "Anyway... I promised to drive you here and hand you a credit card. So, how about I take you to that gift shop and you buy a souvenir for Celia?"

I tensed. I'd survived the thrift store, but here came the real charity. "It's okay. She's easy to please. She loves fridge magnets." I could afford to buy my own souvenirs.

"Okay. You get her one and I get her another one?" He cast me a look that was almost desperate.

I had to let him buy my daughter fridge magnets, to feel better about himself. About the world. It was a nice sentiment, I reminded myself. He wanted to give me something. Whether it was driven by guilt, discomfort, or something else, did it matter? Celia would be overjoyed.

It was a lot easier to let people give things to your child than to receive them for yourself, and Charlie knew it. He kept staring at me, fanning his incredible, gold-tipped lashes that curved so perfectly in the corners, and I lost track. What was he talking about? Something about credit cards... shopping? Gift shopping.

"Fine. You can use your credit card. But only because you didn't get your Pretty Woman shopping montage. That must have been hard."

His face split into a gorgeous smile. "You have no idea. I was fantasizing about sitting in a chair reading a magazine while the shop assistants ran around serving you and then folding under the weight of your shopping bags."

"It's a small mountain town. There's no mall. Not even a proper grocery store. I think you need to adjust your expectations. Also... when does a grown man fold under the weight of one swimsuit?"

"Are you kidding me? The swimsuit was supposed to be the gateway purchase that leads to the next thing and the next thing. That's how shopping works."

"Not how it works for me," I muttered.

Reaching the doorway of the gift shop, I hesitated. "So, what's that fridge magnet going to lead to?"

Charlie's gaze darted around the shop. "I don't know. Maybe we need to update your fridge, so there's more room for magnets." His smile was so mischievous I couldn't help joining in.

"You're out of control."

"You're right." He pulled out his credit card and placed it in my hand. "Here. You're in charge of it now. That's much safer."

Rhonda's words played in my mind. *Someone should confiscate his credit cards.*

It was probably true, but I felt liberated. He wasn't tiptoeing around me, trying to pretend we were the same or that he understood my struggle. The more time we spent together, the more Charlie felt like himself—spoilt and spontaneous, with no filter. I couldn't handle the pity, but I could handle that.

"Okay." I held up his card. "I will find the most ridiculous thing in this shop and you'll have to wear it to your next date, to a fancy restaurant. Promise me and then you can buy whatever you want for Celia."

"Deal. But I also get to buy you something for your next date."

"Deal." I'd win this bet. "But only because I don't date."

He halted at the doorway. "At all? Ever?"

I shook my head.

He stared at me for a moment until his frown gradually melted away and a confident smile broke through. "We'll see about that."

CHAPTER 14

Charlie

"It's all so… ordinary." Bess sighed, browsing the rows of T-shirts and sweaters with the Cozy Creek logo.

The shop had fridge magnets galore, though. I went a little overboard selecting everything that I thought might make her daughter happy. Little rainbows, mountain scenes, a smiling pinecone and a big, fat pumpkin.

What's up, Charlie?

The uncomfortable question hung in the air as I piled the treasures on the counter, blocking Bess from reaching in and returning them. Her soft chest collided with my forearm. "That's too much!"

"They're fridge magnets. Chill."

I needed to chill. What was I trying to do? Buy her child's affection? Erase the ill feeling I got just thinking about their story and what the future held?

Bess stomped off and eventually returned with a Cozy Creek baseball cap and a lumberjack style flannel shirt. "Here's your new wardrobe."

I paid for everything and immediately peeled off my paint-splattered Ralph Lauren henley to change into the flannel. She swiveled to face the display of postcards, waiting for me to get changed. I could have left the T-shirt on, but I was too committed to show her I had no shame.

"It looks a bit small," I said, holding up the flannel. "But I'll take the tags off and if it doesn't fit—"

"Oh, come on!" She turned to me, her eyes dragging over my naked torso before she grabbed the shirt and turned the tags on the outside. "Try it like this."

"Thanks." I smiled, pleased with myself.

She may have thought of me as a privileged idiot, but now she knew I was a privileged idiot with a six-pack, in case that made any difference.

"This is not the true test," she insisted as I buttoned the shirt. "I'm not used to seeing you like this, but it doesn't mean you look out of place here. Wait until you're back in Denver and with someone you're really trying to impress."

I added the baseball cap, turning it backwards. "Is this any better?"

I wanted to impress her, but the rules were different. Everything was different with her.

She swallowed. "Very Luke's Diner."

As we exited the shop, we were already late for dinner. I might have suggested eating in town, but seeing Bess's horror as I showed her the time, I rejected that idea. The retreat price included meals, and I was quickly learning the importance of not wasting anything.

I didn't *want* to waste anything with her. Especially time.

I drove us back as fast as I could, and we headed straight to the dining hall. The heavenly smell greeting us at the doorway turned out to be chicken kebabs and roasted vegetables. We loaded our plates and grabbed a table vacated by two of the ladies, one of them Miranda. She glanced at my outfit and her eyebrows sailed up. "See you in the tub? It's going to be a starry night."

Bess stood frozen, watching them walk away.

"We don't have to go," I whispered. "You don't have to wear that thing you bought. I'm not that mean."

She looked out the window. The last light of the day had turned into intense blue. Cerulean. "It does sound amazing."

"Well, if you're brave enough to put that thing on, I can publicly take the blame. And I'll wear my swimming trunks inside out or something. I'll swim in the flannel."

Bess offered me the tiniest of smiles. "I appreciate your willingness to humiliate yourself." She picked up a chicken kebab, inhaling its aroma before taking a bite. "To be honest, I did bring a swimsuit, but it's old and worn out and I wasn't planning on letting anyone else see it."

"What?" I tried to go for shocked but couldn't quite commit.

I would have taken her shopping, regardless. "You brought a swimsuit you wouldn't wear in public? Did you think you'd have this place all to yourself?" I didn't even try to hide my smile, and her shoulders dropped.

"I thought I could sneak in there by myself, in the dark... to be honest, I don't know what I was thinking. Most days, I'm just trying to keep my head above water. Figuratively." She gave me a wry smile.

"Your swimsuit can't be as bad as the one you bought, though. That's not possible."

"It is!" She insisted. "Or I mean... when I saw what everyone around here was wearing, I decided to pretend it didn't exist. But now I'm thinking it might be less noticeable than the lime green ruffles. I think the fabric dust in that place messed with my brain."

"It can happen."

"I wasn't planning on ever letting you pay for a new swimsuit. I just wanted to replace the one I had with something cheap." She sighed. "It was stupid. There's nothing I can do to blend in with this crowd."

"Why would you want to blend in?"

She shrugged. "I don't want to embarrass you."

I adjusted my baseball cap. "Embarrass me? I'm totally fine with that ruffled number you bought from the friendly ghost. How bad can the other one be?" I was curious now. I needed to see it.

Okay, fine. I needed to see her, preferably naked. I'd been

watching that body in black jeans, band T-shirts and sneakers, the designer uniform, for two years, imagining what she looked like underneath. But if that wasn't an option, I'd take her in a terrible swimsuit.

She winced. "It's black, but really faded and the elastic is starting to wear out so it's kind of baggy in places. I'm positive you've never seen anything that awful on a woman. Or a man."

I stood up and collected our plates. "Okay. Let's go try on both swimsuits and rate them."

"What?"

"Come on. We need to settle this once and for all. Which one is the most hideous? I won't rest until we have an answer."

Her eye roll was adorable. "I'm not parading in front of you in ugly swimsuits," she puffed, heading for the door.

I followed her outside, down the path that led to our cabin. There was enough light to see silhouettes of houses and the outline of the path, but not much else. The stars were winking above us. A perfect hot tub night.

"How else are we going to figure this out, though? You need my infallible fashion sense." I kept poking, spurred by the strange, bubbling sensation that seemed to drive me when I was around her. Sparring with Bess was like drinking champagne without drinking champagne. She'd think me deranged if I told her, which made me want to tell her. Besides, deranged was better than elitist or spoilt. Marginally.

"How about *you* try them on and catwalk across the dining hall?" she suggested, jerking a thumb over her shoulder. "I'm sure we could get some opinions."

"I'll do a private show for you," I offered. "But I can't guarantee the elastic will survive my... um... muscles."

Considering how excited I got firing lines with her, I'd soon be ready to split any swimsuit clean in two.

I took the steps two at a time, determined to keep whatever was happening between us going. Keep her smiling. Keep her having fun. Being brave. I loved that bravery, whenever it flashed behind her eyes. It was absolute magic and held me spellbound. She was all grit and determination; quick wit and curves, and I couldn't tear my eyes away. What was worse, she had no idea what she was doing to me.

CHAPTER 15

Bess

"We're not doing this," I told him as soon as we stepped inside the cabin. "I'll just... get changed." My voice lacked conviction, but I'd made up my mind. As much as I enjoyed the jokes and his poorly disguised interest in my body, I had my limits. Prancing around in ugly swimsuits for Charlie Wilde was not an option.

I ran up the stairs. I couldn't get changed in the loft as it had no privacy. Even the glass-walled bathroom felt too open to his prying eyes, but what choice did I have? I could fake an illness or cancel, but Charlie had practically announced my arrival and part of me felt stubborn enough to show up as I was to enjoy the hot water under the stars. Where could I experience that ever again?

I grabbed both swimsuits and my towel, and hurried back

downstairs. Reaching for the bathroom door, I glanced over my shoulder and froze. Charlie stood by the bed in his underwear, holding a pair of swimming shorts. Earlier in the shop, he'd gifted me with the mental image of his perfect torso, and now his impeccably muscular legs caught my attention.

"Sorry," I muttered, whipping around, and retreating into the bathroom.

"What are you sorry about?" he asked, his voice carrying through the glass door, clear and loud.

Couldn't they have soundproofed the bathroom a little bit?

"I... didn't know you were changing down here," I replied from behind the door, quickly peeling off my clothes and pulling on my black, two-piece suit.

Bracing myself, I turned towards the mirror. It was hung too high for me to see the full ensemble, but I could feel it didn't fit. The bikini bottoms were originally a pair of modest briefs, but the elastic had given up completely, leaving saggy fabric around the crotch. There was enough loose material to smuggle a coconut. I couldn't wear them. I simply couldn't.

I took off the horrible briefs and wiggled myself into the lime-ruffled one-piece. The bottom part of it fit surprisingly well, but the rest was designed for a shorter torso. No matter how I pulled and stretched and adjusted the straps, I couldn't properly cover up my breasts. The material ended right above my nipples, leaving the rest bulging out, my cleavage so on display I could have held all of Charlie's credit cards in there. The ruffles that lined the plunging neckline only added to the effect. How had I not noticed this in the shop?

I stared into the mirror, willing myself not to cry.

"You okay in there?" Charlie called from behind the door.

On a whim, I took a breath and opened the door. "No."

"Whoa!" His eyes went exactly where I knew they would, and I gave the suit another upwards yank, which turned into a wedgie at the other end.

"What's wrong?" He'd already changed into his own swimming trunks and looked like a male model ready for the beach shoot.

"It doesn't fit." My voice wobbled. "And the other one... the bottoms are so loose they'll flap on me."

"Does that matter, though? They'll be under water."

I sighed. Maybe the ugly bottoms were the lesser of two evils. I closed the door and quickly wiggled myself back into my own two-piece. When I opened the door again, I found Charlie outside, smiling victoriously. "I was hoping for high heels, but all good."

I squeezed my eyes closed, mortified. I was giving him the exact show I'd sworn I wouldn't. In ill-fitting swimsuits, no less.

I picked at the loose material sitting on my lower belly and winced.

Charlie cocked his head, still staring at me so intensely my skin sizzled. "So... did you accidentally buy men's trunks?"

I shook my head, an unexpected laugh bubbling in my chest. "They're just stretched out of shape."

"Let's swap." Charlie wedged a thumb under the waistband of

his trunks and stretched the elastic. "You can wear these and I'll wear your bottoms."

"You're not serious."

"I've got the goods to actually fill that front pouch of yours."

I stared at the Patagonia logo on the hem of the turquoise trunks. Before I could form an intelligent response, he'd pulled them off right in front of me. I swiveled around, but not fast enough. Not before I registered the sight of his penis. Charlie's penis. Why was I seeing Charlie's penis? "What are you doing?"

"Sorry. I'm one-quarter Swedish."

"How does that explain you stripping in front of me?" I asked, my voice cracking a bit. Were Swedes particularly well-hung, or was he also one-quarter horse?

"I don't think nudity is such a big deal. I think it's the sauna culture." He tapped me on the shoulder. "You can turn around."

He'd wrapped a towel around his waist and handed me the swimming trunks. They felt silky soft and looked beautiful.

"What if I stretch them out of shape?"

"With that ass?" His gaze flicked down my body and my cheeks heated. "You won't, but I will stretch yours, so let's make a deal. No returns."

"That's not a fair deal for you."

"I haven't seen your employment contract, but I don't think a pair of swimming trunks will tip the scales in your favor."

His words landed like a soft punch to my middle. With no arguments, I took the shorts and stepped back into the bathroom. To my surprise, they fit me perfectly, elevating my black halter-neck swimming top to a whole new league. I opened the door, this time more confident.

Charlie whistled. "Perfect! Ten out of ten."

I adjusted the halter-neck, cheeks burning. "They're really comfortable."

The look on his face caught me by surprise. Just like Jack. Unfocused and excited, his eyes all over me, struggling to stay on my face. The sudden thought brought up a twinge of pain and longing. Was it even possible Charlie Wilde was looking at me like that? Maybe I'd been alone for so long I was starting to hallucinate.

I handed him my awful bikini bottoms. "You'll regret this."

Charlie pulled them on underneath the towel. This time, I didn't turn away, my gaze pinned at his waist, willing for that loosely folded towel to slide open. If he wasn't bothered by his own nudity, I might as well enjoy it.

Finally, the towel dropped, revealing a pair of the most snug and ill-fitting trunks I'd ever seen. Charlie adjusted the crotch, desperately trying to capture his jewels inside the material that could neither contain nor support them.

"Well, the crotch doesn't look so baggy anymore," I said, biting back my laughter.

"I'll be peeking out of these, but that's okay."

"You can't wear those. I'll get changed—"

I was about to go back into the bathroom when he grabbed my arm. "Enough changing. Enough. Let's go."

He handed me a fluffy bathrobe and wrapped himself in another one, pulling me by the hand.

At the door, I halted. "Wait! What time is it? I should call Celia. What if she's asleep by the time we come back?"

"It's eight p.m." Charlie released my arm. "Make the call. I'll find us some drinks."

I fetched my phone from its charger. I thought about going upstairs, but Charlie would have heard me anyway, so I just dialed. Mom answered on the first ring.

"Hey Bess! We're about to have dinner."

"I won't keep you long. I just wanted to say good night. I'm heading off to test the hot tub."

"The hot tub under the stars?" I could tell Charlie heard Mom's loud excitement.

"Yep."

Mom put Celia on the phone, and she babbled for a while about her day, who she'd played with and who'd been naughty. By the time I finished the call, I had tears in my eyes. Saying 'hugs and kisses' without being able to hug and kiss your child was a special form of torture.

"You okay?" Charlie's voice was soft when I finally joined him at the door.

"I just miss her."

"You'll be back home soon."

He was holding two Biased craft beers. An instant memory of photoshopping them for a billboard emerged.

I nodded at the bottle. "Do you actually like that stuff or is your own advertising so powerful you can't help it?"

Charlie chuckled. "I have a lot of samples left. It's drinkable."

With towels under our arms and our feet in complimentary slippers, we made it down the steps and into the dark night. With the help of Charlie's flashlight, we followed the signage around the main building and down a narrow path that turned into steep steps. And there it was—a huge pool of steaming water sitting outside a small cabin, partly shaded by small pines. The cabin porch had rows of fairy lights illuminating the view, but they hardly compared to the glow of the starry sky above. The crescent moon hung low, right above the tree line. And to my huge relief, there was nobody else around.

"This is so perfect," I whispered.

"Worth all the wardrobe drama, right?"

I heard sounds from behind us. "Sure. But you might want to get into the tub before anyone else arrives."

"Damn right." Charlie hurried down the last steps, ditched his robe and towel on a nearby bench and climbed in, holding beer bottles in one hand and his crotch in the other.

I laughed. His willingness to humiliate himself made me like him more.

By the time I joined Charlie at the tub, the darkness spat out three women, including Miranda. We'd taken a long time changing in and out of horrible swimsuits. How had they taken this long?

That's when I noticed the slight wobble in Miranda's step. They must have been drinking.

I greeted them with a smile and quickly folded my robe next

to Charlie's. The cold was digging deep into my bones and all I could think of was getting in the tub. The water felt heavenly on my skin, momentarily pushing all thoughts out of my head. My deep sigh turned into a faint moan.

"I told you she likes tubs," I heard Charlie say.

I cracked my eyelids, just in time to see his arm slide over my shoulders. Ah, yes. The girlfriend act. At least I didn't jump this time as he pulled me closer.

"Sorry to break up your party," Miranda said, sliding into the pool.

The golden detailing of her bikini twinkled in the low light. The other two ladies introduced themselves as Angie and Kathryn. Within seconds, I heard male voices as Matthew and Harry arrived. The tub was at capacity.

Charlie scooted closer to me to make room for everyone else.

"Is this a six-person pool or eight?" Harry asked.

Matthew's voice rose in concern. "Do you think we're over capacity?"

"I'd offer to take Matthew in my lap to make more room, but he's a big guy..." He rolled his eyes, casting a look at me and Charlie.

"Noted," Charlie said, turning to me. "Come here, babe."

He lifted me onto his lap and everyone else shuffled to take up more room. A collective sigh of relief traveled across the water.

"I'm sorry about the wooden seat," he whispered into my ear as the rock-hard erection lodged between my butt cheeks.

What was I supposed to do now? A chilly breeze tickled my

scalp. My bones were still warning up. I didn't want to get out. Not now. Not ever.

I'd have to ignore that boner. It was just biology. It wasn't about me. He was probably turned on by all the women around the pool, batting their eyelashes at him. And even if it was me, this was as far as we'd ever go. Wearing each other's swimming suits and playing for an audience.

Charlie reached over the edge of the tub to grab the beer he'd set down a moment ago. As he moved under my butt, I grabbed the edge of the seat to keep from sliding off his lap. But as his legs spread wider, so did mine. Great. I was now straddling his thigh, and that erection rubbed against the apex of my thighs. "Here's yours," he said, offering me the other beer bottle.

My stomach tightened. "I... can't drink beer."

"What do you mean, can't?"

I glanced around us to make sure nobody was actively listening. The others seemed to have fallen into a conversation about tomorrow's wilderness excursion and the possibility of wildlife sightings this time of year.

I shifted on Charlie's lap so that I could look at him over my shoulder, trying to ignore the fireworks in my core. "I can't burp," I whispered. "That's why I can't drink beer."

"What?" His volume climbed up. "That's not a thing. Is it?"

"It's real. No burp syndrome."

"No burb what?" asked Harry, leaning in. The bear and elk conversation must have run its course.

"It has a medical name, but I can't remember. Retrograde

something. I've had it my whole life. I'm okay if I avoid certain foods and drinks and don't eat too late. Beer is the worst."

"And your boyfriend didn't know this about you?" Harry looked at me in disbelief. "Has he never shared his beer before?" He shot a dirty look at Charlie.

"I mean, I knew it, but I didn't know it was like a medical thing," Charlie improvised, softly grazing my cheek with the cold beer bottle. "I just thought you didn't like beer."

Harry stared at the two bottles he was still holding. "Why did you bring her a beer, then?"

"Yeah, why Charlie?" I raised my eyebrows at him, biting my lip. "You could have brought something I can drink, like white wine with no bubbles." I turned back to Harry with a knowing look. "I think you called it. He wanted to drink two beers and not share."

Harry laughed. Charlie didn't.

"I have a wine bottle in the cabin. I'll go get it." He slid away from underneath me and launched towards the steps, but froze. "Except... I think I just lost my swimming trunks."

My involuntary yelp caught everyone's attention.

"What's happening?" Miranda's head whipped around.

"I think Charlie's going commando," Harry explained to Matthew, beaming with glee.

Everyone's eyes widened. Charlie cast me a meaningful look before addressing them. "It's true. I was wearing Bess's bikini bottoms, on a dare, and let's just say they're now ripped in half and riding down my left leg. And did I mention I need to get out of the pool to fetch her a drink, because I'm still a gentleman."

The entire party erupted in giggles.

"This is better than reality TV!" Harry guffawed.

"I don't suppose you'd all agree to close your eyes for a few seconds so I could…" Charlie tried when the laughter fizzled out and was met by another bout of hysterical howls.

"I'll close my eyes, promise," Harry hiccupped, closing one eye.

I grabbed Charlie's arm under water and tried to pull him back. "I don't need a drink. Honestly."

"I'm going to get you one."

I scooted closer to whisper into his ear. "I'll give you the pair I'm wearing, if you promise to bring them back." I winced at the thought. It was the last thing I wanted to do but couldn't let him go through with this.

Charlie's eyes flashed. "No backsies, remember? I'll get you that drink."

He reached for the handrails and pulled himself out of the pool. I couldn't tear my eyes off him, and neither could anybody else. Backlit by the fairy lights, with a soft moonlight bouncing off his buttocks, Charlie was a sight to behold. He landed softly on the ground and leapt to pick up his towel.

My foot touched something floating in the water. The broken bikini bottoms. I fished them out and tossed them at Charlie. I have a terrible aim, so I didn't even worry about hitting anything. But as luck would have it, the wet piece of material slapped him square on the lower back and he jumped, dropping the towel.

"I'm so sorry," I gasped.

The ladies cheered and Harry whistled. Charlie picked up the towel again, tied it around his waist and slowly turned around, giving us a bow. "Ladies and gentlemen."

"Why do I never have dollar bills when I need them?" Harry moaned.

Charlie took it in his stride, smiling and blowing kisses. There was no embarrassing this guy. I would have been mortified if I'd lost my bottoms in the water. Hell, I'd been mortified by the thought of people seeing my bikini bottoms. He'd known it, too, and made sure it didn't happen.

"I'll be back soon, Bessie-Boo."

He caught me by surprise, pulling my head back against the edge of the pool. Before I could react, his lips were on mine, hot and demanding. The kiss only lasted a few seconds, but it seized my body. For a moment, my lips weren't mine. My mind evaporated into the night sky. All I could think was the absolute takeover. Charlie's lips on mine. His breath on my face. His scent in my nostrils. It made no sense. His fist tightened against my scalp, teasing the nerve endings. And then it was over.

His rough stubble grazed my cheek as he pulled away, smiling. "I'll miss you."

I was grateful for the general darkness and the fact most of me was hiding in bubbly water.

"He's a keeper," Harry said with a dreamy smile as Charlie threw on his bathrobe and slippers and hurried up the steps, disappearing into the dark night. "How long have you guys been together?"

Miranda leaned in, her eyebrows raising in curiosity.

"It's pretty new," I said.

The closer to the truth I stayed, the easier this would be.

"How did you guys meet?" Miranda asked, leaning forward.

"At work."

If I kept my answers short, I'd avoid saying anything incriminating.

"So, you work at Wilde Creative? What do you do?"

"Production."

"Really? That's how I started, years ago. It was so boring. Are you looking to move up to a creative role? Good to know someone on the inside." She nodded at the direction Charlie had disappeared into.

I felt bile rising in my throat. Was she insinuating I was dating Charlie to advance my career?

A woman with a cloud of wild, blond curls, one who'd introduced herself as Angie, shifted closer. "I would marry Charlie for the family jet." Her laughter sounded like tiny little bells.

I gave her a little smile. She looked younger than Miranda. More innocent. I'd heard about the jet, but I'd never seen it. Only Trevor had ever been invited on it, much to Teresa's chagrin.

"I know Charlie from the awards," Angie continued. "We get tickets through work every year, even though I've never been nominated. But I've seen Charlie on stage so many times. He bought us drinks once. Like, everyone at the after party."

I could imagine Charlie there, waving his credit card, fighting off the girls. All those women gunning to become Mrs. Wilde. To live the easy life at his expense.

"He's pretty generous," I admitted.

"He is! Play your cards right and you won't have to work at all. You can just fly around the world and organize parties."

My body tensed. "I'd rather work. I have a daughter and I need to be independent, for her." I couldn't let them paint me as this gold-digging woman.

"Good for you." Miranda patted my shoulder. "How old is your daughter?"

"Five."

"Starting school soon?"

"Yeah."

"Wow. I never imagined Charlie with a single mom. That's so cool." Angie sighed.

Oh, God. I'd have to tell Charlie he was officially dating a single mom. No matter how I tried, I couldn't survive this interrogation without something slipping out. Where was Charlie? How long could it take to fetch one wine bottle?

"Well, I'm off," Angie stood up, wading towards the steps. "But before I go, please tell me how you snatched Charlie Wilde? I mean... give me a hint? Did you go to work in a see-through shirt or something?"

Oh, the horror.

"No. We just... worked late."

She cocked her head as if trying to picture it. "But who initiated it?"

"Charlie." My response was instant because it was true. I would have never made a move on Charlie. I couldn't even imagine us hooking up in his office, no matter how hard I tried.

"Really?" Miranda sounded surprised.

She probably didn't believe me, but there was nothing I could do about it. The more I told them, the less believable it sounded. I needed to shut up, right now.

"Well, I'm off as well. I have a massage appointment." She followed Angie out of the pool.

Kathryn joined them, giving me a smile. The ladies evidently moved as a pack.

"I have one tomorrow!" Harry exclaimed. "Can't wait."

I stretched my achy neck, wondering if I'd ever be able to spend money on that sort of thing. I was getting a little overheated, so I climbed up to sit on the edge of the pool. The guys seemed to have a similar reaction since they got out, too.

Harry and Matthew were still toweling themselves by the tub when Charlie reappeared, holding a bottle of wine and a huge wine glass. "Are you all leaving?"

"Enjoy the privacy." Harry winked, edging past him towards the stairs.

Matthew followed him, leaving me alone with Charlie. Feeling the chill on my skin, I slid back into the water, sighing from relief. No more questions and mind games. I wasn't cut out for this fake dating.

A glass of white wine appeared next to my head. "Here you go, darling."

"Thank you." I took a sip, enjoying the sensation of hot water against my skin and cold drink traveling down my throat. "But you can drop the act now. We're alone."

Charlie peeled off his robe, revealing a pair of boxer shorts. "What act?" He joined me in the tub, sitting right next to me. "This is not an act. This is me being a gentleman."

"Very gentlemanly, thank you." I sipped the wine. It was so good I had to wonder how much it might have cost. "But you shouldn't have left me here on my own. I was interrogated!"

"Really? About what?"

I huffed. "About us. They're all fascinated by the idea of you going out with someone like me."

He gave me an odd look, tilting his beer bottle to his lips. "Someone like... what? You're beautiful and age appropriate." He smiled, igniting a warm glow inside me.

I took a deep breath. "I'm a single mom. I'm sorry, I shouldn't have told them. I just couldn't handle them hinting I was sleeping my way to the top."

Mid-drink, he spat out his beer. "Hinting what?"

I didn't feel like repeating it, so I waited for the words to sink in. He shook his head. "Well, that's stupid. And what does that have to do with you being a mom?"

"I don't know. I guess I wanted to make the point that I want to be independent for the sake of my daughter. I would never rely on a man like that."

It's not safe.

"That's admirable. But don't you think if you... fell in love and

had someone in your life who really wanted to take care of you...
don't you think that could be nice?"

"Sure, but how can I know it will last? My girl's already lost
one father. I can't put her through that again. Hypothetically." I
added the last word in a rush.

He wasn't talking about us, or him. All this pretending was
messing with my head.

"Hypothetically?"

"Well, I don't date, so it's not something I have to worry
about."

"Right." Charlie tilted his head all the way to one side, regarding me with bemused interest. "But what if someone still falls in
love with you?"

"You mean like my garbage man or the landlord?"

"Yeah, totally. You might throw out beautiful artwork and the
garbage man sees it in the trash and falls head over heels."

I laughed. "Yeah, seems plausible. Probable, even."

"Talking about art... what did you think of the Thriver campaign? You prepped that first presentation for us, didn't you?"

I shrugged. "It looked great."

"But..."

Could I tell him? He'd never understand. I took a deep breath,
gathering my thoughts. "It sounded preachy and annoying."

"Preachy and annoying?" He jerked back, hit by my words.

"Yeah, sort of." I already regretted these words. "It's peddling
the idea that you can fix any financial issues by getting better at
budgeting. That if you just plug the holes, the coffers will fill up

again and everything will be fine."

"And... it's not true?" His question hung in the air, challenging me.

I bit my lip, wondering if I'd gone too far. It was because of Jack that I knew anything about economic theories on poverty and everything I knew about rich guys told me this was a bad idea. I took a deep breath. Jack deserved to be understood, even if it was posthumously. "Did you ever see that Ted Talk about guaranteed basic income?"

He shook his head, staring at me, riveted. The quote popped into my head like a dusty old memory I'd accidentally dug up from the back of the storage. "Poverty is not a lack of character. It's a lack of cash."

I expected him to disagree, to challenge me, or call me a communist. But his face split into a grin. "Well, you tell me you're broke and you definitely don't lack character."

Buoyed by his encouragement, I continued, keeping my eyes on the wineglass. "It was a fascinating talk. There was an example of farmers who made all their money during harvest, so they were rich around that time and then poor for the rest of the year. And their IQ went up 14 points when they got money."

"That's a lot."

"Poverty can make you stupid."

I felt his gaze on my skin. "You're not stupid."

"I could be smarter. And more creative." The corner of my mouth twitched. My belly felt warm and fuzzy. "Actually, I feel like my brain's been slowly turning on this week. It's so different to my real life. All the amazing food and freedom to think. No running around. I feel so guilty to sit here and relax, but I also feel like I'm getting back something I lost. Maybe it's IQ points." I covered my face with my hands, to stop myself from continuing.

He was the boss's son. What was I doing?

"Bess, that's amazing." His voice was so soft and excited it drew me out.

My hands dropped and I met his eyes. Those beautiful, glistening eyes that followed me, searching. He'd been looking at me, constantly, making me feel far more interesting than I really was.

"I'm sorry I kissed you," he said. "This fake dating... It never needed to go that far. I have no excuse, other than..." He bit his lower lip, looking simultaneously sheepish, incorrigible and unbearably hot.

"Apology accepted," I said quickly.

Change the subject. Stop thinking about that kiss.

I tilted my glass, watching the fairy lights reflected on it.

We sat in silence, looking up at the starry sky. "Other than... what?" I finally asked. I couldn't let it go.

Some deep, damaged part of me wanted the confirmation. I needed to hear that I wasn't the only one feeling this utterly misguided desire, currently fueled by wine, warm water and the entire Milky Way stretching over our heads.

"Curiosity?" I guessed when he didn't reply.

"No." He shook his head. "I wasn't curious."

"No?" I tried to neutralize my face, to not show my hurt.

"No. I knew it'd be hot." He grinned.

"So what's your excuse?"

His eyes sparkled, reflecting the fairy lights. "Honestly... I was just thinking with my dick. Sorry about that."

Wine sprayed out of my mouth, and a little from my nose. "Seriously? That's your answer?"

"Do you not appreciate honesty?"

Something loosened in my belly and a shaky laughter erupted.

"Oh, Charlie." The words escaped with my out-breath, but they didn't hold the usual tone. More like acceptance.

I felt happy and wanted. I had to enjoy this feeling—it would go away so quickly; I knew it. Memories would twist out of shape, fade, and take on new meaning. Nothing would last. But if I held on tight, I could feel something sweet and delicious here, right now, hiding away from my daily life. Maybe the essence of it would linger like the faint smell of pine and chlorine. And wine.

I drank my wine, maybe a little too quickly, desperate to stay in that bubble.

"I do appreciate honesty," I said. "And I didn't mind the kiss. It crossed a line, but it didn't leave a bad taste."

"Did it taste like this beer? Because it's actually very nice." Charlie took a swig from his bottle. "Maybe that's a way for you to taste beer without getting any bubbles down your throat?" He grinned, and my stomach responded by releasing a batch of hibernating butterflies. So old and frail they could barely fly, blindly bumping into each other.

I leaned in, ever so slightly, suddenly wanting nothing but to taste the beer from Charlie's lips. It was all wrong, but the alcohol had entered my bloodstream, turning off my higher functioning, leaving hormones in charge. And according to them, I wanted to suck him like a popsicle. My gaze settled on the soft curve of his upper lip, following the shape of that slightly protruding lower lip. So perfectly pouty. He wasn't smiling anymore. In fact, he looked concerned.

"What is it?" I asked as my mind registered the shift in his mood.

"I want to kiss you again, but I think we have a problem."

"What problem?" I asked like an idiot. There were a thousand problems with me kissing Charlie.

"You dislike me, Bess."

CHAPTER 16

Charlie

The beer had clearly done its best work, loosening my tongue. I held my breath, waiting for her to respond. For a moment, I thought she might deny it. She'd been hiding it well, but my instincts were usually right.

Bess might have been attracted to me, but she didn't like me.

"I think you disapprove of me," I continued as the words formed on my uncontrollable tongue. "Tell me I'm wrong."

Her voice was so quiet I could barely hear it over the sound of bubbling water. "You're not wrong. But I've been wrong, Charlie. I've judged you based on realities I can't even understand. Your life's so different."

"We work at the same company. We deal with the same jobs. Same clients. We use the same bathrooms."

She smiled. "Yeah, the unisex bathrooms are the worst thing about that place. The seat's always up."

"Is that why you hate me?"

"No! God. I don't even know if it's you. Could be Trevor."

"What is it, then?"

"I don't hate you, Charlie. Maybe I did look at you like that, at work. But it wasn't about you. That's how I feel about anyone with an easier life. It feels unfair. It reminds me of how different my life is and what it used to be. Every time you blow hundreds on some gadget, I think... I could cover a weeks' groceries and gas. And it makes me feel angry and sad. But it's not about you. Everything I learn about you makes me like you." She looked at her empty wineglass, eyes wide. "Good job, alcohol. You really know how to remove inhibitions."

She was slurring her words a little.

"Are you drunk? From one glass of wine?" I had to laugh.

She gave me an unfocused stare. "I'm not great with alcohol, even without the bubbles. And this is a huge glass."

"Yeah, it is." It was one of those bowl-like ones my mom used when she allowed herself only one glass. "Refill?"

"I shouldn't."

"Drink it slowly." She didn't protest when I poured her another one. I liked her honesty. She was real and adorable. If it meant she'd puke and they'd have to drain the tub, I'd cover the cost.

"You're right," I said. "Money brings a lot of freedom and sometimes I don't even think what it's like for someone who doesn't have it. I guess I assumed everyone at work was on a decent income, so I wasn't parading my new toys in front of people standing outside a soup kitchen or something. I never imagined you were in such a tight spot. And now I feel horrible about it."

My mind journeyed back to all the things I'd ordered. The tiny drone I'd been flying over the production floor. The talking vacuum cleaner that could negotiate stairs. That stupid personal robot! I was a douche.

I felt Bess's hand on my shoulder. "It's fine, Charlie. You didn't know. And even if you did, it doesn't mean you're obligated to hide your wealth. Besides, you share it. Trevor and Lee are always so excited when they get your leftovers."

"Wait... why don't you get my leftovers? Sell them on eBay. I know Trevor does. I don't mind."

She swallowed a mouthful of wine, then placed the glass on the edge of the tub. "No more honesty juice for me."

"What? Tell me!"

The pain behind her eyes made my insides twist. "Charlie. Your buddies get your things. Everybody knows the pecking order. I can't rock up there and stick my hand in the Christmas basket before it's my turn."

"Pecking order?"

Bess sighed. "I'm never drinking wine again."

I turned to face her. I could see the effects of alcohol, and maybe tiredness, but she wasn't that drunk. There was a light behind her eyes. Fire. I peeled the wet strands of hair off her cheeks, tucking them behind her ears and held her face, forcing her to look at me. "I love that you're honest with me. I need that.

I can't say it doesn't hurt, because I like you, Bess. I appreciate everything you do. And I guess I hoped I could make you like me, too. That you wouldn't judge me based on my father or the company. That's not me. You have no idea how strongly I feel about that." I held back, swallowing any further comments.

I wanted to tell her. In that moment, I wanted to cry and beg for forgiveness, but fear nailed me in place. She had every right to think less of me, to disapprove or dismiss me. But her glossy eyes told me something else.

"I'm sorry I've thought bad things about you. It feels safer than letting myself feel... anything else." She sniffed, looking away.

I released her face, feeling the loss of that contact like the emptiness itself had a shape and texture. Aching and rough after her soft skin.

"What else?" I asked. "What else do you feel?"

I cringed at the neediness in my voice. This wasn't me. Yet it felt good to be this raw with someone. This was the feeling I'd been looking for. A connection. The absence of emptiness.

She dropped her shoulders and let out a moaning sigh. A sound of desperation. "This stupid pull." She buried her face in her hands.

My arms reached out to her, fumbling under the bubbling water, before my mind even caught up. Because that pull was a good thing. I could work with pull. There she was. My hands found the curve of her waist and drew her closer. Our legs bumped together as we turned to face each other on the awkward bench.

She dropped her hands and cracked her lips, looking at mine.

This time, I didn't catch her off guard. I waited for her to lower those guards, one by one. Finally, I found some words. "If you want to kiss me, you can."

Her lips curled and eyebrows lifted. "I *can*?"

"Yes. But it's your choice, Bess. Only kiss me if you want to. Not because you feel obligated to, or because you feel bad for me. I don't want that."

I could see the war behind her eyes as her gaze flicked between my eyes and lips, tongue peeking between her teeth. She understood.

I waited as patiently as I could, my stomach doing somersaults, my hands tightening around her waist. Her shin pressed against my thigh.

"You're good at it, right?" She bit her lip, staring at my mouth.

"I'll do my very best."

Did she really think I wouldn't bring my A game for her? I was already mentally between her legs, kissing like it was an Olympic sport. There were thoughts running through my head I had to lock up very tightly right now.

"Okay, Charlie. I blame the wine, and the moon and stars, and the fact that I haven't dated anyone in years."

I secured my hand around her lower back, nudging her a little closer. "*Nobody* would judge you."

"You're right. If anyone finds out I had a chance to kiss Charlie Wilde and didn't take it..." She raised an animated eyebrow, licking her lips.

She was teasing me, and it was working. My mind had run

away, waving a white flag. I kept my hands on her waist, but imagined them all over her body, my mouth on every inch of her skin. I desperately wanted to drag us both out of the tub and into a bed. Or any flat surface where I could explore her without drowning.

"You better take that chance then." My voice came out thick and throaty, giving me away. "So you won't be ridiculed."

I deserved to be ridiculed for how ridiculously turned on I was. I released my hand from her waist to adjust my crotch, and that's when she made her move. Her fingers curled behind my neck, and she pulled our mouths together.

Two gusts of hot breath crashed, then fire met fire. Bess had made up her mind and she kissed like she meant it, with ferocity and hunger. Her lips opened to invite my tongue and another surge of pleasure shot through me. There was only so much I could say. So much I could safely reveal. But the sheer intensity of that kiss left nothing between us. No air. No ambiguity or doubt.

Her desire took me by surprise and fueled my own. I let my hands travel underwater, feeling for her body, grazing her breasts. She arched her back, pushing against my hands, moaning into my mouth. We both pulled back to catch our breaths. "Too much?" she whispered.

"Not enough," I said, diving back in.

She tasted salty and sweet, or maybe it was the water. Her nails dug into my shoulders and she swung her leg over my lap to straddle me, bringing my hard-on against her crotch. Oh, sweet

Moses.

She kissed me again, moving back and forth over my cock, buoyed by the water. It was almost too much. What if I came in the tub? Another guttural moan rose from her throat, and I lifted my hips to get closer, grasping her tight ass. This felt better than anything I had imagined. I'd never felt a woman match my movements and energy like this. I always held myself back, staying in control. But with Bess, there was no control. No holding back. Dropping all pretense and caution, we rode the same wave, desperate to stay on this rollercoaster before it all disappeared like an optical illusion.

With superhuman strength, I stopped myself. "Can we continue this in the cabin?" I asked. Pleaded, really. It may have been my dick talking.

She panted against my lips. "I don't know. I might sober up any minute, and this is a terrible idea."

"The worst," I agreed. "I mean, we work together. You don't like me…"

"Charlie, you idiot. I like you too much. But you're the one thing I'm not supposed to like."

"Why not?"

"Because it's not safe." She drew back, eyes brimming with sadness.

I wanted to pull her back in, but she was slipping away, her gaze focusing with clarity. And even though I had a couple of beers in me, I couldn't pretend not to see it. If she didn't want me sober, she didn't really want me drunk, either. I couldn't be one more thing Bess regretted.

"I'd never hurt you," I said. I meant it, even if I doubted my control over these things. I could barely control my body.

But life had already hurt her. She'd been beaten over the head with it. What if I couldn't fix it, no matter how much I wanted to?

"I don't think you'd mean to," she said, sliding off my lap. "You don't mean to hurt anyone."

"But I do?"

"Everybody does. One day you'll die. You won't mean to, but it happens. And that will hurt someone. Many someones, probably."

I sighed. How had our evening turned this morbid? "Your husband died," I said.

"Yeah."

"Did he... mean to?" I swallowed, not sure if I was even ready to hear the answer. But if I wanted to really connect with her, be safe for her, I had to face everything she was holding onto.

She shook her head; her gaze lifting at the sky. "No. I don't think so. He was pulling away from us, sleeping at his brother's apartment. Not sleeping, really. Depressed. I don't think he wanted to die. But he was on too many medications. Doctors weren't paying attention. He wasn't paying attention. And I wasn't there. I should have been there, but I was too busy looking after a toddler, looking for a job, freelancing, trying to keep our condo. We worked on a start-up business that went bust. He took it even harder than me. I was the designer and admin, you know. Not the brains. And then suddenly, I was a 30-year-old widow and a single mom. I had to sell all this random stock, set up payment plans for the debt and move into a cheaper apartment. And then I found the job at Wilde."

"What? Right after?"

"A couple of months later. It was such a relief, even though I felt like I didn't fit in. I wasn't fun and never had money to do anything."

"Not fun? Bess, you were mourning. You probably still are."

She shrugged. "I was so grateful for the job. It was my lifeline. Still is. And you're my boss's son, so this is not okay. I'm risking everything."

I wanted to scream on her behalf. Of all the useless muppets my father employed, this was the woman he wanted to fire. The hardest-working, smartest and insanely beautiful creature with the saddest life story. Not that my father knew her story. She was just a number to him. He didn't believe in getting to know your staff. He didn't believe in sensitivity of any kind. Not like me.

Too soft for business. *Softie.* That was one of Dad's many nicknames for me.

I wanted to be honest with Bess. My insides ached for the words I needed to say, but I didn't want to hurt her. My drunken and horny brain ran around in circles, looking for a way to justify my actions. A way to fix things. Even if we lost this client, maybe there was a way for Bess to keep her job. Then I'd never have to tell her.

I also wanted to extend this moment. Relive the best kiss of my life.

I groaned. "Can I not be the boss's son for one night? I'm not carrying any business cards right now. Maybe we can pretend I'm someone else. Someone you met at this remote spa…" I gestured at the surroundings. "We're not at the office."

"Are you saying this doesn't count? Like, what happens in Vegas—"

"What happens in Cozy Creek, stays in Cozy Creek. That town's not real anyway, right?"

"It *looks* unreal." She gave me a little nod. A hint of a smile.

"So, none of this really happened," I concluded. "Let's go."

I got out of the pool, trying to ignore the partial still straining the boxer shorts I was using as swimming trunks. I'd have to take care of myself tonight, somehow, in a cabin with no walls or privacy.

We wrapped ourselves in our bathrobes and walked back in silence, Bess visibly shivering. I wanted to touch her, reassure her, but I feared anything I said would only make things worse. If I caught her again at a moment of weakness, she'd regret it that much more in the morning. I felt an inexplicable draw towards her, but I had to be patient. She'd already shared more of herself than I'd learned in the two years working with her. That was huge. I could only hope she didn't regret that kiss too much. I knew I didn't. I'd be playing it in my head in vivid detail tonight.

CHAPTER 17

Bess

Charlie opened the cabin door for me and I stepped in on shaky legs. I didn't even know if I was shivering from the cold or something else. Everything felt messed up. Upside down. What was I supposed to do now? He'd made it past my every layer of defense and awakened my body, reminding me of everything I lived without. It had felt so good. He had made me feel so good. Before this, I hadn't thought much about all that I'd lost. Like sex. And now the unfairness of that had punched me in the lungs. I missed it so much. So much that I'd only needed one giant glass of wine to climb on the one guy who was strictly off limits.

"I'm going to need a shower," Charlie announced, traipsing towards the bathroom. "A long shower." He cast me a guilty smile over his shoulder.

Why couldn't I be like that, I wondered. I collapsed into an armchair, staring at the half-empty wine bottle Charlie had left on the coffee table. If I only kept drinking, I might dull my prefrontal cortex for long enough to sleep with Charlie. But that much alcohol would dull my other senses, too, making the sex kind of pointless.

With or without wine, I felt too wired to go to sleep. I thought about my trusty vibrator, currently sitting at the bottom of my backpack, buried under everything else. How could I use it?

I settled into the remarkably cozy chair, rested my head against the soft headrest, and closed my eyes. It was like riding a slowly rotating carousel. I took a deep breath, enjoying the sensation. I heard the bathroom door, then the water running. With the wine still blurring my thoughts, it took me a moment to process Charlie's earlier words. What did he mean by a long shower? How long could it take?

Finally, my addled brain connected the dots and I sat up, my heart pounding. Could it be possible? Was Charlie taking care of himself in a see-through bathroom, a few feet away from me? I listened to the sound of running water, thinking of the way he'd smiled at me. The way he'd elongated the word 'long', and our previous activities.

Of course. Charlie wasn't shy. If he wanted something, he went for it. Why would this be any different?

Sure, this was partly my fault. I'd climbed on his lap and rocked against that hard-on. Could I really blame him for masturbating in the shower? Somehow, having that three-quarter frosted glass as a bathroom wall made things so much more awkward. I couldn't exactly pretend I didn't know what was happening. If I stood up, I'd see his head behind the two sheets of glass, right above the edge of the privacy screen.

I wasn't stupid enough to stand up, was I? The alcohol in my bloodstream loudly disagreed and I pushed myself up from the chair.

There he was, clear as day. Eyes closed, head tilted back, mouth ajar, with water running down his well-formed chest. The blurry image forming behind the privacy sticker gave my imagination everything it needed. Gasping for breath, I stumbled over to the kitchenette, turning on the coffee machine.

I didn't drink coffee at night. I rarely ate, either, to avoid the pain of not burping, but I had to distract myself. I wasn't embarrassed, I insisted. There was nothing embarrassing about pleasure, but the way he embraced it, like he embraced every good thing in life, made me sad for myself.

Why couldn't I kick back and enjoy? Why did I have to be drunk to act on an impulse? And as soon as the effect of alcohol wore off, my brain turned on, keeping those impulses well and truly in check.

My phone pinged and I lunged for it, desperate for distraction.

Teresa: How's it going over there? There's a weird vibe at the office. No sign of Broken Arrow. Guess he's not turning up at all anymore. Trevor is acting odd. Call me!

I stared at the phone, contemplating on what to say. I couldn't risk calling. Charlie could hear me. And if Teresa found out Charlie was here with me, there was a chance rumors would start circulating. Could I trust her?

> **Bess:** All good. Rubie Ridge is beautiful. Food is divine. Lots of art exercises and rich people in expensive clothes having a leisurely time. I miss Celia, though.

> **Teresa:** I think George had a conference up there. Sounds like his kind of crowd. Try to enjoy!

My insides twisted. I needed a confidante, and Teresa was the closest thing to a friend I had. I couldn't keep her completely in the dark.

> **Bess:** Can you keep a secret?

> **Teresa:** Cross my heart and hope to die.

> **Bess:** Charlie is here. We're sharing a cabin because it was the only one available.

I hit 'send' and stopped breathing, watching the three dots dancing on the screen.

> **Teresa:** Whaaaaaat??? CALL ME NOW!

> **Bess:** I can't. He's in the shower. It's open plan, he'll hear everything.

> **Teresa:** Open plan? You're sleeping in the same room? SAME BED?

> **Bess:** I'm in the loft.

Teresa: Why is he there? Is he putting the moves on you? Are you okay?

Bess: I'm fine. It's a bit weird. I'll tell you later.

Teresa: I have so many questions. Call me as soon as you can, okay? Until then, I'll be on tenterhooks, unable to eat or sleep. So, make it soon.

I could only hope she was exaggerating. Teresa had a flair for drama.

Bess: I promise.

My mind going around in circles, I turned on the coffeemaker. It resembled the one in the office, and my hands worked on auto-pilot, making a batch of coffee for the entire production team. Oops.

Well, it had a thermos pot so maybe it would keep for a while. I'd drink the rest cold the next morning, I decided. I counted three complimentary coffee bags. Could I swipe one for home? It'd last me at least a week.

When had I turned into this desperate person with a scarcity mindset? I'd learned about these things. I'd become poor later in life, after being educated, working, and earning decent money. With Jack still working for a shipping company and me freelancing, with no kids to feed, we'd been doing fine. Buying what we wanted. Traveling. Upgrading our phones.

Now, the fear of falling off that metaphorical cliff kept me moving and dictated my decisions. Along the way, I'd stopped enjoying things, even when they were free. Instead, I grasped at everything in desperation. I wanted to try every food they served at this place, or better yet, store it in my cheeks like a chipmunk. My mind screamed, 'Take it! Store it!' but did I enjoy it? I was too worried about running out, being back in that place of panic. Noticing was the first step, right? I could turn things around and make an effort to welcome good things and enjoyment, and try to not worry about the future, if only for a few days.

I took my fresh coffee and tiptoed upstairs, carefully listening to the sound of running water. Charlie was delivering on his promise of a long shower. Had he already orgasmed and was now shampooing his hair? I really needed to stop picturing it.

As I sat on the edge of the sofa bed, the sound of water cut off and the door creaked.

"Do you need a shower?" He called from downstairs.

I was still in my damp swimsuit, wrapped up in the bulky bathrobe. That spa pool probably wasn't the cleanest. "Um… maybe. Sure." I returned downstairs with my coffee and fetched my towel. "I made coffee if you want some."

"Thanks." Charlie stood in front of me, a towel wrapped around his waist.

My eyes dipped to his crotch without my permission, taking in the slight bulge. Did he still have a hard-on? How was it possible?

I left my coffee on its namesake table and hurried to the bathroom, throwing one quick glance over my shoulder. I wasn't even sure why, maybe to memorize the sight of him in a towel, but he took it as hesitation.

"Don't worry. I rinsed the tiles."

Heat engulfed my cheeks like a sudden flame. "Oh, my God Charlie! You don't have to be that graphic."

He raised his brows, the picture of innocence. "I mean there shouldn't be any hair or soap or anything. I know it's awkward to share a bathroom with a guy."

"Ah, okay. Thanks," I said in a strangled voice, hoping the bathroom door would lead me to an alternate dimension, free of all the Charlies of the world.

But before I could step through the portal, he wedged himself between me and the door. "I'm just messing with you, Bess. I came all over that shower cubicle," he whispered, "thinking of you."

His hot breath mixed with mine, creating a whirlpool of confusion. I so wanted to be someone else, someone who seized the moment and ripped that towel off his sculpted body.

"I'm glad I could help," I whispered back. "But didn't we agree to pretend nothing happened?"

He raised his right hand like swearing an oath. "Nothing happened between us. But I can still be turned on by you, right? I can't rip out my eyes. Every new thing I learn about you... I can't help it, Bess. You're an enigma. A sexy enigma."

I felt so warm all over that I could barely stand. I didn't have to, though. My body had already mastered gravity and was floating an inch off the floor. My hands twitched in their frantic need to touch him. To be touched. But as I launched into a movement, he stepped away, a sparkling smile on his face. "Enjoy the shower."

I stepped into the bathroom, heaving in deep breaths. I'd never be able to resist Charlie. I was doomed.

CHAPTER 18

Bess

Later that night, I lay in bed, listening to his breathing. When I finally convinced myself he was asleep, I reached into my bag and grabbed the vibrator. It was fairly quiet, but I still hid under every bit of blanket I could find, hoping he wouldn't wake up to the sound. I kept the toy at the lowest setting and slid it where I needed it, rocking against the buzzing piece of silicone. It wasn't the fanciest model, but it would have to do.

The vibration worked its magic. My mind returned to our kiss in the hot tub, and it didn't take me long to reach the tipping point —the moment reality faded to the corners of my mind. The sweet laps of pleasure turned into waves, building up. It was hot under the blankets, but I didn't mind. I felt safe, hiding from the world, letting myself feel everything I couldn't with him.

Charlie fucking Wilde. I hated him. I wanted him. I couldn't have him. My hips undulated without conscious thought, working against the hot pink wand and its little suction head. I was close, teetering right at the edge. I heard a soft moan and realized it was coming from me. Was I making noise?

He's asleep, I told myself, peeling off the blankets to come up for air. To my horror, I could still hear the buzzing of the vibrator, even through the layers of blanket. In the absolute silence of the cabin, the sound seemed to reverberate and echo off the high ceiling. I listened for any other sounds; any indication Charlie might have been awake. But before I noticed anything else, I heard the most horrifying sound of all. Silence. The battery had died.

When had I even last used the thing? When had I charged it? I couldn't remember, which explained a lot. I threw myself back against the pillow, panting. My entire body throbbed with frustration.

"Can I help?"

His gravelly voice shot through me like lightning. I sat up, clutching the covers.

He stood at the top of the stairs, leaning on the banister.

"Charlie." I was still panting. "What are you doing here?"

"Missing out."

"But we decided…"

"Yeah. I was thinking this could also be something that never happened. In case you need a hand or—"

My body screamed yes while my brain chased its tail, unable to form a coherent thought. "You heard me," I said dumbly.

"Only because I was listening. Intently." He sat on the edge of the bed. "We don't have to do anything, but this is the hottest thing I've ever heard. Ever. So please, continue."

"I ran out of battery," I said, finally closing my dry mouth. "So the show's over, I guess."

I felt grateful for the darkness that concealed my face, but I couldn't stop the flush of embarrassment that engulfed me. He'd heard me. He'd listened to me pleasure myself. It was almost too much to process, yet my body throbbed, disappointed. Unsatisfied. Asking for more.

"Oh, no. So, you do need a hand." He lay down next to me, peeling off the blankets until his fingers grazed my belly. Warm fingers that woke up every nerve on my skin.

"What are you doing?" I asked, my voice so throaty I hardly recognized it as my own.

"I'm not battery-operated, but I do a pretty good job, I promise."

I pulled the covers to my chin, wishing I could disappear. But my body was at odds with my embarrassed mind, refusing to push his hand away.

"Do you want me to stop?" he asked.

"No," I choked out. "But I can't ask you to..."

His fingers slid a little lower, touching the edge of my panties. "Why not? You do things for me all the time." I heard the smile in his voice, but also thickness, like his throat was as sticky as mine.

"This is not some office errand, Charlie."

"No. Because I don't think you've ever enjoyed the errands you run for me like I'd enjoy this."

He sounded out of breath, his voice thick with need, which relaxed me a little. "Come on, Bess. Let me help."

He dragged his fingers along the edge of my panties, and I shivered from head to toe. When did I ever really enjoy myself? Could I let him do this for me? I wanted to touch him, to confirm he really was into this, that I wasn't imagining things. But that's when he shifted closer, and I felt his erection against my hip. A sudden, hard poke that awakened a whole new craving. I wanted him. I needed him. Charlie held still, waiting for my final answer.

I ran my hand down his chest. "So, this never happened?"

"I'm not even here." He pulled back before I reached his crotch but his fingers traced a fiery trail down my stomach, slipping under my panties, reaching the wetness between my legs. He groaned. "Oh, my God, Bess."

He touched me lightly, circling and teasing. But I was too far gone and bucked against his hand, desperate for friction. For a moment, he held back, then matched his movement to mine, stroking my achingly swollen clit. I was no longer holding back my moans. All I could think about was that sensation, rolling and quaking through me, building up until the waves no longer crashed ashore. They drowned me. I came against his hand, letting out a strange, choked cry. The waves of pleasure carried me, taking their time, relaxing every muscle.

As the sweet throbbing gradually settled, I risked a glance at him. "Oh, God. I needed that."

"Me too," he rasped. "Thank you for letting me... not be here."

I sighed. How could I pretend that never happened? "Your turn," I said, again reaching for him under the covers. It was only fair.

But he pulled away, leaving my hand grasping for air.

CHAPTER 19

Charlie

I made it out of her reach, just in time. My self-restraint had never been tested like this. Seeing Bess lose control was hands down the hottest thing I'd ever witnessed.

Forbidden things were always the hottest, weren't they? But there was also something about her... something so tightly-wound that I desperately wanted to see it unravel. Or even feel it, in the darkness. Being able to witness her pleasure, even take a small part in it, felt like a miracle.

"Come on, Charlie. Let me..." Her finger grazed my thigh, voice still throaty and breathless, and it nearly dragged me down.

But I couldn't take what she was offering. Not like this. Not when I hadn't been honest. Definitely not before I had some good news to balance out the bad. I'd turn things around, undo the mess, and she'd never need to know. Or I'd find her a better job.

I pushed her hand away. "I already took care of myself in the shower."

It was true, but obviously bullshit, since I was so hard I'd probably come again in two minutes.

She launched at me, unexpectedly, her fingers closing around my rock-hard cock. "I don't think you did a very good job."

I wanted to pin her against the stupid sofa bed and drive into her until I forgot my own name. I held my breath, riding the wave of overwhelming desire. For a moment I could think of nothing else. But underneath it, a small, insistent voice I seemed to have developed, one that piped up at the most inconvenient times, said something about how I always took what I wanted. How I immediately ordered every single thing I fancied, with expedited delivery. I was a slave to my impulses, already eating the lowest hanging fruit when others fetched a ladder to reach a little higher.

This is why you don't have the great thing. You take every good thing at every opportunity. Great things take patience. Build-up.

I wanted more than the good and the okay. If I wanted it with Bess, I had to be patient. I'd thought our working relationship as a good one, but I was confusing good with convenient. Our relationship had always been one-sided: I told her what I wanted and she delivered. I had to change the dynamic.

Gathering all of my willpower and some I didn't have, I rolled away from her and off the bed. "Don't worry about me. Tonight is about you, Bess. I don't want you to take care of anyone else, okay?"

"Wha… why?" Her voice sounded wobbly like she was close to tears. "Do you not want me?"

I sat back down on the bed, flicking on her night light. Its blue glass shade cast a giant blue ring on the sloping ceiling. Even in the blue light, she looked flushed. Her gaze was unfocused, hair mussed. She'd never been more beautiful.

"I've never wanted anyone as much as I want you right now. But I think tonight should be about you."

"I don't understand." Her lower lip trembled, adorably hurt and sexy. The blue light painted the edge of her face, illuminating her cheekbones.

"I don't want you to do anything with me because you feel like you should. Because you feel… responsible."

She made a small noise of disagreement. "But what if I want to?"

"If you come to me and you want to sleep with me because you want to *be* with me, I'm in. But only if you want more than sex."

I didn't even realize how true those words were before they raced out of my mouth. This is what I needed—Bess with me. I'd be allowed to take care of her. To get involved.

"What?" Her green eyes flashed like jewels catching the light, offset by the flaming red of her hair. Like a fucking goddess.

My stomach somersaulted. Was I ready for this? Someone with this much substance? A real relationship?

"You heard me," I said, my voice sticking to my throat.

Her eyebrows gathered in a slight frown. "But... you sleep around all the time! It doesn't mean anything."

"How do you know who I sleep with?"

She met my gaze without flinching. "Teresa said you leave every party with a different woman."

"I have friends. I entertain people. I date. But I don't sleep with every woman. I haven't slept with anyone in... I don't know. A couple of months? And even that was a one-off after a dry spell. I don't want meaningless sex. I'm thirty-five. I want something real."

"Really?" She sounded like she didn't believe me.

I couldn't blame her. I could imagine what my life must have looked like from the outside. But a lot of it was for show. I entertained the daughters of my father's business partners. I wined and dined clients. Some of them were female and attractive. Some came onto me. But I found myself restless and ended the evening quickly if there wasn't much chemistry. I was searching for something, but always left wanting.

"Is it really that unbelievable that I'd want something meaningful that's also incredibly hot?"

"Have you tried ordering it from Kickstarter? I heard it's where you can find these *unbelievable* things—"

"Ha ha. What's wrong with having high expectations? People who don't aim higher end up settling for mediocre crap."

"People like me?"

Ouch.

"No. Why would you think that?"

She rolled onto her back, staring at the ceiling. Everything in the room felt blue. "I don't have high expectations. Sometimes it's easier to have no expectations."

I stretched out next to her, trying to switch my brain onto a different gear. Because I needed to hear this. I needed to find out more about her, right now when her mind was wandering, eyes soft and lips ready to spill. But I didn't want to corner her. I wanted to give her space. In a way, it was easier to talk lying side by side, not seeing each other's eyes.

I waited, breathing as silently as I could, until she spoke again. "I don't mean I'd take just anyone. I'd much rather have nothing. No one. I know lightning doesn't strike twice and I've already had a love story. I don't expect another one."

"What if you're the tallest tree, up on a hill?"

"Huh?"

"Then you're basically a lightning rod."

She laughed softly. "Well, then my tired metaphor falls apart, doesn't it? But it doesn't mean I'm going to find love again."

"Not with that attitude."

"Are you saying my defeatist whining isn't sexy?" She buried her face in her hand, shaking from laughter.

"I'm saying, you don't date, so how would you ever meet anyone? How would you even give anyone a chance?"

She turned her head and cracked her fingers to peek at me. "Dating means eating in restaurants."

"I'd never make my date pay."

"But I would have to insist that we split the bill. You know how it is... and then there's a good chance the guy won't fight me on it. Not in this economy."

"Then date me," I blurted. "If nothing else, you'll get a free meal and remember what it's like to go out."

"You mean, for practice?"

"Uh huh," I said, trying to keep my tone light. Because I didn't want her to practice. Not for anyone else.

Her eyes turned serious again. "You know this... Whatever this is..." her finger wiggled between us. "It can't go on after this week. Not at the office."

"Why not?"

Her eyes widened in horror. "I... couldn't risk it."

"You think you'll get fired if you date the boss's son?"

If only she knew.

Her mouth twisted in hesitation. I had a strange feeling. An inkling. This wasn't just about her fear of losing her job. "You're worried about what your team would think, right? Because we're not the same..."

I'd picked up on the hints, but always brushed it aside. We were all in the same boat, working for the same company. But we weren't the same. Bess's reaction painted a picture I barely wanted to acknowledge, but part of me yearned for the truth. "Come on, Bess. You don't have to coddle me. You guys talk about me behind my back, right?"

She gave a teeny, tiny nod, looking away. "It's not that bad. Everybody likes you. But you're in a different league. Like a celebrity."

"Celebrity?"

"Yeah. So people are a little awestruck and more than a little jealous."

I cringed at the needy jolt in my chest that made me lean closer, looking for eye contact. "What do they say? Give me the dirt."

She buried her face in the pillow. "No."

"Come on! You're my only ally. No names, just tell me what they say."

I had a reason, I insisted to myself. I needed to bridge the gap between my world and hers.

"What about Trevor and Lee? Don't they keep you updated?"

"They don't get the dirt, either. Do they?" I argued, suddenly sickened by the idea that my closest friends would keep things from me.

"No, I don't think so. They're like your henchmen."

"But you...you're on the production floor. You hear everything."

The realization hit me. My dad was an awful boss. Everyone hated him. Was I awful by association? Did everyone else regard us as one and the same? If Bess heard people talk shit about me every day, no wonder she didn't want to date me. "Please tell me! Tell me what they say or I'll—"

"Charlie's Angels." She held up her hand, alarmed. "That's what they call Trevor and Lee."

"Charlie's Angels." I chuckled. "That's pretty good. But that's not all, is it?"

"No," she said in a small voice, but I saw the corner of her mouth lift.

"If you tell me... you can ask me anything. Anything at all, and I'll give you an honest answer." I could only hope that she didn't ask about her job.

She turned her head a couple of degrees, eyes flashing with interest. So, there was something she wanted to know.

"They call your office Toys'R'Us. And you... I've heard Willy Wonka and... His Highness. Charlie and the Gadget Factory." She winced. "I don't say that, though."

"What do you say?"

I rolled onto my side and after a moment, she did the same, propping her elbow against the bed. Face to face. I felt her warm breath mixing with mine. Her cheeks turned the cutest shade of pink. "Oh, Charlie."

"Come on. Tell me."

"No. That's what I say to myself at work, 'Oh, Charlie'."

"Oh, Charlie," I repeated like a moron. "What does that mean?"

"It's my way of making sense of you. Your toys. Your life. It's so foreign, and I don't want to feel the jealousy or resentment. So, I say to myself, 'Oh, Charlie!'"

The way she breathed out the words sounded almost like a term of endearment. "You say it like I'm a child."

She frowned. "I don't think of you as a child. More like a phenomenon. Something wondrous I can't begin to understand."

"Like... ghosts and goblins? Or astrophysics?"

"Yeah. Like a faraway galaxy." She smiled.

"You're shitting me, right? No way you think of me like that."

Her breath came out in short gasps. "Oh, Charlie. I think of you way too much."

I brushed my thumb down her warm cheek, enjoying the fragile feeling blooming somewhere in my chest, overshadowing my earlier arousal. She was here, opening up to me. Allowing me to see her. "Bess. I don't deserve you. You know how much I appreciate you, right? You know how amazing I think you are."

Her mouth twitched. "I always thought you were exaggerating when you praised my work. You're the real star. You're the creative."

I frowned. Exaggerating? If anything, I'd been trying to keep my silly work crush under wraps. Stay professional. "Bess, I couldn't do what I do without you."

"I thought you were just saying it. You know, like celebrities tell their fans 'you're the real stars!'"

"You think I'm that shallow?" I swallowed my hurt.

Her eyes softened. "It's not that you've ever been shallow, but I've been cynical. Some things you say are so over-the-top I didn't think you could possibly mean them."

There was so much more I wanted to say that my gut churned. Maybe I was over-the-top, but I wasn't fake.

"I'm an idiot, but I mean what I say. I don't talk about people behind their back, either. It's not right."

She sighed. "Then you're a better person than any of us."

"I'm really not," I answered quickly. But her words kept bugging me, and I finally had to ask. "What else do they say about me?"

CHAPTER 20

Bess

I drew a shuddery breath as my eyes roamed the cabin ceiling. This was getting ridiculous. What was he trying to squeeze out of me?

Should I tell him Boris referred to him as Willy Wanker? Or start dropping Teresa's endless selection of nicknames, mostly to do with his attendance—Dr Doo Little, Beer-o-clock, KitKat and of course her favorite, Broken Arrow, because, although useless, he couldn't be fired. Teresa could be a bit harsh.

This wasn't fair. But I wanted my one honest question, even if I didn't yet know what it was. Charlie was a mystery and deep down, I was desperately curious. If I had a chance to find out more about that weird, distant galaxy, I would. For Teresa's sake. And mine.

"Some people call you Mini Fridge."

"I've heard that one. Trevor uses it, too." He rolled his eyes.

"Do you know why, though?" I bit my lip, wondering if he knew. Wondering how he'd take it.

He looked clueless. "Because I have a mini fridge in my office."

I had to force out the words. "Because you're cooler than Fonzie and only there for the beers."

His mouth hung open. "Wow. Okay. Wow. Um…"

This was a horrible mistake.

"It's a stupid joke," I added quickly.

His expression thawed a bit. "Well, it's funny. And pretty obvious. I should have figured that out."

"People are just jealous."

A self-deprecating smile hovered on his lips. "Do you think I'm only there for the beers?"

"No. I know you don't work the same hours, but you do work. I deal with the evidence of your creative process every day."

Nobody could fill the pasteboards with that much junk without putting in some hours. The sheer number of links in Charlie's files told me all I needed to know. And then there were Rhonda's stories of those late nights.

"Bess cleans my mess," he muttered.

"What?"

"That's how I learned your name. I use these silly mnemonic devices. I think it's important to know everyone's names, but I'm so bad at it."

"You don't have horrible nicknames for anyone? Even me?"

He seemed surprised. "No."

"That wasn't my honest question, though. It doesn't count, right? Please!"

A smile warmed his face. "Fine. You can have another. Even though that was an honest answer."

"Do you really think I'd waste my one chance on a yes/no question?"

His smile widened and he laid his head on the pillow, keeping his eyes on me. Lying there, leaning on my elbow, with only a few inches between us, felt strangely intimate. More intimate than him touching me, even though that made no sense.

"You know they call me Buzzkill, right?"

"No! Who does? Why?" He seemed so genuinely upset on my behalf I didn't know whether to laugh or cry.

"Bess Killian, Buzzkill. Now, *that* one's obvious. I... tend to be the first one to get back to work. Last one to leave. First one to remind everyone about the deadlines and ruin their fun." I lifted a shoulder.

"But they respect you. I can tell."

"Boris once told me I'm intimidating."

His eyes had a shine to them. "No. I think you have integrity. You don't blindly follow the herd."

When the herd was bashing a funny-looking temp or sneaking out half an hour early for drinks, how could I follow? And when the guys made snide comments behind Charlie's back, it never sat right with me. Because I saw his brilliance. I saw how much he cared.

"I don't agree with them on everything." I could feel the blush gathering strength on my face. "But I do think you're cooler than Fonzie."

"Does that mean I'm a regular-sized fridge? Good for more than just holding a few beers?"

I paused for a moment, thinking. "No, you're a chest freezer."

"Because I... wait, I can get this." Charlie held up a hand, his gaze pinned at the ceiling. "Because I'm full of peas... and love, and have a wide chest?"

"No. Because there's always room for more stuff you buy on a whim."

"I don't buy that much stuff," he argued, but couldn't hide his smile.

"No. Many people who work for large retailers buy way more."

"I just get excited when I find a new innovation. Like that hammock. I can't wait to try it outside."

"It's October. Why would you buy something like that towards winter?"

"That's the innovation!" Charlie's eyes shone. "It's made of the materials they used for astronauts. You can survive in it in freezing temperatures."

"When would you ever need to survive in freezing temperatures? Your office has central heating. Unless you live in a tent behind the building?"

"Wouldn't that be a shocking reversal of expectations?" He laughed. "No, I live in Belcaro."

Of course, he did.

"I sometimes drive through your neighborhood, even though it's not really on my way," I confessed.

"Why?"

"I get tired of everything falling apart. Feeling like nobody cares. I know it's not that. People are busy surviving so when a trash can falls over or when there's crime or vandalism... it takes a while for anyone to react. We close our eyes and ignore stuff, as long as we can. But sometimes, I feel that getting to me, and I need to see places that people are looking after. So we drive that way and soak in the beauty and order of it. Celia loves pointing out the pretty houses. She counts the flowerpots."

And then she asks 'Can we move here, Mommy? Can we live in that house?' and my heart breaks, I thought. I swallowed, struggling to hold on to my smile.

Charlie didn't struggle. The smile that lit up his face made my insides ache. "She's adorable."

I thought of him showing Celia his Japanese robot. How excited she'd been, not just over the silly gadget, but over Charlie's undivided attention and encouragement. I'd been grateful for that moment—seeing my daughter mesmerized by something she'd never come across otherwise. Charlie was a ticket to a whole new world for both of us.

I did what every mother does, smiled and nodded. Because my child was adorable, obviously.

Letting out a deep sigh, Charlie rolled onto his back. "So, what's your question, Bess?"

What could I ask him? There was a truth to who he was, hiding somewhere underneath those smiles, elusive as a reflection on water. How could I bring it out? What did I want to know?

Deep in thought, I didn't realize Charlie had fallen asleep until I felt him jerk against the bed and a deep breath, almost a snore, escaped his mouth. I turned to look at him, to study his face when he couldn't stare back with those intense crystal blues. He looked so peaceful, almost like he was still smiling. If he thought I was an enigma, so was he.

I lay down on my back, debating my choices. I could wake him up and ask him to return to his own bed, or I could sneak out and sleep downstairs in his bed. Would he mind? And then there was, of course, the nerve-wracking option of sleeping here, right next to him. What would he think of me if I did that? Could I even fall asleep with a man next to me? I hadn't done that in such a long time.

But before I could make up my mind to get up, Charlie rolled over, placing his hand on my stomach, mumbling something. I had to turn my head to check he was still asleep. It seemed so.

The warmth of his touch radiated through me, relaxing my muscles. I hadn't felt like this in a long time. Perfectly safe. Grounded. I didn't want to move. I lay there, a furry mess of thoughts circling my brain, gradually surrendering to the weight of his touch, until I fell asleep.

CHAPTER 21

Charlie

I woke up to something pounding against the cabin roof. Something too hard and tinny to be rain. I turned over, letting sleep slowly evaporate as my mind processed the odd sound. Hail. It had to be hailing. But as my other senses awakened, I noticed something more important. A pair of perfect breasts bursting out of a loose T-shirt, so close to my nose that I might as well have been nuzzling them. Maybe I had. My arm was resting on something soft and round. Bess's thigh. At this point, it could have been raining rodents outside, and it wouldn't have cracked the top ten on the list of things I cared about.

Bess stirred and a niggling thought surfaced.

I'd slept in her bed, uninvited. As the message reached my brain, I softly lifted my hand. I didn't want her to wake up and freak out, but given the racket outside, she was going to. I needed to act quickly.

I took a deep breath and attempted to roll to the edge of the bed. Like an athlete, I visualized the entire series of moves—the smooth roll, swinging my legs over the edge, my bare feet softly landing on the polished wood floor, silently carrying me down the stairs.

Come on, Charlie, you can do this!

But I hadn't accounted for the blanket. Part of it was still tucked under my body, and Bess must have rolled herself inside it like a burrito. As I yanked it, she followed, slamming against my back.

She yelped and I cursed, untangling the blanket burrito from around my legs.

"Sorry. I didn't mean to—"

"What's happening?" Her voice was muffled.

"Not me motorboating you all night, that's for sure." I was out from under the blanket now, sitting on the edge of the bed like a night nurse. "Because I respect boundaries. Consent's my middle name. No, actually it's Vincent. But I—"

"What?" Her head popped up from behind the crumpled blanket, eyes blurry from sleep, hair sticking out on the side.

"I definitely didn't sleep next to you, drooling and groping your ass all night. I'm pretty sure that never happened. Just like a few other things that never happened last night." I flashed her a grin that hopefully conveyed sincerity, as well as the sort of boyish charm that usually got me out of trouble.

She blinked twice and her mouth tugged a little. "I mean, what's that racket?" I could barely hear her over the sound of hail. It made me think of fireworks.

"It's hailing, I think. Steel roofs are loud."

She rolled onto her back, staring at the ceiling. "That almost sounds like gunshots."

How bad was her neighborhood for that to be her first thought?

I adjusted my underwear. I was sporting such prominent morning wood it was probably best to wait a while before getting up. But I couldn't linger. She was sexy as hell and if I wanted to stick to my earlier promise and not touch her, I had to create some space between us.

"I could use some breakfast," she said. "Do you think we can make it to the cafeteria without getting holes in our skulls?"

"It won't last long," I assured her, checking my watch. "It's not even breakfast time yet. Go back to sleep for ten minutes."

"How can anyone sleep in this noise?" She sat up.

"Fair enough."

I adjusted my crotch, psyching myself to get up. Why did I feel so nervous? This wasn't a big deal.

Last night, we'd fooled around, and I'd been confident enough she was into me. Now, I wasn't so sure. I'd asked for more. I'd asked for commitment, something I'd never asked for before, and that one move had thrown me completely off my game.

Was this how it felt like to desperately pine for someone? Was this how pathetic I had to be? Suddenly, even the act of standing up and letting her witness my hard-on, made me a little seasick.

She appeared next to me, placing her feet on the floor, standing up and adjusting the neckline of her shirt, cheeks pink. "Was I spilling out of this?"

"A little." I swallowed.

I'd never wanted to touch anything so badly.

"Well, it's been a long time since I was poked by a hard-on so I can't blame the ladies for going out on the balcony." She pulled a face, brushing the side of her breast.

"What are you doing to me?" I groaned, finally standing up.

It was a good thing I bought quality underwear. Lesser material would have given in already.

"Trying to lighten the mood, I guess." She skipped downstairs and I followed. "I'm still a bit embarrassed over last night."

I caught up with her at the bathroom door. "*You*? You're embarrassed?"

She turned around, leaning against the doorframe. Those cheeks burned bright fuchsia. "Well, yeah. We can pretend it didn't happen, but I don't think I can ever wipe that from my brain. Ever."

"Do you want to?" My voice cracked. "I've already replayed it ten times since waking up because I never want to forget."

"We only just woke up."

I tilted my head and shrugged. What could I say? The sounds she'd made in the darkness, the way she'd rocked against my fingers... those moments now owned the hard drive of my brain. If Google One ever extended their services to preserving sexual memories, I'd sign up for life.

"Why would *you* be embarrassed?" she asked, her voice soft as a whisper.

I stepped closer. "I'm trying not to mess this up," I answered honestly, my heart beating so hard I feared cardiac arrest. Was this how it felt to fall for someone? Dear Lord. This was awful. If I'd been cooler than Fonzie before, that was no longer a problem.

Her eyebrows drew together. "We should have never... I don't know how I'll face you in the office but we'll figure it out, right?"

She looked up at me, so genuinely worried that my heart lurched, crashing into my stomach.

"We'll figure it out," I promised. "But please, don't write me off. I meant what I said. I want to... date you."

She wrapped her arms around my neck, making my heart skip several beats. "I'm yours this week. Going back to work is going to be awkward, no matter what. So, let's not think about that." She reached on her tippy toes to place a kiss on my lips.

It was a gentle gesture and could have turned out that way, had my instincts not taken over. Within seconds, I had her pinned against the door as our mouths crashed together. Like waves against the rocks, turning waters into spraying foam. I craved her like my next breath.

I felt her body melt against mine, pliable, soft, and tense at the same time. I wanted to make her moan so loudly we drowned out the battering of hail. But as soon as I came up for air, my stupid heart spilled words that stood in my own way.

"I want us, Bess. You and me."

She tensed, drawing away. Her lips looked raw and swollen,

eyes unfocused. But her words were clear.

"I've loved these moments with you, but there's no us, Charlie. The only us in my life is me and my daughter."

I nodded, taking a step back. I had to accept it. I couldn't force my way in. Even if she'd taken that first tiny step to kiss me. She hadn't offered me what I asked. Not even one date. She'd offered me a few days, in secret. And that had been enough for me to break my own promise. I was the worst.

Bess gave me an apologetic smile and slipped behind the bathroom door. I threw myself on the cold, messy bed I hadn't slept in, expelling a sigh. It had finally happened. I'd found a woman who made me lose my mind and I couldn't have her.

CHAPTER 22

Bess

I stared into the bathroom mirror, paralyzed. Seeing that look in Charlie's eyes made everything inside me swirl like a sickening soup of pain, pleasure, and endless doubt.

I didn't doubt his sincerity, but I doubted everything else. Because I wasn't an uncomplicated single woman. I was shattered, disillusioned, and terrified to my core. Charlie had no idea.

It was probably a blessing in disguise that he'd gotten into his head he wanted more and wouldn't sleep with me on a casual basis. Maybe that would slow our descent down this slippery slope. Whichever way things played out, I'd get hurt. I could already feel the inevitable end, waiting for me on the other side of this. Waiting with a whip in its hand.

I sniffed, hoping Charlie couldn't hear me. The sound of hail outside had lessened, turning into regular rain. I brushed my teeth and washed my face, pulling deep breaths to calm myself. Hairbrush. Partially dried-out concealer. Mascara that produced clumps if you tried more than one coat. I looked as sad and defeated as I felt. What did he even see in me?

When I stepped out of the bathroom, I found Charlie by the door, dressed in jeans and a grey sweater. "See you in the cafeteria?"

He waved his hand, disappearing through the doorway. The hurt in his voice made my chest feel tight. This wasn't good. I didn't want to hurt him. I'd still have to work with him.

Teresa. I needed to talk to her. She'd be at work already, I realized.

"Can you talk?" I asked when she picked up.

"Hang on a minute." I heard rustling and footsteps. After a moment, her voice returned with an echo. "I'm in the bathroom. Tell me everything."

"This can't leak to anyone else at the office, okay? I'd die."

"Of course not."

"I know you don't exactly like Charlie, so you probably won't approve, but—"

"Bess! If you're telling me you're finally getting some, I don't even care. I'm happy for you. For all his faults, Charlie is hot and single. Hopefully not terrible in bed." Her voice rose like it was a question.

"No! He's... good. But I know we shouldn't get involved. It's a train wreck. I have a child. I have responsibilities. You know I'm not financially stable, right? I need to get my life on track before I can even dream about having a relationship with someone."

"Is he after a relationship, though? We're talking about Charlie here."

"Um... he says so but—"

"This is Charlie. We know Charlie." Teresa's voice carried a heavy dose of conviction. "The only child who's never been denied anything in his whole life. If you want to be his new toy, go for it. Get yours. But I wouldn't expect too much going forward."

My mouth twisted. "Maybe that's a good thing? I'm not ready for anything."

"Then ride that bronco. Have fun. Use protection."

I let out a nervous chuckle. "Would you think less of me if I told you I already... kind of..." I swallowed a gulp of air. That would hurt later.

"Good for you! I hope he treated you right?"

"He did. It was all for me, to be honest. He didn't even... you know."

Teresa fell silent. I heard the toilet flush, then the tap being turned on. Had she done her business during our conversation? After a moment, she came back on. "You're telling me Charlie took care of you and walked away?"

"Well, I'm pretty sure he took care of himself in the shower. And he didn't exactly walk away. We talked and fell asleep. I think we spooned." I winced. "And now things are weird between us."

"Okay. Are you sure you're talking about Charlie Wilde? The

Mini Fridge?"

"I know! It's odd, isn't it? Do you think it's an act?"

"He's very clever. He can talk anyone into buying anything."

I nodded, my mouth dry. "He seems so sincere. I feel like I've misjudged him."

"That's how brilliant he is."

I swallowed a lump and my stubborn heart argued back. "But why would he lie to me? I mean, I'm not asking for commitment. I would have slept with him. He's the one acting weird, saying he wants to date me and now he's all hurt because I can't see this going anywhere. It can't, right?"

"Would you want to date Charlie?"

Teresa's question threw me. "I... I can't."

Another long silence. "Well, be careful, okay?"

"I will."

I ended the call and climbed into the loft to get dressed. After a quick phone call to Mom and Celia, I rushed across the yard in a light drizzle.

At the doorway, I ran into Leonie.

"Good morning, Bess. Just so you know, we've postponed the forest excursion until this afternoon. The weather should improve soon." She looked up at the sky and smiled apologetically, as if the rain was somehow her doing.

"Sounds great," I muttered, pushing past her, my eyes searching for Charlie.

There he was, sitting across the table from Miranda. I felt a strange fire churning in my belly. He'd pulled me into this fake relationship nonsense, awakened desires and messed with my head. Whether I wanted to date him or not, in the context of Rubie Ridge, I already was. Charlie had better remember that.

I marched across the room.

"Charlie!" I smiled sweetly, sliding next to him.

I snuggled up to him, burrowing my face in the crook of his neck, breathing in his scent. Lemon and pine. "The weather is awful. We should go back to bed." I slipped my hand over his thigh, brushing against his crotch.

His breath seized. "Hi, Bessie-Boo."

He weaved his fingers into my hair, then tugged my head back until he could claim my mouth. I'd never been part of such an explicit public display of passion, but I'd decided to commit, so I did. I met Charlie's tongue with mine as his cock pulsed against the back of my hand. Fire coursed through me, surging blood between my thighs. When he finally released me, Miranda had disappeared. Instead, Harry stood at the end of the table, head cocked, a funny smile on his face. "You guys are shameless."

Charlie shrugged, looking a little proud. "Sorry. I can't keep my hands off her."

"No apology necessary. I just thought I'd let you know the nude drawing workshop's about to start."

"Nude drawing?"

"Yeah. I was hoping for a male model, but sounds like they're harder to source around here. Unless you wanted to volunteer?" He raised his brow at Charlie, who rolled his eyes.

"No, thanks. I don't mind drawing a lady."

"Yeah, I figured." Harry shrugged and left.

Alone in the cafeteria, Charlie turned to me. "Thank you for saving me."

"From what?"

"Ms. Whatshername. She's relentless." Charlie exhaled, fanning the front of his sweater.

Relief flooded me at the easy connection between us. Maybe we could get past that awkward moment and return to something resembling friendship. Or at least a working relationship.

I flashed him a carefree grin. "No problem. What are fake girlfriends for?"

But he didn't smile back. He held my gaze, making my skin all hot. "That wasn't fake, Bess."

"Sure it was," I insisted, even if my smile wavered.

"I know you're scared but you can't tell me there's nothing between us."

"That's not what I'm saying, Charlie. I just—"

"I'll get us some breakfast." The hurt look was back, but with a hint of defiance.

He got up and headed to the breakfast buffet. The table was empty. So, he hadn't eaten yet. He'd been waiting for me.

When Charlie returned, handing me my seven-cereal mix, he looked even more defiant. I'd given him hope I couldn't afford to give. I'd given myself room to dream what I couldn't afford to dream. Despite Teresa's words, the idea of being with Charlie haunted me.

I couldn't let that idea grow. I had to focus my energy on something else, and I could only hope nude drawing was the ticket.

CHAPTER 23

Charlie

We spent the morning and a couple of hours after lunch in the studio, sketching a nude model. Contradictorily, staring at a naked lady, trying to etch her likeness on a giant piece of paper, finally settled my hard-on. The model was neither Bess, nor particularly hot, but the act of drawing took my mind off all the things I wanted to do to Bess. Well, not entirely. I was still the average man, thinking of sex every seven minutes. But that sort of frequency allowed other thoughts to enter into the mix, creating the illusion of control.

In the afternoon, we returned to the cabin to get ready for the hike.

I watched Bess fill up a water bottle and fit my empty shoe box she intended to use for leaf collecting inside her little backpack.

"Is that all you're taking?"

She looked up, confused. "What? They said it's only a couple of hours and we're coming back for dinner."

"Yeah. Plenty of time for some snacks, and to try my binoculars." I grinned, lifting the pair I'd hung around my neck. "These have a built-in camera."

She cocked her head, smiling sweetly. "Of course they do."

Something had changed. I'd felt it from the moment we kissed in the cafeteria. There'd been a flash of confidence and challenge in her eyes, and passion that felt at odds with her earlier words. She'd looked at me like she owned me, which felt accurate. But my response to her was so visceral I hardly cared about the power dynamics. I only wanted to touch her.

I'd behaved like a lovesick teenager, giving her the upper hand, and she'd taken it. Not to gloat or reject me, even if she believed we had no future. She'd relaxed into herself, smiling and laughing more, teasing me by playing an obnoxiously PDA-prone couple. I wasn't sure if she felt jealous of the other women or if it was an act, but I enjoyed those touches, sneaking peeks at her at every opportunity. Bess had been drawing her heart out, graduating from soft shading to dynamic charcoal lines. I was so proud of her my heart ached.

"Don't worry, I have trail mix for both of us. The good kind with chocolate." I could only hope my preparedness was a draw card and not another reminder of my privilege and unbridled spending.

"Humans can survive two hours without snacking," she said,

but looked a little pleased as she pointed at my state-of-the-art rucksack. "So, what else did you pack?"

"Well, I've got the basics. A fresh pair of socks, a hydration pack—"

"A what?"

I showed her my portable hydration bag, tucked to the side of my backpack, ready for sipping.

"That's convenient. Are you also wearing a diaper so you don't have to stop for wee-wee?"

"Damn! I knew I forgot something."

"Haha. What else?" She reached for my backpack. "Come on, tell me! I know you want to."

I grabbed her wrists to stop her from going in. Her eyes sparkled like the night sky filled with fireworks, and my chest responded by contracting. I could easily keep her here, locked into me. I didn't want to force her, but the way her lips parted and breath hitched, I knew she wanted this.

"Sorry about teasing you," she said breathlessly. "I'm sure it's all very useful stuff."

I released her arms and threw the rucksack on my back to stop her from diving in. I'd packed the hammock. Not that I expected to need it, but what was the point of buying all these things if you didn't keep them handy?

"A portable espresso maker," I confessed instead.

"What about the milk steamer?" She lifted an eyebrow.

"I grabbed some half and half singles from the cafeteria. It's not a proper espresso, but the fresh air makes everything taste better."

"I was kidding."

"I'm not. Coffee tastes ten times better when you're out in nature. Have you never tried it before?"

She looked down. "I don't do a lot of hiking."

"My family used to have a cabin up here, not far from Cozy Creek. It was sold a couple of years ago."

Because dad wanted to invest in a jet. To show off. I'd loved that cabin, but it hadn't been big enough for entertaining clients, and our life was nothing but a big show, designed to impress. And it did, with anyone else but this woman.

Me in my hiking boots and Bess in her scuffed sneakers, we ventured out of the cabin and onto the path leading past the parking lot, towards our nominated meeting point. The rain clouds had dissipated, leaving the afternoon air fresh and sky blue. The blanket of dark evergreens covered the hills, dotted by all shades of orange—like a fresh painting, hung to dry.

We joined the others, sporting various high-end backpacks and feather down vests and jackets, faces shielded by baseball caps. Bess's faded windbreaker stood out, making me feel like one of the posers. Still, I worried she'd get cold.

Leonie stepped out of the main building, waving her arms like a happy strawberry in her red, puffy vest. "Looks like the weather gods are finally on our side! Is everyone ready? Got your water bottles? Snacks? Cameras? The alpenglow should be amazing tonight."

"What glow?" Harry asked.

"It's the optical phenomenon that makes the horizon glow in reddish tones right after sunset. It's gorgeous!"

"I think I saw it the first night when I arrived." Bess's eyes shone with excitement.

I'd make sure we saw that glow again. But I'd be watching her face, not the horizon.

"Let us begin." Leonie guided us to the far corner of the car park where a narrow, winding path led down a rocky hill, soon joining in with more of a beaten track that dipped into a forest of quivering aspen, so intensely yellow we all gasped.

"It's like I'm drinking the color," Bess said, her voice quietly reverent.

Leonie slowed down her naturally glacial pace, which suited me fine, until we emerged from the aspen, and I saw the endless, gradual climb ahead of us.

"Feel free to go at your own pace," she announced, stepping aside to let the brisk walkers get past her. "Just follow the path. When you get to a small hunting cabin with a red door, please stop there and wait for the rest of the group."

"How far is the cabin?" asked Miranda.

"It's only a twenty-minute walk, roughly." She glanced at Miranda's heeled leather boots. "You have the option of turning around there and coming back if you don't want to walk the loop track."

"Oh, thank God."

Bess traipsed ahead of me at an impressive speed. I had to take the occasional running step to stay at her heels. "Why are we running?" I asked when we'd overtaken the other ladies and were leading the pack.

She whipped her head around, flabbergasted. "What? I'm not running. I'm walking."

"I beg to differ."

"This is my natural pace." She resumed her half-flying walk, hurdling protruding roots and shrubbery like it was an obstacle course and someone was timing her.

I took a deep breath and tried to adjust my stride to match her speed. "It's like we're running away from predators."

"I live in a scary neighborhood. If you amble, people think you're looking for someone to hook you up."

"With what?"

She threw a telling look over her shoulder. "Anything."

"Okay, I get it. But since nobody is chasing us with drugs, religious tracts or fake Rolexes, can we slow down a bit? So, we don't miss the scenery. Weren't you supposed to collect leaves?"

She stopped so abruptly I crashed into her back. "Sorry." I retreated a step, and she turned around.

"You're right. I should get that box out of my bag." She took off her backpack and negotiated the shoebox into her hands, then turned to continue.

The rocky, grassy plain turned into an evergreen forest that closed out most of the sunlight, only letting the occasional beam of light through. The air felt cooler and more humid, the soundscape more intense. With no autumn leaves, we walked in silence for a while. After initially slowing down a smidge, Bess was back to her original speed.

If the distance to the cabin took Leonie twenty minutes, we'd be done in five. But she may have not been using her own pace as the measuring stick, since the path continued for several minutes with no hunting cabin in sight.

Instead, we came to a roadblock. A fallen spruce tree lay across the path like an impenetrable wall of needles.

"Shit!" Bess hopped around, looking for a way through. "We'll have to go around," she finally concluded, pointing at the thick shrubbery. "Heads or tails?"

I followed her gaze, taking in the roots sticking up at one end, and the top of the huge tree, somewhere further along. At both ends, the ground was covered in thick shrubbery of bushes and tree saplings. "Can't we just wait for the others? They might cancel the hike when they see this."

But Bess was already wading through the waist-high growth towards the roots, using the shoebox to shield her eyes from the occasional higher branch.

"I can see the path," she called, her voice filled with excitement. "It's not far. We just have to get through here, duck under these…" she lowered her head to avoid a root and disappeared out of view. "It's here, Charlie! There must be a tight bend in that path right after the tree."

I sighed and followed her. I almost had to get on my hands and knees to make it through, but she was right. The path seemed to continue on the other side.

"I told you!" She grinned as I brushed needles off my jacket.

"So, you did. Do you think the others are able to follow us?"

She tilted her head, a mischievous glint in her eyes. "So, what if they don't? We can check out the cabin and the view and come back, right?"

I shrugged. "Sure."

Bess sprinted down the path, an actual skip in her step. I had to admit, I didn't hate the idea of losing the rest of the group. I quite liked it.

After a moment, we emerged from the forest and the path turned narrower, almost disappearing into the long grass. I saw a hilltop rising behind a stretch of trees, the likely location of the cabin. Soon, we were under the aspens again, drinking in the yellow.

"It's magical," Bess gushed, finally slowing her pace. She even stopped to take photos and gather some leaves, gently placing them into her box.

We continued walking through the forest until the path came to a fork. Bess cast me a confused look. "Didn't she say we just follow this path to the cabin?"

"Maybe she didn't remember this part. Do you want to turn back?"

"It's probably this one, though," she argued, pointing at the slightly wider path leading up. "That other one looks like a dead end. I'll check." She ran down the smaller path and soon called to me. "Yeah, this gets tinier. I don't think it's this one."

When she re-emerged, we continued down the wider track. The aspens gave way to maple trees glowing in orange and red.

Bess took more photos and gathered more leaves. "Have you found any pinecones yet?" she asked me.

I smiled, shaking my head. Pinecones hadn't even crossed my mind since yesterday, even though we'd been walking through a forest. My attention was on her, the sheer joy and energy she radiated.

"I can help you later. I'm sure we'll come across some pines soon." She scooted by a large maple tree, browsing the leaves, and hummed something. Her voice was soft and beautiful.

"What's that?"

"Autumn Leaves. An old song that popped into my head." She looked up, a little embarrassed.

"Do you want to listen to music?" I pulled a pair of earphones from my pocket, offering her the small white container. "I don't think I have that song, but I've saved a lot of music on Spotify."

She gave me an odd look. "It's okay. But you should put them on, so you don't hear me sing."

"I have another pair for me." I dug up a pair of identical wireless earphones to show her.

"My phone battery drains too quickly if I listen to music. And I have nothing saved on my phone, anyway."

"We can both listen on my phone."

I mentally browsed through my playlist, wondering if I had anything romantic. Should I even try something like that? It felt manipulative, and I wanted something real. I wanted us to be for real.

"You serious?" She stood up, her eyebrows pulled together.

"Can you hook up two pairs of earphones to the same phone?"

"Yes." I smiled at her shocked expression, and waited patiently until she picked up the white container from my palm, clicking it open, staring at the standard pair of earphones like it was a diamond ring. "Wow."

I wanted to pull her into my chest and hold her so tight. So, so tight.

You'll scare her off.

"Okay, Charlie. Play me your favorite song." Her eyes bright and expectant, she placed the earphones into her ears.

I swallowed. This was it. Time to share exactly what was in my heart. Choose between playing it safe or playing something real. What did I have to lose?

CHAPTER 24

Bess

I wasn't prepared for what flooded my eardrums when Charlie tapped on his phone. I associated rich people with elevator music and classical orchestras—soothing tunes played at cocktail parties that signaled everything was okay. That the world wasn't on fire, and it definitely wasn't their fault.

What Charlie chose to play for me made no sense. It was rap, or something like it. Musically ambitious, sung in an English accent, incredibly fast-paced and most of all, challenging. After a moment, the infectious beat pulled me into the effortless rhymes, and my mind started paying attention to the lyrics.

The song detailed the tenets of business economics with brutal sarcasm, criticizing greed and capitalism. When it ended, I plucked the earphone out, simply staring at him. "Who is this?"

"Ren. He's a Welsh singer songwriter."

"A rapper?"

"Yeah, that too. He's phenomenal. I discovered him a while back, before he made it big. I always knew he would."

"He sounds amazing. But those lyrics. You..." Words escaped me. I couldn't exactly tell him he wasn't allowed to listen to anti-capitalist songs, but it made no sense. "Do you agree with the message?"

His face stretched into that infuriating, self-satisfied grin. "You mean his breakdown of business economics?" He cocked his head, dropping the smile. "I think he's exaggerating for effect, but it's pretty accurate. Humans are ruthless in their pursuit of power. That's how the money game works."

"But you're playing the game," I insisted. "You're playing and winning."

"Yeah, but it doesn't mean I agree with the system. The rich are getting richer and money sits in assets rather than boosting the economy. The game is rigged against everyone else but the top one percent." He paused for a moment, meeting my eyes. "And I'm not talking about the rich in third person to exclude myself."

"Why don't you get out of the game, then?" I asked.

"Because I like money. I like security. I know I'd be far more stressed without it."

"But... you can't be both. You can't play the game and criticize the game. That's cognitive dissonance, right?"

He looked a bit wary, yet gracious. "Come on, Bess. Human

beings are walking contradictions. You know that."

I considered this, letting my shoulders drop. "I guess we are." If I was ever offered that money, that security, I knew I'd take it. Very few people chose to be poor to prove a point.

I trailed back to the path, continuing up towards a rocky hill. The air smelled damp and crisp and earthy, with a hint of impending snow. "Can I hear more songs by him? Are they all like that?"

I put the earphones back on and Charlie fed me another song— one that sounded very different. I recognized the artist's voice, but the message was more personal. Not about money, but pain.

The music pulled me into its orbit so completely that I felt like my feet lifted off the path, carrying me over the landscape. Song by song, I felt more alive than I had in a long time. So alive that I missed something important.

"Shit! How long has it been?" I stopped so suddenly that Charlie bumped into my back again, pushing me off balance.

He reached an arm around my waist to right me. "What?" he asked, removing his earphones.

"The cabin! Shouldn't we be there by now?"

"Yeah... Sorry, I lost track of time." He found his phone. "We left around four and it's... almost five?" He stared at the phone screen; eyes wide.

"Wait, what? Are we even on the right path?" I squeaked.

"Does it matter? The others probably turned around at the fallen tree, so whichever path we're on, we'll eventually turn around and go back the same way."

My heartbeat settled back to double digits. "Yeah, okay. Should we turn around now? What time does it get dark?"

"Um... I'm not sure. We can turn back if you want to. But I bet if we climb that next hill, the views are going to be amazing." He pointed at the slope ahead of us.

Turning back would have been the sensible thing to do, but part of me wanted to keep walking. For once, I wasn't going to be Buzzkill. "As long as we get back before dark." I turned around, powering up the hill.

The steep climb made my legs ache, but we were rewarded at the top.

Alpenglow.

I'd seen a glimpse of the red, glowing mountains when first arriving in Cozy Creek, but this was on a whole other level. The mountain ranges stretched in front of us like a giant fiery panorama, framed by layers of yellows, rusty reds, and dark greens below.

"Worth it," I announced, removing my earphones mid-song as Charlie reached my side.

"Impressive." He managed between gasps of breath. "And I mean your speed. The view is okay, too."

I'd heard the odd comment about my walking speed before, but hadn't thought about it for a long time. I had a child with only two settings—fast run and sitting on the ground, wailing. When she tore off down the road, I usually had to abandon walking and sprint after her. The rest of the time, I was rushing somewhere, late.

"Sorry. I'll let you catch your breath," I said, throwing him a smile.

"Don't apologize. I'm pretty sure this is good for me. Anything that hurts this much has to be, right?"

He held my gaze for long enough to make it clear he wasn't talking about physical pain. I wanted to look away, but I couldn't. The magic of nature in all its festive colors, the crisp air and the absolute privacy of the wilderness had arrested my senses, along with my words.

"Can we fake-date for two minutes?" he asked. "Just in case you one day give in and decide to accept my offer... Then we'll have this memory of holding each other on top of a hill, looking at this perfect scenery. And if we focus on that moment, it'll be like a real memory of us, together. One perfect moment."

"But we'll know it's fake."

His voice was quiet, struggling to emerge from his throat. "It's not fake for me, Bess."

"One perfect moment," I repeated, spellbound, dropping my arms to my sides. "Okay." I could give him this.

I could give myself this moment.

His arms closed around me, raising a flood of warmth and feeling inside. It wasn't fake for me, either. Even if I couldn't trust the future. My chest squeezed as he kissed the top of my head, his hot breath like gusts of summer wind in my hair. The world lay at my feet, but I closed my eyes, captured by Charlie. Being able to give him what he needed, to make him happy, lifted my heart to my throat. I wanted it to be true.

When he finally released me, I stumbled, searching for balance.

He snapped his hand around mine, saving me from falling down. "That might have been longer than two minutes," he confessed.

"That's okay."

The sun had dipped behind the tree line, reminding us that the day was ending.

"Should we head back?" I asked.

I had to force out the words, since I didn't want to go back. Not even to beat the dark. I'd fumble my way out of the forest. Besides, Charlie would have his flashlight. It probably doubled as a disco ball if needed.

Charlie turned around, scanning the scenery as if looking for an alternative. He must have been praying hard because that's when it happened.

CHAPTER 25

Bess

A high wail, tailed by a low, trembling horn, reverberated through the forest.

"Elk!" Charlie cried out, pointing at a small clearing below us.

I detected some movement, but it was too far away to make sense of. "Are you sure?"

"Yes! That sound was a bull elk. It's mating season so there'll be a harem as well."

"They have a harem?"

"About eight cow elks, usually. We used to watch them when I was a kid. My grandfather was a hunter. They're fascinating. If we get a bit closer, we might see them."

"Is it dangerous?"

"If you get too close, sure. The male weighs about seven hundred pounds and they can attack without warning. But we won't get too close, only close enough to use my new binoculars, okay?"

I was powerless against that pleading look of excitement and simply followed him down the hill, trying to memorize the way. Thankfully, the terrain was mostly rocky, the trees smaller and further apart, allowing us to weave through them in the general direction of the elk.

It wasn't long before we heard them again. The shrill sound, now close and startlingly loud, made me jump.

"That's the bull bugling," Charlie told me.

He'd taken the lead, and I was happy for once to slow down, staying behind him. Heading for the direction of the sound, we made it to a large rock overlooking the clearing. The elk had congregated on the opposite side—one horned male and eight females, just like Charlie had said.

The male seemed to be chasing one of the females, who lazily skipped around the field, letting him get close, then stretching the gap between them before anything could happen.

"Are they actually mating right now?" I whispered.

Charlie grinned. "I think the female's playing hard to get."

As he said it, the cow elk slowed down and circled the male, hopping on its back, then quickly retreated.

"Isn't that the female?" I asked. "Why is she mounting him?"

Charlie smirked. "Maybe she's showing him what to do."

The cow elk strutted off and the bull elk followed, his tongue flicking out. When they got to the edge of the forest, she allowed him to get close, presenting her hindquarters.

"Is he sniffing her...?" My mouth hung open as I stared at the scene.

We were close enough to see what was happening without the binoculars, but Charlie handed them to me anyway. "She's enticing him. Look a bit closer."

"Why does she keep running away, then? She needs to stop and let him mount her, right?"

Charlie drew a breath, blowing it out with bulging cheeks. "Right. I'll never understand females."

"She's already part of his harem, right?"

"Uh-huh. She should give up and accept the inevitable."

We watched for a long time as the two elk circled each other, the female leading on the male. Then, finally, she stopped and the bull elk climbed on her back. With Charlie's binoculars, I caught the moment of almost penetration before the cow elk moved away.

"Was that it?" Charlie asked.

"I don't think so. I saw his thing but... you know."

"What?"

"He didn't hide the sausage," I clarified. "If these are recording, watch the playback." I handed the binoculars back to him.

That's when the elk headed towards us. Charlie crouched to hide behind the rock, pulling me down with him. There was no need for binoculars anymore. We could see them in vivid detail. The giant antlers charged at us as the male swerved by our hiding place. He only had eyes for the female, though. She'd stopped running away now, instead turning back to rub her neck against his, again climbing onto his back as if to show him what to do. They were huge animals. Majestic.

I held my breath as the male mounted the female again, his pointy white erection now on full display. But this time, he rose on his hind legs and thrust into her. The powerful act was over in seconds, after which the animals went their separate ways.

I allowed myself to breathe again. "That was quick."

"You like it to last a little longer than that?" Charlie's voice sounded throaty.

If he was turned on, so was I. Not that I found a bull elk sexy. It was just hard to watch them without thinking about Charlie. What were the human mating rituals? We weren't that highly evolved. We still had those primal urges—behavior so innate that it needed no words or higher reasoning. I wanted him the same way I wanted all the things I couldn't have. Beach vacations, massages, chocolate that didn't cause pimples... Charlie was my pie-in-the-sky dream, and if I had a chance to make it true, why wouldn't I?

"I appreciate more than one thrust, yes." I tried to keep my voice light, but it came out nearly as thick as his. "And a bit of foreplay, not just running around a field, letting him sniff my butt."

His shoulders shook from laughter as he held onto a small tree to keep his balance. "I'm willing to go the extra mile. You like someone going down on you?" He grinned from ear to ear, his cheeks red.

I swallowed. "Are we really talking about this?"

"No, definitely not. Who's talking about it?" He swiveled his head, eyeballing the forest like a fucking owl.

No one was allowed to look that hot when playing dumb.

"We're not talking about it," I confirmed, sliding off the rock and heading in the direction we'd come from.

At least I thought so. After a few minutes of climbing, we came to a path and started following it up and over the hill. But the path kept veering to the left, leading down. We came to a tight bend, then another one. After a while, a large root blocked our way, forcing me to throw my legs over it. I was starting to feel the chill. Not only the cool of the falling night, but the terrifying realization that I'd never been here before.

CHAPTER 26

Bess

Cold dread shot through me. "Is this the right path?"

Charlie reached me. "I don't know. I was wondering that too."

"Please tell me one of your fancy gadgets is a compass."

He shook his head.

"Something with GPS?"

He pulled his phone from his pocket. "It looks like we're too far from the nearest tower. I'm not getting any signal."

I sighed. "And mine died a while ago."

"Your battery life is terrible."

"I'm aware." My iPhone was so old most apps didn't work and the top corner of the touch screen was dead so I had to constant-ly rotate it to do anything. "So, what do we do? It's getting dark. Do we go back?"

He glanced over his shoulder, biting his lip. "I guess."

We turned around and walked for a while.

"We must have gone off course when we went down the hill to see the elk," I said. "Let's go back there and try again."

But when we got to the area where we'd emerged from the forest and onto the path, my plan began to fall apart. We were rapidly losing the last of the evening light, and going back into the woods would have meant diving into darkness.

"You still have that phallic flashlight?"

His mouth twisted. "You gave me so much shit I left it behind. Besides, we were supposed to be back before dark. But my phone has a light."

He switched it on and pointed the light at his feet, making them look vaguely highlighted.

"Well, it's brighter than your average firefly," I said, swallowing my disappointment.

"Stay right behind me, okay? Hold on to my jacket." He took a step into the forest, but I grabbed his jacket.

"Charlie, wait."

He returned to the path, turning to face me.

My stomach churned. "I don't feel great about going in there. It's too dark. There's a bull elk with a whole harem. But I don't know what else we can do." Panic was starting to vibrate through me, tightening every muscle.

"Well... We can spend the night."

"What?"

"We can follow this path up to find a good campsite, make a

fire, eat something..."

"And what? Lay down on a bed of leaves?"

Even in the low light, I could tell his smile was somewhat sheepish. "Or in the hammock."

"You brought the hammock?"

"Just in case."

"What were you thinking would happen?"

"Well, this."

"Is that why you wanted to go see the elk?" My voice rose along with the tsunami of anger inside me. "Did you plan for us to get lost so we could try out your stupid camping gear?"

"No! I also packed a small first aid kit, but I wasn't planning on cutting myself so I can put on a Band-Aid." He raised his voice to match my volume, without the anger.

He was helping me hold onto my anger, to push the fear aside. I could feel my limbs flooding with energy. "Well, I'm glad you brought it, so I'll have somewhere to sleep in while you stoke the fire and keep watch." My voice cracked, but I held my head high, jutting my chin forward.

"Absolutely. I'll keep watch all night."

It was officially dark now, and so cold my thighs were starting to feel numb under the thermal leggings. I was grateful for the two layers of wool under my windbreaker, but cold air was trying to get in through the cracks from every direction. Along with fear. "How are we even going to make a fire?"

"By introducing flame to something flammable." He pulled a lighter out of his pocket and waved it around.

"Why do you carry that? Do you smoke?"

"Are you looking to bum a cigarette?"

"No. I just never thought of you as a smoker."

"I'm not. I took this from Trevor last time he decided to quit."

"And then he bought a new one the next day?"

"Probably."

Trevor announcing he was going to quit smoking was a running office joke.

"Are you one of his accountability buddies?" I asked, desperate to think about something safe and familiar, like the burly Scottish copywriter who smoked like a chimney.

"I think he needs someone like you. Someone who can kill with one look."

I tried to relax my face. I might have been shooting some fairly sharp eye-daggers at him. But only because the alternative was full-blown panic city.

"Let's walk up a bit and I'll use my seventh sense to detect the perfect campsite." Charlie gestured at the path.

"Seventh?"

"I'm already using my sixth sense to monitor your emotional state in the dark."

"Oh, really? What is my emotional state?" I crossed my arms, fighting the chill that crept in through the sleeves.

"Hangry."

I nodded. "I'm also terrified and freezing."

"I was going to say!"

"Your sixth sense is really slow."

I whipped around and started powering up the path, as fast as I could in the faint glow of Charlie's phone light. I could only make out the rough direction of the path. The darkness had already swallowed the details, including the rocks and roots I kept stumbling over. Still, it felt good to move. Do something. The plan wasn't great, but at least there was a plan. We wouldn't die here tonight. I'd decided that much, even if I berated myself for being stupid enough to follow him off the path to see the elk. Why? If I was that desperate to stare at animals, I could always save up to visit the zoo and see the fat gorilla touching himself in the corner.

The path twisted left and right, leading us up the hill. Finally, we came to a small clearing. Charlie took my hand and led me off the path. I heard the sound of water before we found the small stream. "Perfect! In the morning, we follow this down the hill," he said. "That's the best way to get back to civilization."

"How do you know that?"

"It's something my grandfather used to say. If you get lost in the mountains, find a stream and follow it down. Settlements are built around water sources."

It made sense, but first we had to survive the night.

"So, what does your seventh sense say?" I asked, letting him lead me across the high grass.

I should have pulled my hand away, but I couldn't. It was the only part of my body not shivering and terrified.

"I can sense a great camping spot right about... here." He stopped abruptly and I bumped into his side, grabbing his arm for balance.

"Here? Why?"

He lifted his useless phone flashlight. "There's a big rock that way. It offers us some protection. And trees on the other side."

"I can't see anything," I insisted, but after a little while, I noticed the shape of a larger rock. Either that or a black hole that was going to swallow us.

Charlie pulled me closer until we stood by the shape. Definitely a rock.

"And here are some trees we can use to attach the hammock to."

He removed his backpack, and got into work attaching the hammock. I'd never actually seen it in working order, only lying across the floor. I couldn't say I was seeing much of it now, given the dim light, but it looked a lot bigger than I remembered, and puffy like a sleeping bag.

"It has great insulation," he explained as I stepped closer to investigate the material. "Should be good all the way to down to 28 degrees, but we'll see."

"What do you mean, all the way down? I think we're there already." I folded my arms, trying to keep my core temperature from dropping. "Charlie, if this product doesn't work as advertised, we can easily die from hypothermia."

"You won't. I will, if I fail at my fire guarding duties. In that case, take my phone and walk as long as you need to find a signal, then call my dad. He'll send a rescue helicopter."

"Not funny!" My teeth clattered. "Are you not freezing? How

are you able to move your fingers?"

He was wearing gloves and had pulled up the hood of his thermal jacket, which obviously made him better prepared, but the temperature had dropped significantly since sunset.

"Can you help me pick up some sticks for the fire? I have another pair of gloves for you. Mine have this removable lining..."

He peeled off his gloves and gave me the outer shells. They looked like the size ice hockey goalies wore.

I shook my head. "Give me the inner ones, they're smaller."

We swapped gloves and I went off to search the ground. The moon had risen over the tree line, casting an eerie glow over the landscape. Even the stars seemed brighter up here, helping me navigate across the grass. After a while, I found a fallen tree with its branches sticking up. They were dry and brittle and I began snapping them, collecting a pile of kindling. Using my body weight, I managed to break up a couple of larger branches as well, dragging them all to Charlie's feet like a good dog fetching its owner's slippers. I half expected him to pat me on the head.

"Great work!" I heard the smile in his voice.

The hammock now hung between two trees, and next to it, he'd laid a ring of rocks as a base for the fire. After an agonizingly freezing ten minutes, we had the start of a fire. I'd shredded my shoebox to use as kindling, and Charlie sacrificed the printout of the retreat program he found in his pocket.

We watched in awe as the sheet of paper caught the flame, transferring it onto the cardboard and eventually the dry sticks. Gradually, the larger bits of branch caught fire, and I breathed a sigh of relief. Sitting on a log next to Charlie, as close to the open flame as I dared, I held my hands in its glow. "Oh, God. I'm so frozen this actually hurts."

He reached to take my hand, closing it inside his huge, surprisingly warm palms. "I'm so sorry, Bess. This is not what I had in mind."

"What did you have in mind?"

"I just wanted you to see the elk, I didn't even think. I was irresponsible and I'm sorry."

I nodded. "I was, too. I shouldn't have followed you."

Somehow, that part was harder to swallow. Because Charlie was Charlie. Charming, disarming, flighty and irresponsible. But I was me. Blindly following him into the forest to see woodland creatures mating was so off-brand for me I was questioning my sanity.

"You regret it," he said quietly.

It wasn't a question, so I didn't answer. Instead, I accepted the bag of trail mix he handed me, zeroing my focus on fishing out the pieces of chocolate and shoving them into my mouth like it was my last meal. Gradually, the hollow fear relaxed its grip and warmth flooded my belly, slowly making its way down to the extremities.

I didn't really regret anything. Not in that moment. Not when I felt borderline safe again. If I could only close my eyes and transport us back to the retreat, it'd be a wonderful story to tell my daughter.

"I hate that I can't call home," I said between bites of chocolate. "I call every night before Celia's bedtime. She'll be expecting it. My mom will try to call, and she'll freak out when I don't answer the phone."

He dipped his hand in the bag and carefully selected only nuts, no chocolate. "She can call the retreat and they'll tell her we're lost."

I hadn't even thought about what the retreat staff would do.

"Do you think they'll call the police? Send out a search party?"

"I don't know. They might. But it'll be difficult in the dark. They might have to wait until morning." He raised his chin, casting me a regretful look. "But they might also assume we're staying at the hunting cabin if they turned around at the fallen tree. I heard Harry and Matthew talking about how romantic it is."

"And everyone thinks we're madly in love," I finished for him, my gut twisting. "Oh my God! They'll tell that to my mom if she calls."

"You can explain later that it's one-sided."

My stomach lurched. "Oh, come on, Charlie. We've been faking this thing." I tried to laugh, but no sound came out.

I began to feel warmer—so warm, in fact, that I had to lean back from the fire. Why did he have to say things like that? Things I had to forget as soon as I heard them. Or least when I returned to my real life.

I handed him the trail mix. "Thank you. This helped a lot."

"Are you sure there's no chocolate left?" He lifted the bag to study it in the light of the fire, grinning. "There. You missed a piece."

"You can have it." I flushed with embarrassment. "I'm sorry."

"No, I'm glad I could feed you. I also have some muesli bars but maybe we should save those for breakfast." His eyes regarded me with such warmth, I paradoxically shivered.

I felt his hand on my shoulder as he pulled me against him. "We'll be okay, Bess. You'll be okay. I know I'm not the kind of rugged cowboy you'd hope to be paired with for this experience, but I'll do my best, I promise."

My heart fluttered like a trapped moth, blindly flapping towards him, towards the light. Before I knew what was happening, I'd melted against his chest, drinking in the reassuring words, letting my heart rate settle. I believed him, despite everything. I wanted those strong arms around me, keeping me safe. If I could only get a word out to my mom and Celia, letting them know I was safe.

"Are you sure you don't have a signal at all?" I asked.

He handed me his phone. "Keep it. Let me know if it starts working. I've composed a couple of texts and it keeps trying to send them. You might as well write one, maybe walk around a bit and see if you get lucky."

"I don't remember Mom's number."

"I have Rhonda's number. She knows your mom. She'll pass on the message."

A tiny ray of hope lit in my chest. When I saw the time on his screen—only 7.30pm, I sighed with relief. It wasn't even bedtime yet. After a bit of fumbling, Charlie's arm still firmly around me, I found his contacts and scrolled towards 'R'.

"Wait. It's under Gran." His voice sounded restrained and the hand gripping my arm tightened.

"You call Rhonda 'Gran'?"

"She's my grandmother."

"What?" I held my breath.

A medley of every conversation I'd ever had with my office confidante burst through my mind. That last time, I'd complained about Charlie and she'd laughed.

"She doesn't like people knowing, so she tells us to call her Rhonda."

I leaned forward, away from him, and stared at the flickering flames, trying to get my head around this new piece of information. "She told me someone ought to confiscate your credit cards." The line rose from my memory and I repeated it without thinking.

"She's done that before. She asked me to hand in the company card when I bought a new laser cutter."

"What do we need a laser cutter for?" I glanced at him over my shoulder and caught a rueful smile.

"I wanted to experiment. I thought we could develop new products or prototypes."

"But you already have those 3D printers."

"Nothing beats wood as material, though." He took his hand off my shoulder and threw another stick in the fire. "But more importantly, Gran talks to you about me?"

I turned to face him, taking in his amazed expression.

"We're friends." I cleared my throat. "I thought we were

friends."

"But you don't think that anymore?" His eyebrows pulled into a slight frown.

"I guess we are, but I just realized that I've occasionally complained to her about… you." There was something about the cold, dark night and the dancing flames that made the truth flow out, unstoppable. "Nothing mean… it's more like she's someone who understands."

Oh, Charlie.

It was Rhonda who'd said that first. I'd picked it up from her! Although she'd always said it with affection. Or maybe I was attaching a new meaning to her words, making them sound different in my head, now that I knew who she was. I'd been the one channeling my frustrations into that innocuous phrase, trying to hide my anger and jealousy.

Charlie's soft, rough voice rumbled through me. "She would understand. She practically raised me, and I'm pretty sure she works at the company to keep an eye on me."

"What about your mom?"

The sadness in his eyes was instant. "Mom's a… busy woman. She would let me buy anything I wanted to keep me happy and out of her hair."

"That doesn't sound great."

He'd really learned his lesson—spending money to keep himself occupied. But money couldn't replace affection. I'd never thought of Charlie lacking anything, and the thought threw me.

"I really like Rhonda," I said, poking at the fire with a stick.

Sparkles erupted into the night air, dancing their way into the darkness.

It would have been so cozy, even romantic, under different circumstances.

"She likes you, too." Charlie smiled, the flames now dancing in his eyes. "She told me I should get to know you." A smile tugged at his mouth.

"Really? Why?"

I'd never thought of Rhonda as the meddling type. She seemed to stay out of the office drama, happy with her TV drama and cookies. But we'd discussed Charlie a whole lot. I'd always thought it was because she genuinely cared about him, regarded him as a wayward son of hers. Which, it turned out, he was, in a way. It all made sense now, even the fact that I knew what long hours Charlie worked. Had Rhonda been dropping hints about his whereabouts and better qualities for my benefit?

I had to smile, thinking about our fun, friendly chats. It had never even crossed my mind she'd been trying to get us together. She'd succeeded at one thing, though. Charlie had never been far from my mind.

"I'm now replaying every conversation I've ever had with Rhonda," I confessed. "Everything she's ever said about you... it all takes on a different meaning when I think of her as your grandmother."

He nodded solemnly. "I guess it does." For a moment, we both stared at the flames. When he spoke again, his voice had a heaviness to it. "I know what it looks like. I know what people think...

and it's true, in a way. When you work with family, you'll always get special treatment. Either good or bad. People can't be impartial with their own flesh and blood." He let out a deep sigh. "I should have left a long time ago. I should have made my own way. But there's this expectation... My sisters both married rich, took the easy way out."

"Wait... I thought you were an only child?"

He shook his head. "Who said that?"

"Teresa."

"Well. I hope you believe me over her." He gave me a lopsided smile, and I felt ashamed. Teresa was my friend, but how well did she really know Charlie?

"Anyway. My sisters aren't interested, so it's all up to me... the responsibility, taking on the family business. The legacy. I feel like I have no choice." He stared at the fire, arms resting over his knees, a solemn look in his eyes. I could practically see the weight on his hunched shoulders.

I'd never associated Charlie with responsibility. "I thought you had all the choices in the world, but I guess it's not that simple."

"There are choices, but none of them are easy. Me and Dad... we don't agree on a lot. He doesn't want my input when it comes to business, so I tend to stay out of his way and focus on the creative side. That's not his strength and if I left, he'd lose a lot of business. That's why he gives me so much freedom, to keep me at the helm. But I'm not invited to management meetings. The board is basically just him and his sycophants. I'm too idealistic.

Apparently, I'd run the business to the ground if I had my way."

I nodded in understanding. George would regularly go behind Rhonda's back, making us fabricate more hours than we'd worked, to squeeze more money from clients. God forbid he had a down month. I was asked to lie on my time sheets nearly every month since I was faster than the others—an easy target. I'd always thought Charlie was in on it, enjoying the benefits of his dad's dirty tactics.

"I used to think of you as an extension of George, in a way. Nicer, but still on the same side."

"Trust me, we're not." He blew a heavy sigh.

"I'm sorry you're—."

"I don't want you to be sorry for me." His voice had an edge. "Life hasn't been fair to you."

"Yeah, but I shouldn't take that out on you or anybody else." As I spoke the words, I knew how much I needed to hear them. So much, that my eyes filled with tears of shame. "You've been so good to me."

"I appreciate that, but you're currently lost in the forest because of me. I don't deserve a lot of praise."

I had a sudden urge to touch him. I wanted to finish what we'd started. I wanted to be with him, even if it was for one night. What harm could it do? I needed to feel his body against mine, feel all that tension drain from both of us. Stop the apologizing and feeling awkward. Be in sync. Could I argue it was for our survival?

"George doesn't praise you much, does he?"

He gave me a sad smile. "It's not really his style."

"Is that why you praise my work?" My hand landed on his thigh, thumb stroking his jeans, feeling for the hard muscle underneath. "Because you want to be nothing like him?"

My thumb had already made up its mind about sleeping with Charlie. The rest of me wanted to follow... if I could shake the other worries from my mind, I would go for it, holding nothing back.

"I hope I'm nothing like him..." He looked away, tensing under my touch. "We don't see eye-to-eye about many things."

"Like what?"

He turned to look me deep in the eye, so conflicted I wondered if I'd offended him somehow. "So many things, Bess."

CHAPTER 27

Charlie

That was the moment I lost her, even though didn't know it then. I'd been waiting for the right moment to tell her the truth: How much I disagreed with my father and his plans for the company. How I was trying to save her job. But I said nothing, quietly debating myself as she took my phone and walked across the clearing, holding it up, praying for a signal.

I didn't deserve anything from her, not after that. But I took everything because I was weak and deliriously in love.

"Sent! It says the message was sent!" she yelled across the field.

I instinctively stood up as I saw her stumbling towards me. She stopped one step away, her eyes shining with tears. "Rhonda replied. She'll let my mom know. She'll track the cell signal to get our location."

When she jumped into my arms, I was officially lost for words. There was nothing left. I breathed in her scent, the air vibrating with palpable relief and joy. "That's amazing, Bess," I whispered into her hair, every part of my body suddenly awake and alive, blood pumping at double speed to reach all the locations.

I should have let her go and steered us back to that awkward conversation. I should have done the right thing. But that long, tight hug wiped my mind clean. I could only think of her soft body pressed against mine. The smell of her hair in my nostrils.

She'd been pushing me away, probably for a good reason, and I had no idea what had changed. But I didn't want to question it. I only wanted to stay there, locked against her, with no words confusing things between us.

As though she'd read my mind, Bess took my hand and pulled me towards the hammock. I threw the last of the branches into the fire and helped her into it. She removed her sneakers but climbed in fully clothed, disappearing into the padded cocoon. After a moment, her face appeared. "Come on! We can't let you die of hypothermia."

She didn't have to ask me twice. I removed my boots and jacket and climbed in with her, cringing at how the fabric and lines tightened under my weight. But the hammock held in place, gently swaying under the trees. It was pitch black inside it with the covers drawn, but it was warm. We'd survive.

As I settled in, gravity pushed our hips together. I felt her arms against my chest and her hair on my face. It smelled of something sweet, like honey. There were so many things I wanted to do, but the hammock was like a straitjacket.

"Are you okay?" I asked.

"Mmm," she breathed against my chest. "It's so snug. I've never been this close to another person."

"Not even during sex?" I asked without thinking.

"It's different. This is like being tied up, somehow."

"You're not claustrophobic, are you?"

My mind raced, trying to think of ways to calm her down. I couldn't let her out into the night. I had to keep her here. Keep her warm.

"I'm freaking out a little," her small voice piped up as she tried to create space between us using her hands. "I want to give you some space, but it's really hard."

"You don't have to give me space." I stroked her hair. "I don't need space between us at all. But I apologize for my third arm. It gets a bit excited over this much proximity."

There was nothing I could do about that hard-on, not when my crotch was practically pushed against hers. My cock knew where it wanted to be and a few layers of fabric did nothing to dampen its enthusiasm.

"It's okay." She wiggled her hand down to my jeans as if to confirm the situation. "You can take it out if it helps."

I laughed. "I don't think that's a good idea, unless you want to be penetrated."

Her voice turned low and husky. "Do you have protection?"

My breath seized.

I could hardly believe she'd spoken those words. "You'd have sex with me to make room for my cock, Bess? That's very accommodating, but seriously."

Her voice was both breathy and amused as her fingers worked to unfasten my jeans button. "It might be the only way we survive the night. So, do you have protection?"

It was a tough question, because if I admitted to having a condom on me, which I did, I'd also admit to premeditating the strange situation we were in. And I hadn't. Not really.

"If I tell you I have a condom in my back pocket, are you going to judge me? I only keep it on me because I'm an eternal optimist. I wasn't expecting anything, I swear."

"If you'd planned for this, you would've ordered a bigger hammock, right? With fairy lights and mirrors, like an insulated sex swing."

I could hear the smile in her voice before I felt her shake with laughter. She could make fun of me all she wanted if it meant she was no longer terrified. Or mad at me.

"I need that thing. Where can I get it? Does it come with built-in speakers?"

"I'm sure someone somewhere will sell it for half a million dollars."

"Buy. Now."

She hiccupped with laughter and happiness radiated through my chest. "I guess we'll have to make this one into a sex swing." She dragged her hand across my pulsating crotch, her body pressing against my side.

With every touch of her hand, I got harder and the jeans became more uncomfortable. "You need to stop stroking me, unless you're ready to face the consequences," I warned, pushing her hand away.

"Where's the condom, Charlie?" She snaked her hand around me, trying to reach into my back pocket.

I used the opportunity to grab her hips and bring her directly on top of me. We lined up perfectly, her soft body molded against mine. I helped her out of her jacket, then slid my hands under her woolen layers, relishing the feel of bare skin against my fingers. For a moment, the awkwardness of being pushed together in a cramped space disappeared. We were just two people lying on top of each other, enclosed by darkness, desperate to get closer.

When she unzipped my jeans, I froze. I couldn't go back on my word, even if this counted as an emergency, in every sense of the word.

"Wait!" I fought the words out against my will. "I told you—If we do this, it means something, Bess. Tell me this is not casual." My voice rang with desperation.

"There's nothing casual about trying to survive in freezing temperatures," she joked, but I could hear the sadness. The uncertainty.

"Bess. You know what I mean."

I'd never feared silence as much as I feared the seconds stretching between us. The longer she took to give me an answer, the more my stomach twisted.

CHAPTER 28

Bess

My hands froze on the zipper of his jeans. I could feel him fighting hard to slow us down, despite what his body wanted. What mine wanted. Why was this so important to him?

"It's not casual," I finally said, my throat sticky. It was the truth. "I like you too much, Charlie."

His fingers weaved into my hair. "You're with me, Bess. We're together."

His words did something to me, digging under the layers of desire and terror, right into that soft center I'd tried to hide.

"I'm with you, Charlie." In that moment, nothing else could have been true.

Being pressed against his body in a warm, confined space, I felt protected. Shielded from the shitstorms of life. There was nothing casual about that feeling. It was pure and heightened, almost paralyzing.

I tugged down his underwear and wrapped my fingers around that boner, gasping at the girth. I could feel his pulse. I could have kept stroking, to return the favor. But I needed more. I wiggled my leggings all the way down to my ankles and nuzzled that huge erection between my legs. I couldn't resist rolling my hips, riding it a little. Then a little more.

I lowered my lips to his and Charlie kissed me, sinking his tongue into my mouth, one hand roaming under my shirt. He traced my breast and gently pinched the nipple, thrusting his hips forward. The movement made my soaked underwear stretch against my crotch and I gasped at the sensation. I moved with him, momentarily forgetting our confined space and everything else. I was setting the pace, yet he followed my lead, so perfectly in sync with my every little movement that I never doubted his excitement.

"Tell me what you want," he panted, speaking so close to my mouth I felt his hot breath on every word.

"I want you inside me. But I'm stuck."

He grabbed my hips and lifted me a couple of inches. "Bring up your knees."

I fought out of the leggings still hanging off my ankles and shuffled up, wedging my knees on either side of his hips, creating a bit of space between us. The relief! I could move, even if my knees were squished between the taut fabric and Charlie's hips.

"Much better." I reached between us and gave him another stroke, enjoying the way he grunted, his hands tightening around the back of my thighs.

"Stop! Unless you want me to come all over your hands."

"Did you say you had a condom?"

"Jeans back pocket."

I snuck my hand underneath him, locating the jeans crumpled under his thighs, this time successfully fishing the condom out of his back pocket. How did condoms even work? I hadn't done this in ages.

Before I could further embarrass myself, Charlie took it off me. I couldn't see anything but heard the wrapper ripping and I helped him roll it down his length.

I lifted my hips and lowered myself onto him. I had to advance slowly, inch by inch, until my lower belly connected with his. We held for a moment, waiting for the hammock to stop rocking. I felt as stretched and tight as the fabric holding us, every breath releasing a flurry of tingles. I'd forgotten how good it felt to be full. Perfectly invaded.

The hammock's bounce turned into a gentle sway, and I rocked against him, enjoying the waves of sensation. "Is this okay for you?" I asked.

He must have been uncomfortable, trapped under my weight, unable to move.

"I'm trying to... last," he bit out between short gasps, his hands heavy on my hips, steadying me. "I want this to be good for you. Not just good, but—"

"Shush." I traced my finger across his face in the dark and

found his lips. "We're stuffed inside a hammock, Charlie. It's a miracle to even get off."

"Not for me. Not with you."

"Do you really think I'm sexy?" I couldn't stop the question from slipping out.

"Is that your one honest question?"

"Fine. But you must be brutally honest."

He sunk his fingers into my hair and pulled my face to his, hungrily kissing my mouth, then my neck, my ear, the tip of my nose. Mouth again. His voice was low and breathless. "Bess. I'm constantly turned on around you. It's embarrassing. I fantasize about you. I imagine you naked. Sometimes, I don't hear a word you say, I just stare at your mouth."

"At work?" I forced myself to stop moving. My entire body pulsed from desperate anticipation, waiting to unravel. But I needed to hear this.

"At work," he rasped. "I think about kissing you, bending you over my desk, seeing that perfect ass..." He pulled me closer to whisper into my ear. "Am I embarrassing you?" I heard the smile in his gravelly voice.

"I just never thought."

"I try to be professional. You don't dip your pen in the company ink."

I rocked against him, sparkles erupting behind my eyelids. "The ink will never come off your pen now." I'd have laughed if I hadn't been so ridiculously aroused. We held still for a moment. I felt him pulse inside me. He was close, but so was I.

His voice brimmed with emotion. "I'd rather have you. The company can go fuck itself."

Something wobbly moved about my chest, but I could barely process his words anymore. I needed to move. My breath hitched at the intense pleasure radiating through my core. So hot. So perfect.

The pressure built up, taking me higher and higher. A moan erupted from my mouth, louder than I'd ever been in any bedroom. I didn't care who heard us. I wanted to match the sounds of the bugling elk.

I had no routine, but my body took over, remembering everything I'd forced myself to forget.

The hammock swayed. I felt the increasing tightness in my core with no room for anything else. Anyone else. I didn't even have to move. The pressure alone took me over the edge. I shook uncontrollably against him, coming apart, coming down so slowly I felt like I was skydiving, never to reach the ground. I felt the pulse of his release inside me, his fingers digging into my buttocks, claiming me again and again.

It shouldn't have been that good. Not in those circumstances. It was a miracle.

After a moment of catching my breath, I found my voice, deep and a little broken. "Charlie, that was the best I've ever had. Ever."

His reply floated back to me across the enclosed, dark space, whisper soft. "Me, too. But I also can't remember ever having sex before. Sudden memory loss. Come here." He pulled me against his chest, still inside me.

I'd done it. There was no going back. I'd officially had sex with Charlie Wilde and might possibly live to tell the tale.

"I wish I could see you. I need to see you." He shifted underneath me and found his phone from somewhere. Its light hit my eyes like a camera flash and I blinked, blinded, until he turned it to the side.

There he was. Charlie. A goofy smile on his face, eyes soft and gentle as his gaze found me and stayed. "You look happy," he said. "I wanted to make sure you were happy."

"I'm happy," I said, and really meant it.

"You don't regret this." It sounded a little like a question, but only a little.

"No." I smiled.

There are moments in life you want to pause at. Not when you're there, but later, when you find out what comes next. Later, I discovered that was the moment I wanted to pause. My heart full, my body still tender and brain beautifully offline as I stared into his eyes. I would have stayed there forever.

But life's not that kind. Eventually, I lifted myself enough for him to pull out. It felt slippery between my legs. Too slippery. My heart jumped to my throat as I ran my hand across the condom. "It's broken, Charlie. The condom's broken."

He tensed underneath me, pushing up to lean on his elbows and point the flashlight down his body. The condom had torn in half, spilling its contents across his thighs. He removed what was left of it and unzipped the hammock to toss it outside.

"Shit," I muttered. "I didn't notice. I'm sorry."

"How could you have noticed? If anything, it's my fault."

"Why?"

"My condom."

I sighed. "Okay, it's no one's fault. But what do we do?"

This was why I didn't date or take risks. There were always consequences.

"It's so unfair!" I crawled away from him, curling up between his stretched-out legs, putting the hammock out of balance. We bobbed up and down. The lines creaked, tightening on the trees.

"Bess, please come back here. We can't afford to rip the hammock in half."

"We can't afford to rip a condom in half!" I sobbed. "I can't afford another kid."

There was another creak, and the hammock nudged down an inch.

"Please, Bess. Come here. Now!"

My survival instinct won, and I slid back on top of him. He'd tucked his waning erection back into his underwear, but it still nuzzled between my legs, perking up as soon as we made contact. I tried to shuffle to his side, but he locked his arms around me, holding me tight against his chest, like we'd been before. "It'll be fine."

He sounded too calm. Soothing. Either he didn't understand the risk, or he was willing to say anything to stop me from breaking the hammock and putting us both in danger. That made sense.

"I'll get the pill. What is it? The one you can take after, to make sure I don't get pregnant."

"You don't have to."

"Of course I do. I can't risk... I can't afford..."

"I can."

I tried to shake my head, but ended up rubbing my cheek against his thermal shirt. "Oh, Charlie." It came out like a deep sigh. A prayer. Nothing was left of my earlier contempt. Only wonder. "You don't know what you're talking about, but I appreciate it."

His arms tightened around me. "I can afford to buy all kinds of shit I don't need. I can also afford things we do need."

We. My brain fixated on that pronoun, turning it around like a foreign object, examining its shiny edges. Could I really be part of a whole with Charlie? I knew he was generous. Was this him showing off?

"You'd seriously take the risk?"

"It's up to you. I know I want to be with you and I want a family, so I have no reason to make you take some pill."

"You want to buy weird baby stuff from Kickstarter, don't you?" A smile tugged my lips.

"Yeah, kind of." His chest bounced under my cheek as he chuckled.

The sound relaxed me. It warmed my heart that he could imagine himself with a baby, even if he had no idea what he was talking about.

"I hope we find our way back tomorrow so I can get to the

pharmacy. If I take it within twenty-four hours, it should be fine. But if I'm ovulating right now, it's already too late. I can't remember..."

I tried to do period math, but dates and weeks mixed up in my head, disappearing into a fog of tiredness. Judging by the way I'd climbed him, consumed by lust, the chances were high I was ovulating. Shit.

"It's fine, Bess. If it's meant to be, it's meant to be."

That warm, soothing voice was getting under my skin. "You can't really be that relaxed about it." I sniffed. "A baby is a huge responsibility. It changes everything."

"You don't think I'm responsible?"

"No. Yes. I don't know." I groaned.

"That's reassuring."

"I'm in the process of changing my mind about you. It's a messy process."

He weaved his fingers into my hair, stroking down. "Fair enough. I'll wait."

Another thought hit me. "I'll need to get checked up, right?"

"I got tested a few months ago. All clear."

"A lot can happen in a few months."

"Nothing happened in a few months, Bess. Other than me getting a hand job from someone and lusting after you at the office, wondering what you were like outside of work."

"Why? I'm not that much of a mystery. I'm the Buzzkill."

"And I'm Broken Arrow."

My gut twisted. "You heard that?"

"Teresa is pretty loud."

"She doesn't know how much you work. I need to tell her."

"You don't have to defend me. I can take it."

"But she's wrong. They're all wrong. You're far more talented than I am, and you work hard. And you're so much more responsible than I ever thought."

"And you're way more fun than any of them know. You're wild."

I let out a shaky laugh. "I'm full of adrenaline or something. I don't do reckless stuff like this. I don't take risks. Not since..."

"Since the death of your husband?"

I sighed, grateful for the relative darkness. I'd sworn I'd never burden him with the whole story. But as he waited in silence, stroking my hair, the words tumbled out on their own.

"It wasn't the death. Or, it was, in a way. But that was just the grand finale. First, we had this business. We poured everything into it. Jack had invented this new packaging material that was lighter and stronger, derived from corn and cheap to make. It was supposed to be the perfect idea. The perfect product. He never even launched the Kickstarter. There was an investor who wanted in... it all seemed too good to be true. And then he took it and sold it to a huge manufacturer and cut us out. The patent was still pending, and even with all the patents, we couldn't fight back. We didn't have the money for lawyers. We'd burned through our savings getting the prototypes produced, testing and building the brand. I did the design, of course, but there were a lot of costs and we had to live on something." I took a breath, expecting him to say something. Curse. Point out where we'd gone wrong. But he stayed silent, that hand still stroking my hair.

"Jack took it so hard," I continued. "He closed off, wouldn't talk to me. I found out he'd put the last of our money in crypto and had lost most of it. He was desperate to make it all back, but he didn't know how to play that game. He was an innovator, not an investor. When I found out, I lost it and we had a big fight. He moved in with his brother. That's the last time I saw him. He messaged us a few times, apologized. I knew he felt bad. I thought we'd work it out, eventually. I knew he was having trouble sleeping. Anxiety. Depression. But I was too focused on finding freelance work to make rent. I figured if I could get us back on track, with no gambling or risk-taking, only hard work... then he could rest and get better. But..." I swallowed, looking for the right words. "I should have been there. He'd been to three different doctors and had all these pills. I don't think he knew he wasn't meant to mix them. That would have been something I always checked." My throat felt so tight I could barely breathe. "I wasn't there. I didn't check."

After a brief silence, I heard his voice. "It's not your fault. You were busy surviving, looking after your daughter. You were doing the right thing, Bess. You were doing your best."

I'd so badly needed to hear those words that they completely undid me. Powerful sobs shook my body as I soaked Charlie's shirt with my tears and snot. "I'm sorry," I gasped, trying to wipe it with my sleeve. "I'm sorry."

His fingers scooped damp hair from my neck. "I'm honored

you told me."

"I swore I'd never dump this on you. I don't want pity."

"I don't pity you. I admire you."

"I'm covering your shirt with snot."

"It doesn't matter." He wiped my cheek with his thumb.

I sighed, letting the last trickle of tears out. It wasn't like I could hold anything in. Not today. "You're too good to me."

CHAPTER 29

Charlie

My body clenched at her words. Because I knew I wasn't too good for her. I was deceiving her. I had to get the job situation sorted before she found out from anyone else. And I had to figure out what to do with that campaign. I'd made no real progress so far, and time was running out.

"Bess," I said softly, when her sobs had settled. "What would you do with that financial literacy campaign? What would you do if it was up to you?"

She tensed a little. "The whole thing is a bit of a mismatch, isn't it? Offering financial classes to people who simply need money. In many cases, if someone paid off your loan… if you had money left to invest, then you'd want to learn about investing. But not when you're barely surviving. When your life is so lean and mean there's nothing to play with. Nothing to invest."

"But some of the adjustments you can make will pay off in the long run. You don't need to have any more money. They might help you restructure your loans and save hundreds or even thousands a year."

"Really?" she asked, lifting her head.

Did she not know this?

"So, the question is, how could we reach people who don't know that? Who could really use some savings like that."

"I honestly didn't know that program could help you get more money."

"They teach budgeting. What did you think that was about?"

"I don't know. Whenever I read an article with budgeting tips, it's someone telling you to buy in bulk and put it in a chest freezer when you can't afford to buy bulk or have a chest freezer."

"That sounds stupid. I'm pretty sure the Thriver guys help you apply for cheaper loans and better-paying jobs and financial assistance. And get all the tax deductions you qualify for. They're passionate about helping people. That's why I wanted to work with them. I had to convince Dad that it was worth it, and now I'm failing the campaign and he'll rub it in my face." It felt good to lay it all out in the open. Even if there was no solution. Even if I didn't get to win this one.

Bess lifted her chin against my chest, peering at me. The faint light from my phone cast shadows across her face, adding a touch of drama. "So, money? They help you get money?"

I wasn't sure why I felt so uncomfortable. "Yeah, essentially."

"Then why don't we tell them that? Why talk about financial literacy or budgeting, which implies people are financially illiterate or can't control their spending?"

I drew a sharp breath. Something finally made sense. "You're right. It's like we're telling them they're in financial trouble because they're stupid."

"Some are," she said with a sigh. "But not all. And it's probably not a good angle, either way. We should drop the word 'literacy'. It sounds like you need to go to school to learn something rich people learned a long time ago."

"Yeah," I agreed, my insides rearranging themselves as my mind accepted the new reality. "Let's pitch them something else."

Bess's voice lifted in excitement. "How about we tell them... we know it's expensive to be poor. You're not stupid, but you're stressed. You're tired. You're constantly playing catch-up, always a little behind. You need a break... more than that, you need a lucky break. We're on your side. Our financial experts have helped hundreds of people improve their bank account balance." She lifted her hand off my chest, gesturing with it, her voice rising in excitement. "I don't know how many people they've helped, but it would be cool to know, wouldn't it? Even get some data on how much money they've saved or earned or what they've managed to do with it. Like putting their kid through college. Getting their teeth fixed. Real goals that might feel unachievable."

"Yes!" I grabbed my phone and quickly typed in her words to keep them safe. "Bess, you're a lifesaver."

"We could use real stories of people. Maybe with silhouettes and different names if they want to remain anonymous. But it'd still be impactful to see people who've turned their lives around and hear their words."

"That's brilliant!"

I could hardly contain my excitement, even if the hammock was containing most of my movement. I'd been right about Bess. She had ideas and passion. So much value even Dad couldn't dismiss it.

"You'll need to pitch this," I said.

She stiffened. "I couldn't! You do it. Don't even mention my name. I'm totally happy to be in the background. I'm glad if I can help."

"No, you must. I can't do this one."

"Why not? You can pitch anything."

"Not this one," I insisted. "They need to hear it from you."

Otherwise, they won't see your worth.

If I told her the truth, she'd freak out. I couldn't risk her jumping up and down and destroying the hammock that was separating us from death by hypothermia.

"Can we do it together?" She finally suggested.

"Yeah, sure." I'd make sure she took center stage and shined.

She relaxed against my chest and we both sighed. Sudden exhaustion swept over me. "This has been the strangest, most terrifying, but also the best night of my life." I meant it with all my heart.

"Me, too." She shifted, reaching her hand down my leg.

It took me a while to realize she was looking for her leggings. She helped me find my jeans as well, and we both dressed up with slow, careful movements to avoid rocking the hammock too much. Once fully dressed, she bundled her jacket under her head. Then she slid next to me. There was no room. The tight fabric pinned us together like hot dogs in a bun, but I was tired and deliriously happy. Happy for her and her ideas. Happy to be alive. And that's how I eventually fell asleep, dreaming of everything we could do, together.

CHAPTER 30

Bess

I fell into strange twilight sleep, too exhausted to move, yet too uncomfortable to truly relax. Each time I cracked my eyelids, I saw the same darkness. The night was as long as it was uncomfortable. Like sitting on a crowded bus, desperately trying to respect everyone's personal space when there simply wasn't space. So, you eventually gave up and became part of the human wall, shoulder to shoulder, moving in unison at every turn. Charlie was a good sport, resting his hand against my back, not once making frustrated sounds. Unlike me.

It was one thing to hug and cuddle while we were awake but sleeping in such a tight cocoon put us in danger of cutting off each other's circulation. At some point, I woke up with a numb arm and had to turn around. "I'm turning to even things out," I grumbled. "To make the other arm numb as well."

Charlie grunted in response and turned to spoon me, carefully resting his hand on my hip. I fell asleep again.

When I woke up, I could finally see a faint light. The sun was rising. My every limb stiff and a little cold, my armpits oddly sweaty, I reached up to unzip the cover. "Charlie," I whispered. "I think it's morning."

"Thank God!" He tried to stretch his arms overhead, but there was no space.

I tried to move over him without crushing him to death. "I'll get out and walk around. Maybe restart the fire if I can find the lighter. You can go back to sleep."

"No, I'll go," he protested, eyes half-open. "You don't know how to use my travel espresso machine."

"Seriously?"

He opened the rest of the cover, letting the freezing morning air into the hammock. I burrowed down into the padded fabric, every muscle tightening against the cold. Feeling a little embarrassed but ultimately grateful, I let him get out and zip up the cover. Without him, the hammock felt like a giant, soft cloud that hugged me from every direction. The warmth slowly returned, and the gentle swaying made me sleepy again. Before I knew it, I'd drifted off into a deep, vivid dream. In it, we walked around the empty office floor, got lost and camped out under his desk.

I woke up to the smell of coffee and the crackle of fire and discovered one thing. There is no better way to wake up than swaying in a hammock in the middle of wilderness, smelling an open fire and coffee. Nothing beats it. The absolute bliss lasted for about ten seconds, before my mind began cataloguing things to worry about. Being lost in the forest. Not having cell phone reception or enough food. The possibility of being pregnant. Having to present my half-baked campaign idea to clients that I normally wasn't allowed to talk to. But, despite all the bombarding thoughts, the smell of coffee still helped.

I pulled on my jacket and unzipped the hammock. Pale morning light had transformed the scenery into something fresh and serene. I could hear the babbling creek and saw the clearing we'd stumbled across in the dark, covered in long, dewy grass and one hundred percent less scary. Near the blazing fire, the air didn't feel as cold as before. Charlie sat perched on a log next to the fire pit. Seeing me, he raised his steel cup and smiled. "Coffee? We'll have to share this cup."

By the time I'd climbed out of the hammock, he'd made me a cup, handing it over with a flourish.

"That was fast." I sat next to him, at the far end of the wonky log that sat so close to the ground my knees were up against my chin.

"I had boiling water ready to go." He gestured at a small kettle next to his feet.

"You packed a kettle for a two-hour hike?"

"I heard the hunting cabin had a fire pit and I need it for making coffee, so..."

"What else did you bring? Continental breakfast?" I cast him a hopeful look.

"Sorry. I only have those muesli bars we didn't eat last night."

"I was hoping you were rationing things." As if on cue, my stomach growled.

"I went through my whole backpack in case there were any forgotten treasures. And I found... drum roll, please."

I rapped my hands against my knees, turning it into a vigorous rub to keep them warm. With a cheeky grin, Charlie stuffed his hand into his pocket and pulled out a half-eaten Snickers bar, presenting it to me like a gift from the gods.

"What kind of maniac eats half a Snickers bar?" I stared at the leftover chocolate, then at him. "Explain yourself."

He shrugged. "I guess I forgot to finish it."

"What happened? Earthquake? Bear? The only time I don't finish a chocolate is when Celia steals it from me. Or rather, she reminds me that sharing is caring."

"Teaching kids to share can really backfire." He pulled a silly face.

I nodded. "It really can." Unable to wait any longer, I unwrapped the chocolate bar and tucked into it. "Oh, my God, it's the bigger half!"

"Sharing is caring." He cast me a comically pleading look, his lower lip protruded.

"You already ate half of this," I argued, laughing, but broke off half, carefully catching any crumbs on my palm.

Charlie hesitated a moment but took the chocolate and ate it in one piece as I worked through mine bit by bit, washing it down with the surprisingly strong coffee. When the chocolate was finished, Charlie presented me with the muesli bars. It wasn't exactly the breakfast of champions, but the quick caffeine hit evened out the effect of poor sleep and stiff muscles, making the prospect of venturing back on the path feel possible.

"Any messages on your phone?" I asked.

"One from Gran. She told your mom and they're on their way."

"On their way where?"

"Cozy Creek and Rubie Ridge I suppose."

"Oh, shit." Mom didn't even have a car. She currently spent so much on keeping mine on the road she couldn't afford her own. "We need to get back. They must be worried sick."

"We can't be that far. Let's follow the creek down the hill."

We extinguished the fire, and I helped Charlie pack up the hammock. Having abandoned the leaf-collecting and my shoe-box, my bag was essentially empty, so I offered to take some of Charlie's items. Once we had everything on our backs, we exchanged a meaningful look and headed to the creek.

"I hope you're right, because this is not the easiest path to walk," I said, picking my feet across the terrain.

Rocks and tufts of long grass dotted the creek banks. There was no path at all, only the small stream that took twists and turns as we followed it down the gentle slope. Soon, the stream split into two smaller ones. We picked the stronger one and continued, dodging trees and shrubs and occasionally climbing over larger rocks. Inside the forest, our visibility was limited to a few yards ahead. The cold humidity of the shade settled on my skin, making the air feel cooler. When we finally emerged from the woods, we found the sun had climbed higher and I relished its warmth on my face.

The open plain also offered us with a view, albeit not one I recognized. The mountains rose ahead of us, but the stream seemed to curve to the left, running down towards a dip between hilltops. Soon, the terrain turned steeper and the stream turned into a mini waterfall, gushing and gurgling down the rocks. I could see all the way to the bottom where the ground flattened out again, but there was no easy way down.

Charlie grabbed my arm, holding me back like he thought I might fall. "We'll have to climb down. I'll go first."

He released my arm and began edging down the rocky surface, holding onto a young tree for support. Once he made it to the next tree, I took a deep breath and followed, making sure to trace the exact path he was mapping out below. But he was a lot taller, with longer legs.

As I reached for a rock ledge to find my next footing, I fumbled. A smaller stone came loose under my foot, and I rolled down with it, scraping my ass along the bumpy surface until I landed against a large pine like a downhill skiing cartoon character. I only realized I'd hurt my ankle when I tried to take another step and it buckled. Pain seared through my left foot, all the way up to my calf. If I hadn't still been holding onto that pine, I might have fallen all the way down.

"I can't walk!" I cried. My voice echoed back from the rock wall, amplifying the panic. "I think I twisted my ankle."

Charlie climbed back up to meet me until I could wrap my

arms around his neck.

"Hold on to me," he said, carefully inching his way down the slope, holding onto trees and exposed roots. "This feels like the ninja training at the gym—which is a piece of cake for me, so don't worry." Judging by the way he panted, the words were meant to reassure himself as much as me.

When we made it to level ground, he set me down on a mound of soft grass and rolled up my pant leg to examine my ankle.

"It's just a sprain," I said, although I had no idea. Either way, what could he do?

"It's starting to swell up." He felt around my ankle, gently pushing his finger into the skin. It felt tight, like a water balloon being filled. The ankle throbbed in sync with my heartbeat.

Once the initial shock wore off, the reality of the situation dawned on me. I couldn't walk. How were we ever going to get out of this forest?

"Leave me here and keep going, get some help." I gestured at the direction of the stream. "You can follow the stream to get back up here."

"Absolutely not. I can carry you."

I sighed, fighting tears as the pain pulsed through me. "No, you can't. You already have a backpack."

"I'll leave it behind."

"What? Your fancy hammock and coffee maker..."

"I don't care. Give me your bag. I'll put my phone and valuables in there and we'll leave the rest. We can come back for it later."

"Unless the elk find it and use the hammock as part of their mating rituals." I tried to smile. If I joked, he wouldn't see how much pain I was in.

"In that case, I'll let the elk have it. Although I might take the binoculars, so they don't find the sex tape."

I laughed a little through a film of tears. I handed him my small backpack, and he transferred a few items into it. Finding his weird water bag, now half empty, he offered me a drink. "We can probably fill it from the stream. It's bound to be clean. But first..." He went back to his backpack and pulled out the first aid kit. "You're in pain."

I took the painkillers he offered and washed them down with the water.

Charlie hung his rucksack on a low tree branch. "Let's go."

He crouched down to get me on his back. I couldn't remember the last time I'd had a piggyback ride, but it must have been in my childhood. Jack wouldn't have offered—he'd had back issues throughout our relationship. But Charlie lifted me on his back as easily as he'd thrown the rucksack over his shoulder, locking his elbows behind my knees. I wrapped my arms over his shoulders and rested my chin against his neck, feeling like the biggest nuisance on the planet, yet deeply grateful. If he'd left me sitting here by myself with only pain to keep me company... I didn't even want to think about that option. But Charlie wouldn't leave me behind.

"If I'm too heavy, put me down and take a break, okay?" I said into his ear.

"I'm fine."

Crossing open fields, he kept a good pace, leaping over rocks. But when we entered another forest, he slowed down, taking care when passing trees so I didn't bump my sore ankle on anything. After a while, my pain turned into a manageable dull throb. The ankle must have been pumped full of fluids now as I could hardly move my foot, but as the pain subsided, I found it harder to ignore other sensations, such as the familiar scent of his skin and hair, and the way his muscles flexed and moved under his jacket.

I was desperate to find a way out of the forest, yet equally desperate to never again join civilization. Never again to return to the office. Mom was driving here, bringing my daughter. I missed Celia so much I ached, but I knew what that meant. The retreat was over. The fake dating was over. I'd have no reason to ever again share a cabin, bed or hammock with Charlie Wilde.

I inhaled his scent—pine and wood fire mixed with the familiar lemon, trying to memorize every note. This was my last chance. We'd make it out of here. I'd find those morning-after pills and go back to my old life, hoping that Charlie agreed to keep our shared retreat a secret. If word got out that we'd spent a few nights up in the mountains sharing a cabin and drawing nudes, the rumors would follow me around. And if Charlie insisted that I pitched the campaign idea to our client, it would look like I was sleeping with him to advance my career.

I cringed at the thought. I'd lose everyone's respect. Apart from maybe Teresa and Rhonda. I wondered what Charlie's Gran must have thought about the messages we'd exchanged.

"Your phone, Charlie." I tapped his chest with my hand. "Is it working?"

"It's in your bag."

"Should we check?" If nothing else, I wanted him to take a break.

Charlie helped me down onto a large rock. He didn't audibly groan, but I noticed the way he straightened his back and rolled his shoulders. I was a burden. Literally. I handed him my backpack, and he found his phone.

"No signal." He stared at the screen, frowning.

Were we going deeper into the dead zone with no cell phone coverage? Did that mean we were getting even more lost? There was no way we could return, not with me hanging on Charlie's back.

"And now it's dead," he informed me after tapping the screen a couple of times. "I don't have a battery pack, sorry."

"We went for a two-hour hike, Charlie," I reminded him. "No more apologies."

"I feel awful that you're hurt and hungry and we're lost... This is so not what I wanted for you."

"Don't worry about me. My ankle doesn't hurt that much anymore." I slid off the rock and placed my foot against the ground and leaned on it to test how it felt. The sharp pain made me wince.

"Stop that! You can't walk."

"Yeah, okay."

Charlie filled his water carrier from the stream and we both had a drink before I climbed back on his back and we continued our way down the hill. After a few more minutes of frantic praying, I spotted something shiny between the trees. A roof! It had to be a roof.

"Charlie! There's a house. I think there's a house. Or some sort of building. Or hallucination."

He picked up speed, nearly jogging over the bumpy landscape. As we got closer, the building took shape. It was small and rusty red, maybe a shed of some kind. But where there was a shed, there was a house.

Once we reached the shed, I saw a small, windy path leading from it towards a larger farmhouse with a wraparound porch. After our long journey, the house looked so homely and inviting that I blinked, half-expecting the vision to vanish like a mirage. But as we got closer, I noticed the dirty work boots and flowerpots by the front door. Signs of life!

Charlie lowered me onto the steps before rapping on the door. I held onto the banister, balancing on my healthy foot. After a moment, we heard footsteps and the door cracked open a little, then all the way. A middle-aged woman with kind eyes and an apron tied over a blouse looked at us quizzically. "Hello?"

"I'm sorry to bother you, but we got a bit lost when hiking out there and followed the creek down the mountain, hoping we'd find our way back."

"Oh, dear Lord!" Her eyes widened with compassion. "How long have you been out there?"

"Just one night," I clarified. "We had water, we're fine."

"Except Bess here hurt her ankle and can't walk."

"That sounds like a rough journey." She blew a breath, shaking her head. "How can I help?"

"If I could charge my phone, I could maybe call an Uber or something."

"There's no Uber in Cozy Creek. There's Huber, though."

"There's what?" Charlie angled his head like he hadn't heard that right.

"Jimmy Huber's rideshare. He doesn't let his drivers come all the way here, though. Says it's too far. Anyway, come in from the cold. I've got a fire on." She stepped aside and Charlie helped me into the house.

"I'm Charlie. Charlie Wilde."

"Anna McCreedy. Welcome to our ranch!" She shook Charlie's hand in the doorway and led us into a spacious hall, closing the crispy air outside.

I breathed a sigh of relief. Traveling on Charlie's back, stealing his body heat, I'd kept reasonably warm, but I'd stopped moving. Without the exercise keeping my blood flowing, the cold had crept up my arms and legs, making the non-injured foot feel so cold it was almost numb.

The living room was cozy, a fire blazing in a small stove. Judging by the paneled windows and worn-out wood floors, the house had history. Charlie set me down in a cozy, quilt-covered armchair, then followed the lady to a large shelf of books and board games. And there, right at the edge, a collection of tangled cables grew out a multi-plug like an electronic hanging plant.

"Lightning cable. Perfect." Charlie threw me a smile over his shoulder, immediately plugging in his phone. "It's charging, Bess."

"Thank you so much," I said as I caught our host's eye.

She smiled. "You two are from out of town, aren't you?"

Charlie looked a little flustered but returned her smile. "Is it that obvious?"

She cocked her head. "Well, Cozy Creek's a small place. And I don't know any locals who'd venture into the forest this time of year with nothing on their back." She glanced at the small backpack I was hugging.

"The backpack! Charlie, we have to go back and get it."

"No, we don't." He shot me a stern look. "We need to get you to the doctor." He turned back to Anna. "We had to leave my backpack behind when Bess got injured. I couldn't carry both."

He sounded disappointed with himself, like he'd supposed to. *Oh, Charlie.* The sigh floated out of my chest like a silent prayer. He so desperately wanted to do the right thing, to fix everything. He'd saved me.

"I can send someone out to pick it up if you give me some coordinates." Anna nodded at the door.

I was about to protest, but Charlie jumped at the chance. "It's by the creek, close to the small waterfall."

"I think I know that one. We can get it for you. Where are you two staying? Cozy Creek? I'd take you back myself, but I've got a pie in the oven and two more I'm baking for the Fall Festival—."

"That's okay." Charlie waved his hand, staring at his charging phone. "If I can wake up my phone, I'm sure we can organize a ride."

"Oh, don't worry. I'll call one of my boys to give you a ride. Nash should be done with the horses now. Remind me to give you Jimmy's number, too, if you need a ride later. Tell him I sent you. He doesn't drive tourists." She pulled a cell phone out of her apron pocket and left the room to make the call.

CHAPTER 31

Charlie

I stared at my phone, waiting for the screen to light up. When it did, I picked it up immediately.

"Did it turn on?" Bess craned her neck in my direction. "Can I call my mom? If she's driving here, I need to tell her where we are."

"I think it's best I call Rhonda first."

"Why?"

I was glad she was confined to the armchair, because I had a sneaking suspicion I needed to confirm. "Rhonda is the only person we've had any direct contact with."

"What do you mean? She said she told my mom."

I nodded. "I'll double check."

Gran was a wild card. The phone rang twice before she picked up. "Charlie! Are you out of the woods yet?"

"Yes, we made it to a farmhouse outside of town. Getting a ride back from here."

"So, everything's alright? I can call off the search party?"

"You sent a search party?"

"A small one. I asked your father's PI to trace the text message to the nearest cell tower, and we mapped out your likely location based on that and the coordinates of the retreat. Your father's old buddy is canvassing the area in a helicopter. "

"Who? John? Yeah, let him know." I glanced at Bess who was listening to our call, leaning forward. "Now, you called Bess's mom, right?"

"Of course!" There was a telling pause. "I told her you were camping with the group and out of cell phone range. It was late last night, after dark. I thought, why worry her unnecessarily? What can she do? She doesn't have a helicopter."

I felt like shouting 'I knew it!' but kept my voice calm. "That's okay. We'll handle it from here."

Gran harrumphed at my clipped tone. "Think about it, Charlie. You've been through quite an ordeal. I thought you two could use some time alone before the family arrives."

She was not wrong, and, irrationally, that made me even angrier. I ended the call and approached Bess. "I'm sorry. She told your mom we were camping. So, not the whole truth."

"But, she said." She looked up at me in disbelief.

"Welcome to my family and a whole new level of puppet mastery. If Gran thinks something is best for you, she'll do it."

"And how is it best for me that my mom doesn't know what happened?" Her voice rose a bit.

"Think about it," I urged her softly, sitting on the rug next to her chair. "Gran has been playing a bit of a matchmaker." I winced. "She gets a message late at night that we're lost in the forest but safe. What does she think?"

She blushed. "Well, she's not far off, is she?"

"No," I admitted. "So, she's excited and wants to let things play out."

"But it's not like my mom was going to barge in."

"No. But she will. And we're safe now. We'll be back to the retreat soon enough. Do you want her here? If you do, I'll call her myself, right now. But I think Gran wanted to give you the choice."

"But... she said she told my mom." She huffed, gently moving her swollen ankle, her hand protectively around it. "I was so relieved."

"Which, again, was her goal, I bet." I shrugged apologetically. "And she relayed the message that you were okay so your mom wasn't worried, either."

She huffed, and I saw the anger dissipate.

"Gran traced the cell signal," I continued. "She figured out our approximate location and organized a family friend to canvas the area with a helicopter."

Bess's jaw went slack as she stared at me. "Really? A helicopter? For a couple of fit, young people spending a night in a hammock?"

"My family sends helicopters for less. John was probably on the way to his cabin. Searching for us would have put him an hour out of his way, tops."

"Is he a local?"

"Someone we know from here; from the time we still had the cabin." I stared out the window, at the mountain range ring-fencing the secluded farm. Mountains high enough to stop clouds in their tracks and change the weather. A constant presence. "I miss that place."

"I'm sure you could buy a place up here if you wanted. How much do those cabins go for?"

I hadn't even thought about it until she said it. "How much money do you think I have?" I chuckled.

She blushed. "I don't know. I'm so broke I think everyone else is loaded, sorry. I have no idea what real estate costs up here, or even in the city. It's one of those things that's so far out of my reach that I don't even try to keep up. I tell Celia it's gazillions, every time she asks.

"She asks about real estate?"

"She asks 'Can we buy that house?' or 'Can we live in that house?' and I have to explain that we don't have a gazillion dollars."

I cringed at the thought. I didn't have cash at hand, but I had investments I could pull. If I really wanted to buy a cabin in the woods, I could swing it. Something she saw as unattainable was very much attainable for me. I waited for the familiar urge to shop, to find the perfect cabin and buy it, but nothing ignited in me. The cabin felt meaningless, unless it was for her. With her.

My phone pinged with other missed phone calls and messages. I skimmed through them, catching up on work and sending quick replies to Trevor and Lee, making sure I didn't hold up any jobs. I checked my investments and noticed I'd made five grand on a wild bet. I thought about riding it out to see if I could make more, but as my gaze snapped back to Bess, my fingers itched to cash out. Five grand could probably cover her rent for a while. Why was I risking it for a quick thrill?

As I sent through the sell order, another message pinged. It was from the office and made the hair on my neck bristle like I'd plugged myself into a socket. My eyes scanned the text in a frantic hurry.

...restructuring ... economic downturn ... refocusing our priorities...

It was the warning shot. The first cue before the redundancy packages were rolled out. Bess would be on that list.

Anger fizzled in my chest as I thought about my father, casually flicking through an email like that on a Thursday afternoon. He'd promised to wait until next week to announce the job cuts, but apparently the panic-stirring couldn't wait. And he was probably hanging out at the golf club as his staff worked themselves into a frenzy. In a way, I felt grateful to be far away. But he had no idea how much him jumping the gun messed with my plans.

I needed more time. Could I stop Bess from checking her email? Her phone was useless and there was only one charger, so it made sense for us to charge mine first. Maybe I could delay the inevitable until I had a chance to talk to her. Why hadn't I done it in the forest?

"Are you okay?" Bess asked. "What is it?"

I tried to relax my face. "Nothing. Stupid work stuff."

"That campaign?"

"Yeah," I lied. "But it's okay. Once we present your ideas, they'll change their tune."

She said nothing, only watched me in silence.

Our host, Anna, barged in, wiping her hands on a tea towel. "Good news! My son Nash is on his way over. He'll take you to town."

"Thank you so much." Bess smiled at her.

"Don't thank me, thank him. See if you can get more than one word out of him in response. He can be a bit moody." She rolled her eyes. "But I've bribed him with pumpkin pie so you can expect a swift journey."

I inhaled the aroma coming from the kitchen and my stomach growled like a ventriloquist dummy.

Anna's eyes widened. "I'm so sorry! When did you last eat? Stay for pie. It'll be done in a minute. Nash can have his reward in advance."

I saw Bess's head about to shake and jumped in before she could politely refuse and ruin this chance for both of us. "That sounds amazing! We had some muesli bars, but it's been hours."

"Hours of carrying your girlfriend? You're quite the hero, Charlie." She gave me a warm smile, her head tilted.

My brain kept searching for hints of sarcasm, but there seemed to be none. Yet those words twisted like a knife in my gut. "I'm really not. I'm the reason we got lost. I wanted to see the elk mating, so we followed the sound of bugling and then it got too dark."

"Oh! Did you see them, though? It's quite the sight. Might be worth a bit of extra trouble. Drop a good video like that in the town chat group and people go nuts!" She chuckled.

"We got a video, didn't we?" Bess looked up at me. "Maybe we can share it."

Anna clapped her hands. "Fabulous!"

I brought up the videos I'd taken on the binoculars and let Anna have a look.

"This thing records video? What do you know!" She held the binoculars to her face. "Can you send this to me? My email is up on that board because I keep forgetting it."

The oven timer rang. "That's the pie. I'll bring it over, so you don't have to move with that sore leg."

We chuckled at her email address, printed, and laminated, on a corkboard by the shelf.

The front door opened and a huge guy with a dark beard stepped in, eyeing us with suspicion. "You're the young couple who got lost up the hill?" He made it sound like we'd walked in circles in his backyard like confused toddlers. Which we kind of had.

I straightened, offering him a friendly smile and a handshake. "That's us."

I introduced myself and Bess, and by the time we'd confirmed this was Nash, our ride, Anna barged in with a tray of pumpkin pie and plates. My mouth filled with saliva and Nash's expression thawed considerably.

Maybe it was best he got his reward in advance, so he didn't eat us.

Anna poured us cups of coffee and cut us generous pieces of pie. We dug in, too busy stuffing our faces to engage in small talk. Nothing had ever tasted so good. I couldn't remember the last time I'd eaten something home baked, anyway.

Feeling a lot more alive, we said farewell to our host and gathered our things.

"I'll bring the car closer, so you don't have to... you know," Nash gestured at Bess's leg. As he traipsed across the yard towards a freestanding garage, I handed Bess my phone. "Here you go. It's got enough charge now. Call your mom."

Leaning on the banister, she turned the phone in her hands, looking conflicted. "Maybe it's best that I don't get her all worried. Celia is still at kindergarten... She'll have to pick her up. Does she even need to drive up here? She'd have to borrow a car."

"Your mom doesn't have a car?"

"She uses mine. We sort of share." She glanced up and I could practically see the thoughts crisscrossing in her brain. "What if I can't drive my car back? How do I get it back home? Even if Mom comes here, she can't help. We won't have enough drivers." She dipped her chin, studying her feet as she tried to move her ankle up and down.

"I'm sorry to burst your bubble, but you can't drive anything without a functioning right foot. I can give you a ride back. We'll pick up your car later."

She released a sigh, and her gaze drifted out to the mountains. "I really screwed up this whole thing."

"What thing?"

"This retreat. I was supposed to help you with the campaign, but I don't think I've been much help at all. Instead, there's all this unnecessary drama."

"You didn't deliberately throw yourself down the mountain, did you?"

"No. But I'm clumsy."

"So am I. I once fell off a boat."

"Drunk?"

"Yeah," I admitted. "But you were sleep-deprived and delirious from hunger. It's basically the same thing."

"Where are you guys headed?" Nash called from an open window of his Range Rover. "Rubie Ridge?"

Bess's eyebrows sailed up. "How did you know?"

"You have that... look," he said, looking at me rather than her.

I glanced at my high-tech hiking gear. Despite all the walking, my clothes looked relatively unscathed. Bess had muddied her already worn-out leggings rolling down the hill and her sun-faded jacket had a button missing. For once, I was the odd one out.

"That clueless, out-of-towner look?" I smiled. "I need to get Bess to the doctor. Is there a clinic in Cozy Creek?"

"Sure is."

He didn't elaborate, but jumped out of the car to open the door, helping Bess onto the front seat. I took the backseat on the other side, urging Bess to put her seat back if she needed to.

The windy road navigated a thick forest which sucked us into its shadow. The journey felt longer than I'd anticipated.

"How far are we from town?" I asked.

"Bout twenty miles."

"We walked twenty miles?" Bess frowned.

"We're closer to Rubie Ridge," Nash added.

Bess glanced at me, her eyes filled with worry. "Take us to Rubie Ridge, please. Charlie can drive me to town from there."

I picked up my phone, relieved that the internet was working again. I quickly discovered there was one medical center, which claimed to be well versed in sports injuries—probably because of the nearby ski resorts and the constant stream of tourism. Even better, they were still open for an hour. "Let's go straight to Cozy Creek, if you don't mind. We need to get to the clinic before it closes."

Nash shrugged. "No problem."

I could see the conflict on Bess's face, but as she locked eyes with me, I gave her a warning look. We were at the mercy of kind strangers, but it didn't mean we had to act like doormats. She needed help, and I'd make sure that she got it.

CHAPTER 32

Bess

We made it to the clinic with ten minutes to spare, and were met by a frustrated-looking receptionist.

"We're closing!" she called us, scrambling to push a button somewhere to disable the doors.

"Good thing we made it," Charlie countered with a smile, settling me down in a waiting room chair before he approached the counter. "You'll get rid of us as soon as someone qualified takes a look at my girlfriend's ankle."

The word 'girlfriend' messed up my breathing pattern, and I coughed a little. I could barely see the receptionist behind the plastic safety barrier, but after a moment, I heard a rustle of paper and Charlie joined me with a clipboard full of insurance forms. "I'll need your help with filling these out."

I'd been bracing myself for this moment. I'd tried to divert us back to Rubie Ridge, hoping I could manufacture a miracle healing. Anything to avoid this. But Charlie had been adamant, so here we were.

I filled my lungs. "I don't have health insurance."

He stared at me for a long time. "But... we offer health insurance. It's part of your contract."

"Yes, for the full-timers. But most of us in production are part-timers."

Was he not aware of this?

"Wait, what? You're there all the time! You work full-time."

I lifted a shoulder. "I get offered extra hours on a regular basis."

"So, you essentially work full-time but don't get the benefits?" The confusion on his face was starting to morph into anger.

"I appreciate the extra hours," I added. "I need them."

"But... even part-timers are offered insurance, right?"

He really didn't know. Charlie, who wanted everyone to be happy and everything to be good and fine, had no clue what was going on right under his nose. I almost didn't want to burst his bubble.

"The premiums are more than I can afford right now, so I opted out," I explained carefully. "I can only afford to cover Celia."

"How much?" he asked breathlessly.

"Five hundred per month," I answered. "I know it's not that bad. I'm just in a tight spot right now so I can't do it."

His eyes were dark. "Because of the debt?"

I nodded; my voice lost somewhere deep inside.

"Bess. I need you to be honest. Are the debt collectors threatening you?"

"No! Of course not." I frequently received threatening letters informing me of the down payment schedule, but so far nobody had turned up at my door with a baseball bat or mentioned my kneecaps. Jack had been smart enough to not borrow from the worst of the sharks, even if the interest and late fees were ridiculously high. But as long as I kept on top of my payments, I'd make it through. If I worked extra hours on the weekend, I could even put a little aside and start paying for health insurance. I had a plan.

Charlie stared at me, his mouth a straight line. He may have doubted me, but didn't push any further. Instead, he returned the clipboard to the counter and pulled out his credit card.

I buried my face in my hands, praying for my ankle. Please, no fractures. Nothing requiring a cast. I needed this to be a bone bruise, nothing more.

God heard me, but must have stopped listening half-way through.

An hour later, we sat on a park bench by the town square, my foot in a moon boot. There was no fracture, but possibly a torn ligament. Terms 'physical therapy' and 'surgery' had been thrown about and resolutely ignored by me. I was choosing to focus on the rest, elevation and wearing the boot—three things I could manage on a low budget. I'd already figured that with the boot on, I could put a bit of weight on my foot without screaming from pain. The crutches helped, too.

Now, a little high on painkillers, watching the yellow and orange leaves gently float down from the mature trees, I felt hopeful.

"I called Huber." Charlie bit back a smile. "They should be here soon."

I nodded, my gaze still on the leaves. Falling slowly, gently towards the ground. "It's so beautiful."

"Absolutely perfect," he agreed, but he wasn't looking at the leaves. He was looking at me.

Later, I blamed the painkillers for messing with my head. It was easier than blaming some deep, dark part of myself. Because I didn't think about the morning-after pill. I briefly thought about it when the radiologist asked if there was any chance I could be pregnant. No, I said. Too quickly. But she didn't notice, and it didn't matter. Because I was going to get the pill. Then they offered me some codeine, and after that I didn't think about it at all.

I didn't think about it when I sat outside the freaking pharmacy, waiting for Charlie to pick up my prescriptions. I didn't think about it when he carried me to the park bench, past a group of kids playing in a pile of fallen leaves.

I still wasn't thinking about it when a blue Bronco claiming to be our taxi arrived or as I listened to the cute driver named Noah chat about his new life in Cozy Creek. In fact, he sounded so genuinely excited about small-town life that I got swept away into the fantasy of it all, imagining myself living here.

I made it all the way to our cabin, still floating in that light-headed lull, feeling like everything would be fine. Like everything would always be fine. Until the rainbow-haired receptionist barged in, her voice shrieking from panic. "You're back! You're here."

"Yes, we are," Charlie confirmed, collapsing at the table. "Did we miss dinner?"

Rainbow-hair blinked, confused. "What? No. I don't know. You've been away for twenty-four hours! Everyone's freaking out. I had to inform your families." She turned to me. "Your mother is on her way."

"What? Right now?"

"She just called from town, asking for directions." She turned to Charlie. "And your father—"

"Told you he already knows and sent a helicopter?" She nodded, and Charlie gave her a wry smile. "So, you're saying if we go right now, we might still get dinner?"

He got up and helped me to my feet. Or rather, one foot.

"Excuse me." He pushed past the receptionist to get out the door. "We're a bit hungry."

My eyes caught her name tag again. Harley. She must have reprinted it. Harley followed us outside and all the way to the main building, asking endless questions of our night in the mountains. Charlie gave her terse answers with enough information to satisfy her curiosity until she finally left us alone with the Malaysian curry. Its heavenly scent had already infiltrated my brain, making me half-float towards the pile of plates, gently bouncing on a dispenser.

Finally, with my mouth full of delicious chicken, my body decided to send me a terrifying message. A tiny twinge deep in my abdomen.

The morning-after pill!

My fork-holding arm halted in midair and everything I'd already eaten started second-guessing its intended direction. I took a deep breath, determined to keep my food down. I'd have to figure this out.

"Charlie," I whispered as my stomach gradually settled. "The pill."

Charlie put down his fork and swallowed. "What pill?"

It was a reasonable question since he'd earlier picked up a bag of them for me.

"The pill. The one I need within twenty-four hours."

His eyes widened in understanding. "Sorry, I totally forgot."

My face felt hot. "Me too. This is a disaster."

"Mommy!"

I turned towards the sound and saw my daughter. She ran across the floor with her arms outstretched. Behind her marched my mother, eyes wide with worry. "You're here! They just called to tell me. I'm so relieved!"

Celia climbed into my lap, snuggling against my chest and holding on so tight I could barely breathe. I felt Mom's hand on my head, patting my hair. Too many emotions crowded my heart and mind, making it difficult to speak. How much my child had missed me. How much they cared. And how sweet it felt to hug her, despite everything. Through my turmoil, I heard Charlie greeting my mother, asking her about knitting. Where had he learned about her hobby? Mom was part of a Ladies Yarn-Bombing group that covered trees in colorful knits and was always happy to talk about it.

Listening to their chatter, I regained my equilibrium. After a moment, my eyes searched for Charlie. It was like my body knew I needed to see him, even when my mind was undecided. He smiled at me across the table, then waited to catch Celia's eye. She gave him a shy smile.

"Did you miss your mom?" he asked.

Celia nodded, burrowing her head into my chest.

Charlie offered my mom a seat at the table and we shuffled to make room for her. That's when she noticed my moon boot.

"She's okay." Charlie jumped in before Mom could react. "The foot's been X-rayed. It's not fractured, but there's possibly a torn ligament. She needs a lot of rest and some physical therapy, but she'll be fine. I'll make sure she gets any treatment she needs."

"Good." Mom sighed, fixing her wispy strawberry blond bob as she collapsed in her seat.

She'd always been a hopeless romantic. She'd fallen for the Irish poet, lived in Dublin and believed everything would work out. Until it didn't. But, despite her own misfortune and my horrible luck in love, she still believed in fairytales, insisting that I should look for true love. Or failing that, a dependable wage earner who I'd grow to love. And there, watching her carefully assess Charlie from head to toe, I wondered if the ankle injury had made me telepathic, because I could hear the thoughts in her head.

Handsome. Wealthy. Responsible. Hang onto this one.

A week ago, I would have scoffed at 'reliable', but now the word slipped through without raising any alarm. I'd been relying on Charlie. I'd been hanging onto him for dear life and we'd made it out safely. But I couldn't hang onto Charlie by getting pregnant. I had to get that pill somehow, from a town where nothing seemed to be open after five p.m. My eyes felt teary, but it was probably some sort of panic sweat from my brain.

Panic was contagious though, and I had to make sure Mom didn't get onboard.

"I'm sorry you had to come all the way here." I gave her my most reassuring smile, under the circumstances. "I tried to message you, but my phone died and Charlie didn't have any reception. But we are both fine, I swear."

Mom studied me for a moment, trying to decide if she could trust my words. My delivery was a little shaky, but the message was one she wanted to hear, and that helped. She grabbed my napkin and tried to fan herself with it. "I'm so relieved! The thoughts I had running through my head on the drive..." She sagged lower in her seat, sniffing dramatically.

"That must have been awful. I'm sorry." I offered her my half-eaten plate. "Are you hungry?"

In my family, we fixed everything with food, as if low blood sugar was the primary source of emotional upheaval.

Charlie jumped to his feet. "Finish your meal, Bess. I'll get your mom a plate. Celia?"

"Cheese sandwich and apple juice, please," my daughter announced, looking up at Charlie like he was a genie who granted wishes.

"There's only curry." I pointed at my plate. "Take it or leave it."

She dropped her chin, a picture of sadness. "Okay."

"I'll see what I can do." Charlie disappeared into the kitchen.

Mom didn't waste any time leaning in with prying eyes. "So, what is the situation? Are you two...?"

I shook my head. "It's not a good idea. I have to work with him. I can't risk my job."

"Some things might be worth a bit of risk-taking." She raised her eyebrow, sneaking a piece of cauliflower off my plate.

"You know I can't. Not right now. And speaking of risk..." I glanced at my daughter, spinning on her chair, taking in the huge, light-filled space, walls adorned with paintings. I could only hope she wasn't listening that carefully. "I need to find a morning-after pill, but the pharmacy in Cozy Creek is closed. If we drive back right away, I could find a 24-hour one back home," I whispered, half-terrified, half-relieved to get the truth out.

Mom stared at me for a moment, mouth ajar, eyes huge. Her fingers clasped the cross around her neck. "Oh, dear. Oh, dear. Well, we better get going then."

I gave her a grateful nod. I knew she'd understand.

We were about to get up when Charlie barged through the

kitchen door and placed the grilled cheese sandwich and a tall glass of apple juice in front of Celia. "Here you go, madam."

"I'm not madam," she giggled. "I'm Celia."

"I'm sorry, of course you are."

Charlie rushed back to the buffet and filled a plate for my mom.

"You don't have to..." Mom protested half-heartedly, but accepted the food.

As she tucked in, I finished my meal and made a move to stand up. Charlie blocked my way. "What do you need? I'll take your dishes away." He took the plate off me. "Sit down. Rest that leg and keep it elevated. I'll get you an extra chair."

"Will you also go to the bathroom for me? I left my crutches in the car."

Charlie didn't miss a beat. "I'll take you there."

He helped me up and wrapped his hand around my waist, supporting me better than the crutches ever could. "We'll be back soon," he called to Celia and Mom.

As we exited the cafeteria, we ran into Miranda.

"You're back! What happened? Everyone was so worried!"

Charlie gave her a quick rundown of our mountain adventures and she made appropriate noises of sympathy, frequently glancing out the window, staring at the mountain range in horror. "I can't even imagine."

"It wasn't that bad," Charlie said. "But Bess needs to use the bathroom and I'm on duty, so..."

"Oh, of course." Miranda flashed us an exaggerated smile and leapt ahead of us to open the disabled bathroom door.

As Charlie helped me through the doorway, I heard Miranda's heels click on the hardwood floor. She was heading towards the art studio, presumably to update the others on our survival.

Locked inside the large bathroom with safety rails, I turned to Charlie. "So, I'm peeing in front of you?"

Charlie pressed his ear against the door. "I can hear them coming." He winced. "Don't make me go back out there."

"I thought you liked talking to people."

The way he vividly recounted our night in the wilderness to the captivated Miranda, I imagined him as an actor poised behind the theater curtain, eager to return to the stage and dazzle once more.

He cast me a desperate look. "But... I just did. I'm done. They'll come and ask me to tell the same story again, and I don't like *that* story."

"What story?"

He stared at his hiking boots. "You know ... the sanitized version. I don't want to tell that story because every time I do, the real story fades."

And just like that, he made sense to me. Painfully. Completely. Because it was all the things I couldn't tell that mattered. All the moments we'd shared that I wanted to keep forever. I didn't want them morphing into funny anecdotes or mortifying mistakes, downplayed to keep the tone light.

"I like our real story, too. The uncensored one." I caught his eyes, and a fire rushed through me until I remembered where I was. "This isn't part of that story, though. Right?" I glanced at the toilet bowl.

There were romantic locations, and then there was this.

He grinned. "Okay. We can edit this out." He shifted between me and the toilet bowl, blocking my view. "Let me stay on this side of the door. I'll close my eyes and block my ears and sing."

I sighed. I'd given birth in front of three strangers. I could pee in front of one Charlie.

Despite my full bladder, I held still, suddenly aware of the opportunity I had. We were alone, maybe for the last time. I had to update him. "Charlie?"

"Yeah?"

"I need that morning-after pill. I told my mom. She'll drive me back to Denver."

His eyes flashed with alarm. "What, now?"

I nodded. "I can't risk it. What happened out there was the most terrifying and magical thing in my life." I bit my lip, forcing myself to look into his eyes. "I don't want it to become a cautionary tale."

CHAPTER 33

Charlie

My heart hammered, and I felt the panic tightening my chest. Time was up. She was leaving, and I hadn't told her the truth. If she returned to work, she would hear about the restructuring. If she got her phone working, she'd probably hear about it on the drive home. And she'd instantly know I'd kept it from her.

I couldn't let her leave.

I grabbed my phone and began searching through my contacts. I needed a favor, and there was only one guy I could trust.

"Can you turn around?" Bess asked, using the safety rail to limp her way to the toilet bowl.

I found a rain soundtrack on Spotify and maxed out the volume, making it sound like someone was showering.

"I feel like I'm peeing on a lower deck of the Titanic."

"Did the lower decks have plumbing?" I asked, focusing my eyes on the phone screen.

Trevor was online, as usual, the three dots immediately popping up as I messaged him. The giant Scot wouldn't leave me hanging. Thankfully, he was one of the irreplaceable ones, and not worried about the restructuring.

Charlie: Are you at work?

Trevor: Yes. People are going bonkers over here. Stay away.

Charlie: SOS. I need you to drive to Cozy Creek. Via a pharmacy.

Trevor: On my way. Send me the deets.

My shoulders dropped and typed the instructions.

I heard the tap over the rain soundtrack and turned around, holding up my phone. "There! I organized a driver to pick up the pill and meet us here. ETA two hours."

She stared at me like I'd summoned a spirit out of the toilet bowl. "What? How?"

"Don't worry about it. But now you don't have to leave, right? We're not in a hurry." I took a tentative step closer, grasping her damp hands over the washbasin.

I wanted to lose myself in those eyes and experience even an inkling of what we'd shared in the forest. I would have taken ten percent. A few more minutes.

"What about my mom and Celia? They came all the way here."

I'd already thought of it, and the words rushed out. "Invite them to stay! The cabin is paid for and has enough beds. I'll clear out and book into somewhere in town. We can take Celia there tomorrow to see that Fall Festival. It looked cool. Do you think she'd like it?"

I thought about the hay bales, cute stalls, and the carousel. Kids loved that stuff, right?

"You'd do that?" She breathed the words in utter disbelief.

She had no idea what I was willing to do. No idea what an idiot I was.

"I'd rather do that than go back to our lives in Denver. Am I the only one?"

She placed her hands on my chest, her lips a breath away from mine. "No."

Relief flooded my body. Suddenly, she was so close that everything became blurry. All I could think of was that mouth on mine, her spine curving against my arm as I pulled her flush against me. I held her slightly off the floor, making sure she didn't place any weight on that injured leg, placing kisses down her neck and collarbone, inhaling deeply. "Bess," I murmured. "Stay with me. Give me time. Let me show you..."

I lost my train of thought as she softly moaned under my touch.

Tears stung deep behind my eyes. I was holding on too tightly, too desperately. I feared hurting her, but at this rate, I was also going to get hurt.

Be cool, Charlie. You're not like this.

My heart would not listen, and my arms grabbed onto her, holding even tighter.

It wasn't only the upheaval at work I worried about. I'd seen the look in her eyes when she held her child. Despite all her challenges, her life was already full of meaning. She had a mother who loved her enough to personally show up. She was the entire world to her child. My family would send a helicopter, but I would go back to an empty apartment. Without her, I had nothing.

She wouldn't risk even the tiny possibility of my seed growing inside of her, and that pained me more than I cared to admit. Not because I wanted a baby right now. But because it didn't scare me like it scared her.

I knew I couldn't make her see things from my point of view. We lived in such different realities. To her, another child equaled bankruptcy. And it was her body. But, I was desperate to hold on to what we had, now that she still responded to my touch. So, I kissed her again and again, working up a level of excitement that could only lead to frustration, enjoying every little sound from her throat, every time she relaxed a little more into my touch. Her tongue met mine in a slow game of chicken, neither of us willing to back down.

Maybe she wanted to hold on, too?

Finally, we ran out of breath and held there, her forehead pressed against mine, panting in unison.

"In different circumstances," I said, "Would I be such a horrible candidate for a baby daddy?"

She let out a shaky laugh, pulling away to look me in the eye. "What?"

Hiding my gnawing anxiety under theatrics, I threw my arms out, eyes wide. "I'm serious! Am I such a horrible choice?"

Embarrassment reddened her cheeks. "I'm not looking for a

baby daddy."

"So… never again?" I wanted the truth. Even if it hurt.

"No, I mean… I wouldn't want a baby daddy. Isn't that someone you breed with who gives you money?"

I wanted to kick myself. "Fuck. I didn't mean it like that. I meant… me, as a father. I don't know. Maybe I'm totally delusional. It's a lot harder than it looks, right?"

Her smile disappeared, and she looked at me for a long time, eyes narrowing and then widening again like she was having trouble reading something. I swallowed. Could she see the ball of anxiety in the pit of my stomach that reared its ugly head every time I thought about starting a family? I'd chickened out so many times, discouraged by my parents' example. I didn't want to breed children to heap them with money, privilege, and expectations. I didn't want to be the father who used financial carrots to control their offspring.

"You really want a family, don't you?" Her eyes regarded me with a sense of wonder. "But you're scared."

My lungs deflated. "Yeah."

She smiled the sweetest smile I'd ever seen, one that crinkled the corners of her eyes and painted her whole face with sunshine. "Oh, Charlie! You'd be wonderful."

"I hope so. I haven't had the best role models. Except Gran."

"Me, neither," she admitted. "My father lives in Dublin with his new family. I barely see him."

My heart squeezed. "That sucks." I pulled her in for a hug. "Thank you for believing I could do better."

"Easily." She breathed deeply against my chest.

I inhaled the flowery scent of her hair, now mixed with pine and earth. I could smell the entire forest and mountains embedded in my Bess. She was my greatest adventure, and one day she'd accept it. I wanted to stay there forever, but we both knew the time was running out.

Reluctantly, I turned toward the door. "Shall we?"

She halted, looking at me for one last time. Silently acknowledging everything that had happened and that it'd be there, even when we found ourselves back in the real world, separated by work and responsibilities. At least that's what I chose to believe.

I cracked the bathroom door, peering into the hallway. At first glance, it seemed empty. Whoever had been out there had become tired of waiting and left. But as I swung open the door, it hit something. Someone.

We rounded the door and discovered Ilme, our Estonian art teacher. She must have been running down the hallway at that exact moment, blindsided by the opening door. Her long, paint-adorned lab coat was open and her top knot had unraveled, hanging over her shoulder. Her eyes were red-rimmed, matching the color of her nose that appeared to be bleeding.

"Oh, my God! Ilme?" Bess hopped to the side to lean on the wall so I could help the teacher.

"I'm sorry!" I popped back into the bathroom to get her some tissues.

"Thank you." She stuffed pieces into her nostrils to stop the bleeding. "It was my fault. I wasn't looking. I'm quite upset."

"Why? What happened?" Bess asked.

I sighed. There were only so many people whose problems I could handle at that moment. My troubled ladies' dance card was full. But I could tell Bess had a soft spot for the Estonian teacher. And if she cared, I cared.

"I was fired." Ilme sniffed. "I wasn't pushing their products and catalogs. I told you guys to pick things from nature. Apparently, that's not good for business."

"That's terrible," I said lamely, lending one arm to support Bess and the other to pat Ilme on the shoulder as we made our way back to the dining hall. "I'm sure you'll find another teaching job. There are lots of art schools."

"So unfair!" Bess huffed. "Why would they do that? Why?"

The dining room was empty now, the buffet cleared away. Bess's mom and Celia sat at the corner table, looking at something on a phone screen.

"Come sit with us," Bess told her. "Let's talk."

Ilme nodded gratefully and joined our little table. Bess introduced her to her mom.

"Kathy," she said, offering her hand. "Nice to meet you. I've never met anyone from Estonia."

"That's understandable. There are only 1.3 million of us."

Kathy laughed a little, noticing her bloody nose, red eyes, and general shakiness. She exchanged a quick glance with us. Bess nodded at the same time I did, vouching for the misunderstood artist.

"I'm so glad you got back safely!" Ilme cast us a grave look.

"They said it was my fault. If we'd ordered those expensive items from the catalog and never went outside, you wouldn't be lost in the mountains and eaten by a bear." She added a rare half-smile. "I'm being dramatic, sorry. I added the part about the bear."

"It was definitely not your fault!" Bess's eyes burned. "We didn't get lost because we were collecting leaves or pinecones. We got lost because we were reckless."

"I was," I added, earning a sharp look from Kathy.

"But to lose your job over that... it doesn't make sense!" Bess frowned, eyes flashing with the injustice of it. "I'd be furious." She paused for a beat and the color drained from her face. "I'd be screwed."

I swallowed a swelling lump. If she was this worked up over someone else's temporary teaching job, what would she do when she found out about hers?

"It's okay." Ilme patted Bess's hand, sensing she'd triggered something. "I'll get paid. I'll be fine, but I won't be asked to come back. They don't feel *comfortable...*" She flashed her eyes, elongating the word.

"Their loss," Kathy said decisively. "I've been making art installations in public parks on a tiny budget for years. It's so rewarding. Using nature as part of our creation... I love that! And being in a location like this, you should absolutely connect with the natural environment and use found materials. That makes so much sense." She cast a dreamy look out the window, sighing at the scenery, and I saw my opportunity.

CHAPTER 34

Bess

I noticed the spark in Charlie's eyes before he spoke, and my whole body tensed in anticipation.

"You should stay! The cabin is paid for until Saturday morning. There are two double beds. The meals are included. I already booked myself into another place in town so it's all yours."

Mom raised her delicate brows, staring at him in disbelief. "Cabin? Here?"

Charlie got up. "I'll go sort it out with the front desk."

"But we don't have anything. I mean, I packed a change of clothes but not much else. I wasn't sure how long it would take." She threw me a questioning look. "And I was under the impression that Bess really needed to get back to Denver tonight?"

Her look turned exaggeratedly meaningful, and Charlie responded with similarly over-the-top eyeballing. "That has been taken care of. She can stay."

Mom looked a little confused. "What about Celia?"

"She can skip one day of kindergarten, can't she? We can go to the Fall Festival in Cozy Creek tomorrow. I looked it up and they have a cotton candy stand and a petting zoo with bunny rabbits."

Celia looked up from the phone, her eyes so huge she could have passed for a cartoon character. "Yes! Please, Mom! Please, Nana!" Her little head whipped back and forth between us.

"Well played," I told him wryly. "Sugar and baby bunnies."

"I play to win." He grinned back, impervious.

Mom was warming up to the idea, her gaze frequently flicking to the mountains, which were beginning to take on that red evening hue. The sun hung low behind the trees, sending golden beams through the branches. "This is an exceptional place. I do have our knitting group meeting on Saturday morning, but I guess I could reschedule."

"Perfect!" Charlie enthused. "Two nights of fresh mountain air, outdoor spa and catering. You'll come back a new person."

She blushed, giving him a shy smile. "You know how to convince a lady."

"He works in advertising, Mom." I flicked Charlie a bemused side-eye.

My mother was already sold. "I am borrowing Gail's car, and I know she's not fussy about it, but I could return it on Saturday since we're meeting at her house." Her eyes sparkled with excitement as she batted her lashes. "Did you say there was a spa?"

I rolled my eyes. Mom had spent more time studying Rubie Ridge website than I had. She knew exactly what the place offered.

"A hot tub under the stars," Charlie confirmed with a grin.

"I have a swimsuit you can borrow," I added, sharing a quick smile with Charlie.

"It is a gorgeous location," Ilme echoed. "I wish it wasn't run by pretentious moneybags."

Charlie looked out the window, eyes hard. "I know the type."

Listening to my mom and Ilme chat about the healing properties of the mountain air, my face softened into a smile. Despite everything on my mind, I was feeling hopeful again, almost giddy. Even the dull ache in my ankle couldn't dampen my spirits. Charlie had done it again. He'd somehow turned everything around and saved the day.

"Do you want to see the cabin?" He asked Celia, who nodded vigorously, finally dropping Mom's phone on the table.

"Will you be okay?" I asked Ilme as we got up. "Do you have to go back to Estonia?"

Her eyes met mine, sharpening. "There's an Estonian saying—the brave wolf has a fat chest." She frowned. "Okay, it doesn't translate well. But it means if you want to be fed, you have to go hunting. I'll hunt for a new job."

"If I ever open an art center, I'll hire you immediately," Charlie said.

"Watch out. I'll make people uncomfortable," she warned him, whisking a long strand of dark hair off her face.

He laughed a little, then gave her a focused stare. "You're an artist! Art is supposed to make us uncomfortable. Artists are the gatekeepers of truth."

Before we left the dining room, I caught a glimpse of Ilme's face and knew his words had hit home. Charlie had sprinkled his magic all over the room.

How did he do it?

A few minutes later, we'd dragged Mom's bags into the cabin. Celia familiarized herself with every piece of furniture, jumping from the chair to the couch to the bed, squealing with delight. I couldn't remember the last time we'd done an overnight trip anywhere. She occasionally slept on Mom's couch. That was it. Witnessing the pure joy she drew from this adventure brought tears to my eyes.

"I'll take this," Mom announced from the loft, testing the sofa bed. "You, your giant boot and Celia can sleep in the big bed."

"I'll ask them to change the sheets," Charlie said, already on his phone.

"No." I placed my hand over his phone, enjoying the excuse to touch his fingers. They were so warm. "Unless you peed the bed."

"Did you pee the bed?" Celia asked him in earnest. "I sometimes do. But not anymore because I'm a big girl."

"That's great," Charlie said, struggling to keep a straight face. "No, I didn't pee the bed this time."

"Then it should be fine. You've only slept there for three nights."

"Three nights pining for you." He raised a meaningful eyebrow, and I nearly choked on my saliva. I'd forgotten how men could be shameless and disgusting and charming, all at the same time.

"Okay, yeah. Let's change the sheets. Maybe on both beds." I looked up at the loft, then locked eyes with Charlie. From the look on his face, I knew he was thinking of that first night.

"Good call," he said, his voice a little husky.

"So, where are you staying?" I asked.

I wanted to stay there, too. Not that I didn't want to cuddle my child. Only those cuddles would progress to her kicking me in the shins all night long. I'd carry her to the toilet, disoriented and violently thrashing in my arms, so she wouldn't have an accident, since Mom hadn't packed any diaper pants. Despite the fear of hypothermia and other complications, I'd enjoyed the respite from my usual nighttime routines. I'd enjoyed myself so much, despite everything. I felt lighter than in years.

"I... it's a small place, just outside Cozy Creek."

"Are you coming here for breakfast tomorrow?"

"I wouldn't miss it! Seeing you mix all the cereals is the highlight of my day. I can only imagine what your daughter will do."

"Is it okay if she eats there? What about Mom?"

"It's all sorted. They're more than happy to let them stay, knowing that I won't sue them."

"Seriously? What would you sue them for? Your own stupidity?"

He lifted a shoulder. "A poorly organized excursion, failure to provide instruction, general health and safety. It doesn't really matter if you can afford the lawsuit."

"Did you threaten them?"

"Not in so many words, but they know my family." He sighed. "Look, it's complicated. The main thing is that I won't be suing them, as long as they treat you and your family like royalty. So, let me know how they're doing." He flashed me a cheeky smile.

The rules really were different for rich people. My mind boggled, but I couldn't deny it felt nice to know Mom and Celia would get preferential treatment. They never got that.

"Are you joining the art classes?" I asked.

He looked down, a little ashamed. "I'd love to, but I'm running out of time. I need to work on the new campaign. I'm trying to set up a meeting to present it first thing on Monday."

"I'll help you. Mom can watch Celia. What time is the festival?"

He looked up something on his phone. "It starts at midday and goes until sundown."

"Maybe we'll go after lunch?"

"Sounds good." He smiled.

I bit my lip. "Sorry, I'm in mom mode. It's mostly scheduling, with some health and safety thrown in."

His smile widened. "I can see the spreadsheets reflected in your eyes."

I made my eyes comically large, staring at him. "It's my default setting. Sexy stuff, eh?"

"The sexiest," he said, licking his lips.

There was no joke that could ruin the mood for this guy, and I kind of liked it. The way he looked at me left no doubts. I no longer wondered what Charlie thought of me, or bothered to hide the way my body responded to him. It felt good to be open about it, even if I now worried how I was ever going to reel it in and act professionally around him.

The stairs creaked as Mom returned from the loft, grabbing Celia off the bed where she was doing somersaults. Charlie waved his hand, retreating to the door. "I'll be off then. See you in the morning!"

"Text me when you get there?" I asked him. "I'll charge my phone. It's still somewhere in my bag." I gestured at my backpack lying on the couch.

Charlie's expression shifted, and he leapt to the couch to grab my bag. "I totally forgot!"

"Oh, right. Your wallet!"

I walked over to the kitchenette to give Celia a drink of water as Charlie retrieved his valuables from the bottom of my bag.

Suddenly, I heard his alarmed voice. "Your phone's not here!"

"What?"

"It's not here! It must have dropped somewhere. The bag was open on the side. Did you ever tip it over?"

"No. I don't think so." I rushed to examine the bag.

I turned it inside out, sticking my hand into every pocket. The phone was gone. This couldn't be happening! "Where the heck is it?"

He gave me a pained look. "I don't know. Sorry."

"Did you lose anything? Your wallet?"

"No, all good." He lifted the wallet to show me it was safe before slipping it into his back pocket.

Deep breaths, I told myself. The phone was worth nothing. I only had to replace it somehow.

"Kathy?" Charlie called from the door. "Can I have your phone number? Just in case, since we've lost Bess's phone."

Mom appeared by my side, Celia in tow. "You lost your phone? How?"

"I don't know," I said, my chin wobbly. "Maybe in the forest? Maybe when I fell?" I turned to Charlie. "Was it in my bag when you put your things in there?"

He looked away, thinking back. "I'm not sure. I guess I didn't really check. I just dropped my things in there."

"Then I must have lost it when I fell," I decided, not that it made any difference. I'd never see that phone again.

"Anna from that ranch emailed back. They found my backpack in the forest. I'll send someone to get it. I'll let you know if your phone's in there. If it's not, I'll get you a new one," Charlie said decisively, opening the front door. "Let me know if you have any preferences."

"What? No!"

"No preference? I'll choose, then. Judging by your wardrobe, I'm going to go with something black." He glanced at my black jeans and dark sweater. "With amazing battery life."

"Get purple, Mommy!" Celia yelled, hanging on my arm.

"No... I'm not arguing over the color! You're not buying me a phone. I lost it. It's my problem."

"It'll be my problem if I can't call you."

"Here's my number." Mom interrupted, sticking a piece of paper in Charlie's hand. "You can contact us on this. And my daughter is most grateful for your offer to replace that phone if you can't find it. She's having trouble remembering her manners."

"That's okay. Tell her it'll be my pleasure. I love shopping."

Charlie winked at me, pocketing the note. He crouched down to say good night to Celia, teaching her an elaborate handshake that involved some slapping and clapping and lots of giggling on the girl's part. Finally, he stood up and gave me the saddest smile I'd ever seen. "Are you okay?"

I nodded a little shakily. "Are you?"

He looked like he was about to say something, but instead waved his hand and pivoted on his heels, rushing down the steps. I watched him jog down the path towards the parking lot, eventually disappearing into the shadows.

For a moment, I felt his absence like a tangible void, a vortex of negative ions that seemed to suck the joy right out of me. How was I supposed to neutralize the effect of Charlie fucking Wilde?

I'd made myself a cup of tea when I heard knocking. Had he come back? I put down the cup, my heart pulling me toward the door until I realized it wasn't him.

It was Trevor.

The burly, bearded, six-foot-five Scot with a distinctive laugh I could both hear and recognize from anywhere in the office. But he wasn't laughing. Swiping his mop of curly hair off his eyes, Trevor handed me a paper bag with a pharmacy logo on it.

It took me embarrassingly long to figure out what it was. The morning-after pill! The delivery man Charlie had arranged was his star copywriter who worked with our biggest clients and had a way with the words that could turn every woman's knees to jello—he'd proven that on one slam poetry open mic night I'd uncharacteristically taken part in. Now, staring at his slightly hunched frame and apologetic face, I thought of the haunting lines he'd written for his deceased mother.

"Please, don't tell anyone," I asked breathlessly.

"I already promised Charlie. I'm not a gossip."

"Of course not."

"Well, I better get back."

"Right away? It's such a long drive." I frowned, staring at the paper bag. At work, I struggled to order more toner for the printer and now I was getting one pill hand delivered. The whole thing seemed insane.

Trevor flicked his wrist to dismiss my worries. "Trust me. Right now, it bodes well for me if Charlie owes me a favor. The bigger, the better."

"Why? What do you need from him?"

Trevor looked a little startled, like he'd remembered something. "No reason. Nothing. Um... It's just something I like to have in my back pocket to pull out at an opportune time." He flashed a cheeky smile, wiggling his eyebrows, but I couldn't shake the feeling he was hiding something.

I didn't have time to figure it out, though, before he excused himself, jogging back to his car.

I closed the door as Mom appeared. "Celia's ready for bed.

Who was that?"

"A delivery guy," I said, too tired to explain. "He dropped off the morning-after pill."

"Wow! That's an amazing service. You wouldn't think it's even possible in such a remote location." She nodded appreciatively, wandering off.

"It's not," I said quietly to myself.

But with Charlie, things seemed possible. How would I cope with my old life after tasting such freedom and ease? I'd begun to believe in good things in a way that was most certainly foolish, and likely to cause pain. I was also growing attached to the beautiful things. The cabin was filled with them. It was the kind of space I would create if I'd ever had the money. The kind of space I wanted to be mine.

For a long time, I'd told myself it was best not to want for or even dream too much. When you weren't moving towards those dreams, they became irrelevant, even hurtful. But having the front-row seat to Charlie's reality had stirred up the old dreams. I'd caught myself mentally identifying with his world, sensing those same possibilities. If I wasn't careful, I'd succumb to my old Pinterest addiction.

While I feared the impending reality check, I also loved that glimpse of the old me. The person I'd been with Jack in the good old days. We'd shared so many ideas, our heads in the clouds, minds full of excitement and endless belief. Well, him more than me, always. But I'd been far more trusting. So much more optimistic. I'd been ready to take risks.

The brave wolf has a fat chest.

I tried to laugh at the ridiculous Estonian saying, but it niggled at me. I'd been the brave little wolf. I'd ventured off the familiar path, chasing something elusive and exciting, and that's why I no longer had a phone. That's why my heart fluttered around Charlie and I couldn't even think about returning to the office. That's what risk-taking brought me: trouble on top of trouble.

CHAPTER 35

Charlie

Driving down the mountain in the waning evening light, I felt sick to my stomach. Bess's phone, still dead as a dodo, sat heavy in my pocket, reminding me of what a horrible human I was. But once the first lie had left my mouth, I had to keep going. I had to commit. Otherwise, she would have never believed it. And now I had her for two more days, incommunicado. Well, I could hope. Even if she used her mom's phone, Wilde Creative required everyone to generate complex passwords and store them with a password manager. Without access to that, she probably wouldn't remember the login details to her email.

Was it worth it? Could any of this be worth it? Because the phone wasn't the only thing I'd lied about. I didn't have a place to stay. I only had the addresses of one inn and one motel, as well as the knowledge that every Airbnb in town was fully booked. It wasn't looking good.

When I arrived, darkness had fallen. Main Street glowed under rows of old-fashioned streetlights, decorated with hanging baskets of mums. The Fall Festival preparations were clearly underway, bunting flapping in the gentle breeze and hay bales piled up on the sidewalk. For a moment, I felt as though I had stumbled onto a historical film set where the buildings were mere facades, with nothing behind the charming paneled doors.

That illusion was broken as I reached the inn. Finding the front door unlocked, I stepped inside the time capsule of heavy drapes and floral patterns. The sweet smell of baking added to its homey feel. I introduced myself to a woman dressed in shiny fabrics, laden with jewelry. She looked like she was on her way to a gala in the 80s—which might have been her heyday.

"Nice to meet you! I'm Ruth Hickey, the owner." She circled the reception desk to shake my hand.

"Do you have any available rooms?"

"For tonight?" Her eyebrows shot up in shock and sympathy. "No. We're booked solid for the next two months."

I nodded. "Oh, okay. Do you know any other place that might have availability? Anything at all?"

She cocked her head. "Levi Carmichel has a place that he's meant to be renting but who knows what's going on with that guy. One minute he's a recluse, the next minute he's got some pretty young thing up there."

"That's okay. I'll check the motel."

I made for the door, but she blocked my way. "Stay for a cup of tea? On the house. I hate disappointing people." She took me by the arm and seated me in the corner of the small waiting area. "Let me order for you."

"It's really not necessary—"

"Nonsense." She called out to someone, ordering the tea, then took a seat across the small table.

"So, where are you from, Charlie?"

"Denver."

"Oh… That's nice." She made it sound like it certainly wasn't.

"Not as nice as Cozy Creek," I conceded.

"Of course not. And what do you do?"

"Advertising, mostly. I'm a Creative Director."

She cocked her head, studying me with even more interest. "Would you consider relocating? We could use someone with your skill set. I mean, the town really sells itself, but it doesn't hurt to put the word out there, does it?"

"I suppose not."

It was the most laid-back attitude to advertising I'd ever heard. For a moment, I allowed myself to imagine having a client like that and almost laughed out loud.

My tea arrived, and I sipped it quickly, answering Ruth's questions and listening to her elaborate sales pitch for Cozy Creek. Who needed advertising when you had a lady like this in your corner? She seemed to have her fingers in every pie around town. If I ever decided to leave my troubles behind and relocate to the mountains, she'd be my first port of call.

"Thank you." I set down my empty cup and stood up. "I better go check that motel."

"Best of luck, dear! It's the Fall Festival week, so the town gets a bit crowded. If everything falls through, come back. I'll make room in my bed." She winked. "Oh, don't look so shocked! I'm only joking."

I gave her an awkward smile and deliberately slowed my pace so it didn't look like I was running out the door.

Holding onto hope, I drove to the motel, a little outside of town. It looked dark. Too dark. When I got to the front door, I saw the notice. The building was closed for renovations.

I was about to leave when I noticed the small figure stepping out of the side door. The movement activated an overhead light, revealing a hunched woman holding a pack of cigarettes. "We're not open!" she called in a raspy voice.

She didn't sound friendly, but I was desperate. I took a step closer, raising my hand in greeting. "Hi! Would you happen to know any place in town, anything at all? I really need to find something for tonight. I'm not picky. Happy to pay what's fair."

She let out an audible sigh, lighting her cigarette. "You picked the worst time of year. You won't find anything. And you look like you're used to something a bit nicer?" She glanced at my latest model electric Porsche, a gleam in her eyes.

I sensed a glimmer of hope.

"You're right. If I have to, I'll sleep in my car. But it's not that comfortable, so if there's anything even slightly better, I'll make it worth your while."

I might as well have said 'please rip me off'.

"Let me make a call." She put out her cigarette, saving the rest of it, and stepped back inside.

I waited. After a couple of minutes, she reappeared with a piece of paper. "Go to this address. It's my son's house. He has accommodation at the back of his property. It's not convention- al, or strictly legal, but it works. There's heating, but no running water. It used to be on Airbnb, but some idiots complained, and they took down his listing." She coughed for a while as if purging her body of the horrors of Airbnb.

"Perfect!" I feigned excitement. I could already tell this wouldn't be perfect.

The address was only a two-minute drive away, but down a windy dirt road that seemed to get narrower at every turn. When I reached the mailbox, I paused for a moment. Would sleeping in my car be that bad? It was the sport model, so not that spacious, but if I laid down the back seat, there might be enough room. No, there wasn't. Unless I wanted to sleep with my feet hanging out the window. And the nights were freezing. I already knew that much.

I parked in the driveway and stepped out, filling my lungs with that chilly night air. An outdoor light flicked on and a lithe man in his fifties descended the steps of an old villa. "You must be the Porsche man?" He said brusquely, sticking out his hand.

"Charlie Wilde."

"Hank…" He started, then decided against adding his last name.

This was going well.

"Your mother said you have a... room to rent for a couple of nights?"

"Not a room. More like a... you'll see." He pivoted on his wool slippers, motioning for me to follow. "Five hundred a night. Non-negotiable."

"Sure," I said, mentally counting how much cash I had in my wallet. Five hundred might have been pushing it. "I can pay for one night in cash, get you more tomorrow."

"Okay, fine."

He led us around his house into a backyard that backed into the forest. A floodlight on his back porch illuminated the row of trees. A rope ladder caught my eye. As my gaze followed it up the trunk of a sturdy maple, I saw a small door. "Is that a treehouse?"

"It's a luxury treehouse. Glamping."

Oh, dear.

"Go on, see for yourself. It hasn't been cleaned recently so some dust may have settled, but it's perfectly livable and romantic, I've been told."

I set my foot on the first rung of the ladder, wondering if the guy was going to shoot me in the neck and use my skin for binding rare books in his basement. The ladder stretched lower and creaked under my weight, but it held. I climbed to the door and pushed my way in, landing in the low-ceilinged crawling space on all fours. It was exactly as cold inside as it was outside, which didn't surprise me. I saw the exposed wiring coming up the exterior wall, connecting to a switch. Definitely not legal, I thought, flicking on the light.

There was a bed with sheets on it. It looked unused. Everything else looked well-worn and recycled, from the shelves full of comic books to chipped cups hanging on hooks and a rusty microwave tucked into a corner. I turned around, calling down from the doorway: "Your mom said there's heating?"

"There's a space heater on the other side of the bed."

If I turned it on, I'd risk burning in a fire; If I didn't, I'd risk hypothermia. I might have been safer on the ground, in my hammock. Was it worth driving back to that ranch to pick it up? It was dark. I was bone tired. Would I even remember the way?

I climbed down the ladder. "Who did the electrical wiring? It doesn't look kosher."

"I did," he said defensively. "Anyway, it's a small space. Heats quickly and keeps the heat for a while, so you can turn off the heater if you're too worried."

"Alright," I said. "I'll take it."

I could always sneak Bess in here to see if she thought it was romantic. I wanted to share this ridiculousness with her. I wanted to share everything with her. But my stupid lies had brought me here, and I was currently enjoying the consequences of my actions. This treehouse would be my punishment. I could only hope the culmination of that punishment was the discomfort of repeatedly hitting my head on the ceiling, not death by fire.

I paid the man and went to my car to get my things, heaving my overnight bag up the ladder. Once I'd made it inside, I investigated the heater. It seemed relatively new—safer than the microwave—and turned on without an issue. The room, or half-a-room, heated in minutes, and I relaxed my muscles.

I waited until the room was toasty warm before turning off the heater and crawling under the blankets. As I settled in, my phone pinged.

Trevor: Package delivered. She was quite shocked to see me. I told her I'd keep things between us, but maybe you need to have a wee chat with her tomorrow?

I let out a deep sigh, cursing the fact that I couldn't contact Bess. Not without involving her mom. After a moment of debating, I took out my phone and called Kathy.

"Hi! It's Charlie Wilde. Can I speak to Bess, please?"

"Hang on a minute."

I heard a rustling, and after a moment, Bess whispered. "Charlie?"

"I wanted to check in on you. Trevor said he scared you."

"Scared me? No, I was a bit surprised, that's all. He knows about us, Charlie!"

"Yes. I couldn't trust a random stranger with something like this. I wanted to make sure you got that... pill. Did you? Was it the right kind?"

"Yeah."

She sounded unsure. Sad.

"Does it have bad side effects?"

"I don't know. There's usually a long list, but that's okay."

"You don't have to—"

"I know."

"I lo—miss you." I caught my tongue in time, but my tone betrayed me.

The silence stretched between us. I listened to her breathing. It was erratic, with long gaps between sharp intakes and exhales. As erratic as mine.

"I miss you, too," she finally replied. Her sigh made the phone mic rattle. "I'll miss you so much." There was a long pause, then another sharp inhale. "Good night, Charlie."

She ended the call, leaving me to listen to the treehouse creaking as the wind shook the trees. It was a solid enough construction, and I didn't feel any draft, but the way the floor shook beneath me was unsettling. Nothing like the gentle swinging of the hammock, but a lot less confined, with an actual bed to spread myself across.

My muscles still felt stiff from the night in the hammock. Carrying Bess on my back added a layer of soreness to the mix, but I found it hard to enjoy the comfort of the mattress. My arms kept stretching out across the bed, searching for her shape and warmth. I wanted Bess more than I wanted a bed to sleep in.

She was considering us, on some level, I told myself. I'd seen it in her eyes. My mind kept returning to those moments in the bathroom, willfully ignoring the unsavory setting, hyper-focusing on her expressions and the way she'd responded to my touch. The truth was somewhere in there. It wasn't in her words. And it certainly wasn't in my words, I thought with a pang of disgust. I had to make things right, as soon as possible.

Tomorrow. I'd fix everything tomorrow.

CHAPTER 36

Bess

I woke up at dawn, my heart pounding. Within seconds, my mind caught up with my body's panic.

The morning-after pill sat in its bag on my nightstand, unopened.

I'd fallen asleep.

The late-night phone call with Charlie had left me reeling, but with one sleepless night already under my belt, the exhaustion had won over. I must have gone out like a light. I was still in my hiking clothes and, judging by the rotten taste in my mouth, hadn't brushed my teeth. Miraculously, Celia had slept through the night, lying across the bed with her head propped on my moon boot. She hadn't peed the bed, either, I realized in relief.

Frantically counting the hours since unprotected sex, I got up, took the pill packet, and hobbled across the cabin as quietly as I could, to get a glass of water. To buy time, I stopped to brush my teeth and wash my face.

It was still dark outside. With any luck, Celia would stay asleep for another half hour. I settled by the window with my water glass and pill packet, watching the sky above the dark trees gradually turn lighter, signaling the coming day. The moment felt special, like a gift I wanted to store away. The blue moment of dawn.

I popped the blister and dropped the pill on my palm, frozen in my indecision.

Did I want Charlie's baby? Or did I just want him to take care of me? If, by some miracle, I'd already gotten pregnant... would that be the worst thing in the world? Charlie would take care of me, of us, and I'd be far better off than I currently was, all because of one mistake.

But if I didn't take the pill, I was willfully making that mistake. I'd be the conniving woman trying to trap a wealthy man by getting pregnant. I could never do that.

Yet, the pill remained in my hand.

Why was it so hard to swallow one tiny tablet?

This was my Matrix moment. This pill would detach me from the fantasy and face plant me back into my real life—back to un-inspiring sceneries, tiny rental apartments and the daily strug-gle. It would sever the ties between myself and Charlie.

I'd take it. I just needed time to say goodbye.

I watched the sunrise make the sky glow, softening the shad-ows and revealing colors upon colors. I'd never forget Rubie

Ridge. I'd judged this place as a pretentious upper-class resort, which it arguably was, but it had also slipped past my defenses, pulling me into its strange, invigorating, soothing orbit. Making me feel like I belonged. Like Charlie.

Without realizing it, I had my eyes trained on the parking lot, right when Charlie's red Porsche Taycan rolled in. It was an ostentatious car, shining like a jewel in the faint morning light. But I couldn't commit to my usual judgmental tone. Instead, my heart jumped to my throat. Charlie was here.

I didn't even ask myself if I should go outside to meet him until I stood by the door in my bathrobe, my one healthy foot in a slipper, ready to limp towards him. Every part of me fizzed and bubbled like it was made of champagne. I opened the door quietly and slipped onto the porch, gasping at the chilly air.

Wait! The pill was still in my hand, but the glass of water sat on the table inside. Could I swallow it without water? Quickly now, I told myself. Just do it!

But with only one solid leg to stand on and my limbs stiff from sleep, my movements weren't as swift and precise as I visualized. As I swung my hand, the pill rolled off my palm, hitting the porch with a faint clink.

Where had it gone?

Holding onto the baluster, I maneuvered down to my knees, scanning the wide wooden planks in the low light, but the pill had vanished. I stuck my finger into the crack between the planks. Was it wide enough for the pill to fit through? Surely not.

My heart pounding, I pulled myself up, feeling like the stupidest person on earth. I'd had one job.

I'd find that pill, I told myself. I'd take it a little later. Nobody would have to know.

I negotiated the stairs and advanced down the path, peering at the Porsche. But Charlie must have hopped out of the car while I'd been kneeling on the porch. When he appeared in front of me, seemingly out of nowhere, I jumped like a frightened bunny.

"Bess!" He grinned, wrapping me in the tightest hug of my life.

I felt his strong arms and the hard chest under his soft jersey. The scent of lemony soap and pine. So much pine, like Charlie had somehow become one with the evergreens.

I hugged him back a little awkwardly, a thousand doubts and worries rushing through my mind. But gradually, the warmth and conviction of his squeeze overwhelmed me, pushing those thoughts away. Charlie held me like I was his life raft and only hope of survival. My muscles relaxed and I settled against him, breathing in his scent. It felt so good I could only surrender.

"How was your night?" I asked when he finally released me. "Where did you stay?"

He looked at me for a moment, as if contemplating something. "One of the inns in town. It was fine." He rolled his shoulders, stretching his neck.

"Terrible bed?" I guessed.

"No. It was fine."

"Then why are you here so early?"

He cocked his head. "I couldn't wait to see you. Why are you up so early?"

"I don't know. I fell asleep quite early." My hands flew to my face in embarrassment. "I slept in my hiking clothes."

He laughed. "It's okay. I'm glad you're up. I was worried I'd wake you guys."

"What time is it?" I reached for his left hand to look at his watch. 7:15 a.m. "The breakfast buffet opens in fifteen minutes, and I really need a shower."

The cold air travelled up my sleeve, inducing a shiver.

He glanced at the cabin. "Are Celia and your mom still asleep?"

I nodded.

"Let's go sit in my car. Just for a minute." He pulled me down the path towards that shiny Porsche.

The interior smelled of leather, still warm from the drive. Charlie flicked on the power, adjusting the heat until I felt the blissful warmth of the seat warmer through my bathrobe. "This is nice."

"It's not a family car," he said grimly, looking out the window. "We can trade to something more practical."

"Trade? What? Why?" My brain spun in circles, grasping for meaning.

"I mean, I'm not a huge fan of minivans, but I'll go for whatever—"

"What the hell are you talking about?" I stared at him, feeling a little ill. I had to find that pill. Maybe another one for Charlie. "Nobody is asking you to trade cars. We're not even supposed to be together, right? Not publicly. Not at work. I've loved this week, but I don't know how we can go forward.

I'd tried my hardest not to think about the future, but staring at the new dawn behind the windscreen, with my mother and child a few yards away, I could no longer hold the sobering thoughts at bay.

I could see my own pain reflected in Charlie's eyes, but coupled with a dose of obstinance I wasn't capable of. "What does work have to do with any of it? We found each other! There's something between us. You can't deny that." He shot me a look of challenge.

I shook my head, lost for words. There was so much between us I could barely make sense of it.

He took my hands in his, staring at them. "We have one more day in Cozy Creek. Can we just enjoy it? Pretend all the work stuff doesn't exist. We're just two people traveling in the mountains."

Outside the window, the tips of the spruce trees glowed in the morning sun like a row of bright teepees. It was going to be a beautiful day.

"What about my mom? I told her we're not dating."

"You also told your mom you needed a morning-after pill. If she still thinks we're platonic buddies, I don't think we need to worry about her skills of detection."

I let out a sad chuckle. "Yeah, okay. She knows we slept together, but I kinda told her I can't risk getting involved."

"You're already involved, Bess, and you know it. I know I'm involved up to my eyeballs. Even your mom knows that."

I nodded. He was right. Whatever I'd told Mom, she would have seen through it. I'd lost my heart to Charlie and there was no going back. Everything had changed.

"It'll be so awkward in the office." I bit my lip.

"It's worth it, though. You're worth it."

I nodded, tears in my eyes. "So are you."

I knew it now. I'd endure anything to stay with him. Whether it made sense or not.

"One more day in Cozy Creek," I said, a smile spreading across my lips. "Let's make it a great day."

This week was a gift. I had to make the most of it.

Charlie held up one finger, grabbed his phone off the hands-free stand and opened Spotify. 'What a difference a day makes' by Dinah Washington flooded through the car speakers, filling the space between us with its old-fashioned charm.

Charlie crooned along as the song reached its crescendo. He had a nice voice.

I couldn't help smiling and he used the opportunity to pull me against his chest, whispering into my hair. "I'm so glad I found you."

"Me, too. I'm sorry I misjudged you. You're good a man, Charlie. You have a good heart."

"I'm not perfect," he said, his eyes glistening with gravity. "I make mistakes and I'm going to mess this up. But I'm hoping, by then, the good things weigh more."

"I'm not perfect either," I said, swallowing hard. My mistakes could cost us dearly. More than he knew.

I wrapped my fingers around his neck, reaching to kiss him. The way he kissed me back, slowly and tenderly, spoke volumes.

I allowed myself one last moment of bliss, forgetting everything else, letting that affection pour through me and flood every corner of my body.

When I felt the need building up in my core, I pulled away and clambered out of the car. "Let's go."

He caught up with my slow limping and helped me to the cabin. I could hear Celia's squeals through the door. My eyes did a quick scan of the porch as I stepped across it, coming up with nothing.

"Mom! Where did you go?" my daughter yelled as Charlie opened the door.

"I saw Charlie's car, so I went out to meet him."

Mom appeared from the bathroom, looking freshly groomed. "Good morning! This place is so quiet, I can't believe it. No traffic, no sirens, no neighbors... nothing."

"Breakfast?" Charlie gestured at the door.

"Isn't this amazing?" Mom looked at us in awe. "I hope they have coffee."

"And cereal!" Celia's eyes shone like stars.

"Of course, they do." Charlie chuckled. "Your mom can show you how to mix all the different cereals in one bowl and create a whole new breakfast dish."

"All in the same bowl?" Celia looked at him like he'd suggested it was going to rain Froot Loops.

When we arrived in the cafeteria, the kitchen staff was still setting up the buffet. Only Harry sat at a corner table, raising his hand at us. "Good morning, early birds! Are you ready for the big reveal? Three p.m. today."

"What's that?" I asked.

"When we're revealing everyone's artwork. Should be fun."

"Ah." I glanced at Charlie. "We kind of missed half the week lost in the forest, so we have nothing to show for ourselves."

"There's still time." Harry wiggled his eyebrows. "The winner gets a free week's stay at Rubie Ridge."

"A free week here?" Mom's voice vibrated with reverence. "You should do something, Bess. You could win it."

"You could do it together," Harry suggested. "I'm sure that'd be fine, given you've lost so much time. Let's ask." He raised his hand, looking over my shoulder. "Good morning, Leonie! A question."

Leonie appeared by his table, wearing a yellow kaftan and a tired smile. She turned to us, lowering her voice to a hush. "I'm so sorry about what happened. I didn't want to bother you last night as it was late. I thought it best to let you get some rest. How's the leg?"

"It's okay." I waved at the moon boot. "I'm sorry we missed so much of the classes."

"They could present their final artwork together, right?" Harry nodded at us. "There's still a bit of time."

"If you'd like to participate, that'd be fantastic!" Leonie clasped her hands together, her clunky bracelets clanging like cymbals. "I was worried you wouldn't get to be part of the gallery opening this afternoon. That's where we vote for the winners. I'd hate for you to be left out."

Charlie cast me a questioning look. "What do you think? Before we went into the forest, I had an idea of something we would build with pinecones and a bit of glue. Might be fun with Celia."

"But don't you need to work on the campaign?"

"I can do that tomorrow. Today is… a special day, remember?"

"Cereal!" my child yelled as Tag the kitchen helper poured cornflakes into a dispenser.

I nodded. "Okay. First cereal, then pinecones."

We filled our trays and took the table Harry had vacated, after he rushed back to finish his artwork. As we sat down, more people arrived. I heard them talking about their art pieces in excited but hushed tones, careful not to reveal their ideas to the wrong people. I wondered when the relaxing week of art classes had turned into this sort of competition.

Celia shoveled multi-colored cereal into her mouth, her face shining with excitement. "Can we have this every morning, Mom?" she asked between mouthfuls.

"That looks like Froot Loops," Charlie observed.

"It's not. It's some sort of fancy, organic alternative. The brand names and ingredients are all written on those little cards." I gestured at the buffet.

"Great." He left to take a photo of the card.

"What is he doing?" Celia asked us.

"I think he's finding out what it is so he can buy it for you," my mom explained helpfully, an approving smile hovering on her lips.

"No, sweetie. He just likes it, too," I corrected, shooting Mom a warning look.

"If he likes it, why didn't he take any?" Celia pointed at Charlie's tray with a piece of toast and a coffee.

Mom raised her brow at me, siding with my daughter. But they didn't know Charlie like I did. As much as my heart fluttered around him, I had to look at the big picture. I had to consider the Charlie I knew from work. The spontaneous, excitable guy with a major shiny-new-object syndrome. I'd seen the fads come and go. The robots and 3D printers, cars and girlfriends. Charlie got excited, then he got bored. Some boxes didn't even get opened as his interests shifted to something else. As much as my heart screamed otherwise, I couldn't stake my daughter's happiness on someone like that.

I could enjoy the ride. That was the best anyone could get with Charlie, and that's what I was going to do today.

After breakfast, Charlie lifted Celia on his shoulders and carried her back to the cabin. The girl giggled with excitement as they reached the door and Charlie had to scoot down to fit them both through.

"Ready to fly?"

"Yes!"

He lifted Celia off his shoulders and heaved her onto the bed. She squealed and laughed so hard she got the hiccups. I had to remind her to breathe so she wouldn't start coughing and throw up. Still, I couldn't help but smile, a lump in my throat, as she got up and yelled, "Again!"

When had I seen her like this? I didn't really play with her. I could only hope she had these moments in kindergarten.

"What was the pinecone idea you had?" I asked Charlie, plopping on the edge of the bed, lifting my leg up on it. "How many do we need for it? Because I might not be of that much help."

Charlie ran his fingers through his hair, a cheeky smile on his face. "I was actually hoping Celia could help us." He turned to my daughter, now climbing over the back of the couch, then sliding down on her tummy.

"Help with what?" she asked, looking up.

"I'll show you. Put your shoes and jacket back on. Let's go!" He picked up my backpack. "Can we use this?"

"Where are you going?" I asked, watching Celia pull on her purple puffer jacket and booties.

"Outside to collect pinecones. We won't go far. Don't worry."

I tried to get up, but Charlie motioned me to stay put. "Stay. Rest that leg. Take a shower. Do you need help with that?"

"I should be fine." I glanced at the bathroom, letting myself imagine the bliss of warm water. "Are you sure?"

Nobody took my child off my hands to give me a break, not even Mom. Not unless I asked.

Mom followed them to the door, throwing me a reassuring smile over her shoulder. "He's right. You won't be of much help like that. Stay back and rest."

Charlie turned to Celia. "I think *you* have some great ideas about what we can do with the pinecones. Let's find some good ones first, and then you can tell me what you think we should do."

I pointed at the bowl of pinecones on the table. "He's talking about those, Ce. They've probably fallen off the trees around here. Look!"

Mom took one of the large pinecones and handed it to Celia. She turned it in her hands, head tilted. She had my natural urge to say the right thing. Be honest. And right now, Charlie, her hero, was asking for her help.

"We should put it back in the tree," she decided, handing it to Charlie.

"Hang it back in the tree? Why?"

"Because it fell, and maybe the tree wants it back. Maybe it misses it."

"But what if we can't put it back? What should we do then?"

She thought for a moment. "Make a new tree for it. Just like the old one, but purple!"

"A purple tree. Interesting." Charlie cocked his head. "Should we paint them all purple?"

"Yes!" Celia shouted, clearly visualizing the incredible display of purple, her favorite color.

"But we need lots of pinecones like this. Big, beautiful ones. Can you help me find them?"

The girl vibrated with energy and enthusiasm, bouncing against the door. Charlie opened it for them, flashing me one last smile before disappearing outside.

"Don't worry. I'll make sure they don't wander off into the forest," Mom told me, closing the door behind them.

Suddenly, the room felt deafeningly quiet. Never in a million years had I thought that our last special day would include having a cabin to myself. It took me a moment to get my bearings, but I eventually made it to my feet and into the shower. As I stood under the hot stream of water, leaning on my one good leg, it hit me.

Charlie wasn't just playing a couple. He was playing a family. Could I let him go on like this? Could I enjoy the break and having another adult around, one who was strong enough to carry my child?

One day wasn't long enough to get too attached, I decided. Celia would be fine. She already knew Charlie, the man with the gadgets. He was the fun uncle. It was me who was getting far too attached. Going back to my life was going to hurt, but that was still the plan. What else could I do? I couldn't risk my whole life on this man, no matter what my heart was blabbering about.

And if I didn't find the lost pill on the porch, what would I do then?

CHAPTER 37

Charlie

We'd found a dozen beautiful pinecones, when I finally worked up my courage.

"Kathy?" I cleared my throat. "Can I ask you something?"

The older woman raised her expressive eyebrows. They made me think of Bess, but the friendly look in her eyes was more like Gran. Always ready to listen.

"I'm in love with your daughter." I held my breath.

"I figured." She glanced at the cabin, tiny in the distance, a dreamy look in her eyes. "You know she's been through a lot, right?"

"I know. And I think that's why she doesn't quite trust me, yet. We work together, so it's complicated. But there's something she doesn't know."

"What?" Her eyes flashed with alarm.

"My father has decided to restructure the entire agency. To reduce the production team to a bare minimum. Make it AI-assisted and automated."

Kathy's eyes flooded with panic, and she clutched her scarf. "Bess will lose her job?"

"At present, yes. But I think she's got the chops to work in the creative team. She has the ideas. A fresh perspective. I just need the others to see her talent. So, we've been working on a new campaign together. I think the client will love it. But I need her to feel safe enough to present it with me. I was afraid that if she found out about the job cuts, she'd freak out and we lose that opportunity."

"Wait, she doesn't know?"

"No." I swallowed a lump that felt like a giant pinecone. "I should have told her, but there's been a lot going on and she was doing so well with that campaign I didn't want to lose momentum."

"I see." Kathy bent down to pick up a beautifully symmetrical pinecone and handed it to Celia. "What do you think of this?"

She turned in her hands, looking at it like a goldsmith studying a piece of jewelry. "Pretty good." She lifted her chin to look at me. "Charlie, is this a good one?"

"Yes," I told her, distracted. "I'll pay you five bucks each if you go find some more."

Her eyes widened, and she nodded solemnly. "I'll find all of them," she announced, rushing off.

Watching her grandchild skip away, Kathy frowned, deep in thought. "Bess doesn't want to take any risks. Not after what happened. She's been a bit closed off. I mean, it's good that she's careful. We don't need another Jack in our lives, thank you very much. That man was all big talk and mighty plans. No realism." She shook her head. "I was so anxious, watching them. I had to go on medication."

"He was an entrepreneur?" I asked, feeling the sting. Jack sounded too much like me.

"A dreamer."

"Most are," I said carefully. "You have to believe in what you're—"

"I was trying to be kind and not speak ill of the dead." She rearranged her scarf, hiding her mouth behind a gloved hand. "Jack didn't live in the real world. He was up and down. All or nothing. Flying high one minute, then down in the dumps. It's okay to fail. It's okay to feel depressed. But if you're not honest. If you don't communicate..." She shot me a sharp look and my gut tightened.

I couldn't spin this any other way. I'd been keeping the truth from Bess.

"Well, at least you're not lying on your brother's couch, drugged up," she concluded. "Maybe it's better that Bess doesn't know. It would have ruined this vacation, for sure. It's a good thing she lost that phone, I suppose."

I felt another bout of guilt, but held my tongue.

"She'll find out eventually," Kathy continued, casting a grave look at me. "Then what?"

"I was hoping that by then, she'll see that we belong together, and it doesn't matter either way. If she's fired, I'll resign and start a new business. I'll take my clients with me. She won't be left unemployed, I ensure you."

I had a new plan. It was still on taking shape, with too many question marks, but I felt good about it.

"That's ruthless. Are you a ruthless man, Charlie?"

"I can be," I admitted. "For a good cause."

She huffed, looking at me like she hadn't quite decided what I was good for. "You seem more resilient, though, or am I completely off?" She tilted her head, and I noticed her eye color matched Bess's. The crow's feet bracketing them deepened as she smiled. A beautiful woman, like Bess.

"Bess is resilient. I am… fortunate. I haven't needed all my resources. But I'm not afraid to ask for help."

At that moment, I saw the acceptance on her face. She'd made up her mind. "Bess is lucky to have you. She hasn't had a lot of luck lately, or resources. But are you sure you're in this for good? She has a child." She nodded at Celia.

"I love them both."

I'd just have to prove to Bess that I meant it.

"Fair enough." She looked at the cabin again. "Let me see if I can help you a little."

CHAPTER 38

Bess

I'd never spent so much time on my knees. After a blissful shower, I'd forced myself to dress up and look through the porch, again. If I licked the stupid thing clean, surely, I'd end up consuming the required pill. After fifteen minutes of awkward searching, moving every flowerpot, decorative sculpture and the welcome mat, I'd discovered something that looked like an old Tic Tac, as well as two white pills that looked eerily similar.

Why were there so many discarded pills lying around on the porch? What kind of pill-poppers did Rubie Ridge host? To be fair, I'd also unearthed a piece of condom wrapper, a stick of gum and three dental floss holders, so it was pretty obvious the porch hadn't been cleaned for a while.

Satisfied that I'd scoured every inch of the entranceway, I sat on the steps, staring at the two pills in my hand.

What the fuck was I supposed to do? Without access to the internet, I couldn't check what my pill looked like. I remembered it being round and white. That was it. But did it have a groove in the middle? How deep a groove? Was it chalky or shiny? Why was my memory useless?

I fetched the foil blister the pill had been in, trying it with both pills. They each fit in fine, although one had a tiny piece missing on the side. It could have broken off as I'd dropped it though, so I couldn't rule it out.

It was likely my pill was one of these two. If I took both, I'd get the right one, but also risk ingesting something else harmful. Chances were it was just a painkiller. But what if it wasn't?

How bad could it be? I was on no other medication. Was there anything that could interact with the morning-after pill?

This is how Jack had died—mixing medications that shouldn't be mixed, thinking he was doing the right thing.

The thought punched me so hard my lungs flattened, and I fought to draw another breath. I should have been there. I was the cautious one who thought of everything, who constantly assessed the level of risk.

Except this week, with Charlie, I'd taken a risk after risk and ended up here with an injured leg and two terrifying pills.

What was worse—a pregnancy or unintended drug side effects? Even if it was Adderall or Vicodin, one pill wouldn't kill me. What did those pills look like? Why, oh why didn't I have internet?

As I stared at the glory of autumn colors on the horizon, the answer came to me. I'd have to tell my mom or Charlie what I'd done. That was the only way. Instead of pills, I'd swallow my pride and out myself as the clumsiest idiot in Colorado. Jack had been alone and too proud to ask for help, spiraling deeper into his stupid risk investments, too wired to sleep.

I was not going down that way.

I heard Celia's bubbling laugh from somewhere behind the cabin. They must have been on their way back. I made a half-hearted attempt to get up, but what was the point? I'd made my decision. I'd say the awkward thing, even if it made me burst into flames. I could try to avoid risk, but I couldn't hide. I'd be the brave wolf with the fat chest. Oh, my. If all these blunders made me fall pregnant, I *would* have a fat chest, I thought, and an odd, uncontrollable laugh escaped.

Charlie found me on the porch steps, holding two pills, laughing with tears streaming down my face. He lifted Celia off his shoulders and sat next to me, his voice cracking with concern. "Are you okay? What happened?"

"No. I'm an idiot. Charlie, I lost the pill. I dropped it on the porch and then I scoured every inch of this area and I found these two. And now I don't know what to do."

He stared at me in horror. "Yes, you do! You flush those down the toilet, right now."

"I mean, I need to take it. I should have taken it last night, but I fell asleep putting Celia to bed." I looked up at him, my eyes blurring with tears. "It was right after our phone call. She stirred, and I curled up next to her to settle her down and then I must have fallen asleep. Didn't even brush my teeth. I'm so sorry."

"Sorry about what? You were exhausted. We both were."

"But I should have taken that pill right away when I got it. When I was still functioning. I was so stupid. I thought I'd get Celia to bed first..." I sniffed.

Celia crawled into my lap and wrapped her arms around my neck. "I love you, Mommy. Don't be sad."

Charlie smiled, stroking my hair. "She's right. We love you. Don't be sad."

Tears flowed freely now, completely distorting my vision, which made it easier for Charlie to remove the pills from my hand. "But seriously, we're flushing these. You never swallow random pills you find on the ground, right?"

"Mommy doesn't let me pick up candy in the street, even if it's still in the wrapper," Celia informed him.

"Exactly! This is the same thing. Right?"

"Right," I finally answered, my mouth sticky, hands limp.

"We can pick up another one in town this afternoon when we go to the festival."

I nodded, and relief slowly trickled down my spine. Of course, that was the sane thing to do. Not having an emotional breakdown over two dirty pills.

Charlie leaned closer to whisper in my ear. "Or we can take our chances, because we're okay either way. We're fine."

"Stop that," I hissed. "You don't want a baby. You have no idea—"

"Nobody does. It's one of those blind jumps, isn't it?"

I nodded. I'd been the blindest of all. I'd jumped and crash landed as a broke single mom. Still, I couldn't imagine life without Celia. She had so much light in her. Even in the darkest times, she never let me slip into the void. I told myself I had to keep it together for her, but I drew strength from her shining green eyes like some sort of life force vampire. Her hugs, wild dreams and enthusiasm sustained me.

"We're all going in blind, I guess. Nobody knows what's coming."

I glanced at my daughter, tugging on Charlie's hand. "I want to do the loopy loop."

Charlie got up and held her hands, letting her climb up his body and somersault over, landing back on the ground. My little monkey. I clapped obligingly.

Mom reached us, blowing out a breath. "She's got a lot of energy, that one."

"Sure does." Charlie lifted his arm so that Celia could swing from it.

"I think I need to lie down for a bit." Mom edged past us to get inside the cabin.

Charlie set Celia down. "Do you want to go check that tree for pinecones? Five dollars each, remember?"

"Five dollars?" I eyeballed him, watching my daughter skip away with the backpack.

"Is that too much? Too little?" Charlie looked alarmed. "I wanted to motivate her, and she said she's saving up for an iPad."

"No, she's not! She *wants* an iPad. She also wants a swing and a jungle gym. She wants her own personal unicorn! She's not saving up for anything. She doesn't even have a piggy bank." I couldn't help the frustrated shudder.

"Chill. I'll get her a piggy. She can start saving."

"I don't want her to have an iPad. She's five."

"Sweet. We'll get the unicorn. How much do those go for?"

I rolled my eyes. "Why don't you look it up on Kickstarter?"

Charlie lifted his hands in surrender. "Okay, I admit. I know nothing about kids. I'm hopeless. I need guidance. But I think she's amazing." His face softened and a genuine smile broke through as he gazed at Celia's slight frame, combing the ground under the old pine tree.

"She is," I confirmed. "She's the reason I didn't lose hope. That I keep trying. People say they work hard to give their kids anything, but it's not just that. It's the way she believes in better times. The way she keeps dreaming about everything, trusting that she'll one day get it. I try to inhale that faith every day. I'm faking it, but even that helps sometimes. Because I never want to break her spirit, so I must believe a little bit more and try a little bit harder."

I could feel Charlie's eyes on me. Studying me. "You used to be like her, didn't you? I can see your spirit in her. The original one that life hasn't smacked around."

His words hit me hard, and I had to turn away to compose myself. "I was a lot more naïve," I said. "I had all these plans and goals. We were professional dreamers."

"I sometimes wish I had that. I haven't found that much to dream about. I guess that's why I shop on Kickstarter. I want to feel like I'm part of someone else's dream."

"But you dream up new campaigns and visuals all the time at work."

He huffed a sad laugh. "They're not my dreams. I don't have that much skin in the game. I mean, it's fun to win, but it's not my purpose." He paused, drawing a deep breath, holding it for a moment. "I don't think I have a purpose."

Something flamed inside of me. "You want to make everyone happy. You want to discover amazing things and elevate them. You care so much! That's a lot of purpose, Charlie."

"You think?" He gave me a lopsided smile.

"Yeah. When I was planning our Kickstarter campaign, I was dreaming of a backer like you."

"You planned a Kickstarter campaign?" He blinked.

"I didn't get very far before the lawsuit and everything else happened."

Charlie's eyes flicked at Celia, still searching the ground under the pine tree. "Did you ever plan to have another one?" he asked softly, "you know, before…"

"Yeah, sort of. We planned a lot of things, but it was all conditional. Like, once we get the business off the ground. Once we had enough money and a bigger place. You know…" I shrugged.

"I have money, you know. My place is… not small."

I looked down. "I couldn't casually have a baby with someone. It feels wrong."

"Casually? What's casual about it? Labor?"

I laughed at my stupid word choice. "I meant relationship-wise."

"Despite what you've told yourself, I'm not commitment-phobic. I've been... picky."

"Meaning you've never dated anyone long enough to be considered commitment-phobic." I gave him a lopsided smile.

He nodded. "Well, it's not a topic that gets raised on the first or second date. But I don't want to waste anyone's time. Dating someone you don't see a future with is a waste of time."

"And you see a future with me?" The question came out too fast, unfiltered, full of wonder.

"I do." He pulled me for tight side hug, making my chest expand. So much warmth.

But I couldn't help the niggling thoughts. "How do you know you won't change your mind? You can't even commit to a cell phone. You order a new one every two months."

"Because then I can give the old one away," he said quietly, cheeks coloring.

"You want to give your phone away?" I watched him poke a small rock with the tip of his sneaker, and my puzzle of Charlie gained one more piece. The impulsive, infectiously enthusiastic, neglected, spoilt, genuine, creative, easily bored... and now, with a gravity I hadn't noticed before.

"People are proud. They don't want charity. But if you throw something away, they'll catch it."

"You get bored with stuff, though. Don't try to deny it." I threw him a cheeky smile.

"Of course I get bored! I buy shit I don't need and change my routines and order food from a new restaurant. It doesn't mean I throw away something I love. I've had this one pair of jeans since I was eighteen. They're pretty worn out, but I'd never throw them away." He turned to look me in the eye. "Life is full of risk. Unavoidable risk. You might get bored of me. One of us could die..." He bit his lip, his gaze dark. "I'm sorry. I didn't mean to dredge up—"

"It's okay. It's never that far from my mind, anyway. I guess that's why I don't like taking risks. Because 'risk' is not just a word. It's a precursor to pain."

He took my hand, squeezing it between his own. Making it warm. "I don't want to cause you pain. Ever. I'm not saying I'd be an amazing father or partner or anything. I'm scared shitless of that. But I still want you and everything that comes with it."

I believed him. Charlie might have been naïve, but he wasn't lying.

My breath felt hot on my lips—hot air rising from my churning guts. "There's little chance I'll be pregnant anyway, from one time. That'd be quite miraculous."

"Exactly. So, why stress about the pill?" He smiled.

I couldn't give him an answer, but I felt so good sitting next to him, touching him... like he was filling my heart with faith.

Charlie released my hand, peering over my head. "Oh, my God!"

I followed his gaze and saw Celia dragging a backpack full of pinecones. It was open, with the contents spilling over as she tried to move it across the bumpy grass and walking path separating us. Celia stopped in her tracks and burst into tears. Charlie jumped to his feet and caught up with her as she tried to lift it over a rock, spilling more cones. I stood up on autopilot, but something held me back. I wanted to see what Charlie would do.

He helped her gather up the fallen cones, slipping some into the hood of her jacket. Then he lifted the backpack onto his shoulder and Celia into his arms, whispering something into her ear. She looked over at me, then back at Charlie. The cries stopped, and he carried her across the path and to the cabin steps, lowering her onto my lap.

"She's done a phenomenal job," he told me. "I think we should get to the kitchen and stick these in the oven. They need to dry up and open before we can paint them."

"What are we making out of them?"

Charlie grinned. "No idea. We'll let Celia decide."

"Me?" The girl looked up, blinking away the last tears.

"Yes, you. You're an artist."

"I am?"

"Of the purest form," Charlie confirmed.

The girl beamed. "I'm an artist, Mom."

Her tears had dried, somehow transferring into my throat. I swallowed down the lump and smiled. "Yes, you are."

Everything we didn't dare to believe about ourselves was present in our children.

CHAPTER 39

Bess

We spent the rest of the morning in the kitchen, then in the studio, gently baking pinecones, then mixing paints and dipping the cones into different colors.

There were no teachers around, although Ilme made an appearance. She seemed in higher spirits after some promising leads from two other art schools and a gallery that wanted to display her work. Seeing our pinecones, she praised Celia, making her glow from pride.

For the first time, I felt at ease in the art studio, enjoying the experimenting without the nervous feeling I'd had during the earlier art classes. I wasn't being judged for what I created. I was part of the creation, like an active spectator.

"Is this what it's supposed to be like?" I asked as Charlie

picked up a dried, pink pinecone, examining it by the window. "Art. Creativity. It feels more fun like this."

I'd spent a while browsing Pinterest on his phone, looking for the right technique for attaching the cones together to create a sculpture of sorts.

"You should always work at the edge of your ability. So that it's not too easy or too hard. That's the key to achieving the state of flow."

"Maybe the edge of my ability is googling pinecone wreaths. Everything else we did before stressed me out." I glanced at Celia, playing with a piece of wire. "It's more fun to work together."

He smiled. "Not quite so egocentric."

Everyone else was working solo, many in secret. The only other people sharing the studio with us were Harry and Matthew, both painting on large canvases on the opposite sides of the room. No peeking was allowed, but Celia had checked out both works-in-progress and reported her findings to both us and them. "The other one has lots of color on it," she piped up at Matthew, who sneered.

"One hour to go!" Harry called over to Matthew, waving a paintbrush. "I'm done, how about you?"

We worked together, Charlie asking Celia's thoughts and opinions, letting her make the decisions, gently culling the unfeasible ideas, reminding her of limitations like gravity. Leonie did a walk-through, taking 'behind the scenes' pictures, but I barely heard her enthusiastic commentary, or noticed Miranda and her posse arriving. I was too engrossed in the act of creation.

Half an hour later, we'd fashioned a rather gravity-defying spiral of pinecones in pastel rainbow tones that kept falling over.

"We'll have to attach it to something," I said, peering at the high ceiling. "One of those beams, maybe? We need a ladder."

"Look at you thinking big!" Charlie grinned at me, supporting the fragile structure with one hand. "Can you hold this? I'll go find one."

"Where?"

He shrugged, giving me that carefree smile that said he'd find a way. After a few minutes, when my arms were starting to ache, he returned with a paint-splattered step ladder and we managed to tie our creation to one of the beams using a bit of fishing line. I stared at it, astonished. Despite trying to manage Celia's unrealistic ideas, we'd achieved exactly what she had described—a gravity-defying display of magic, like a pastel hurricane in the freeze frame. The pinecones were attached to each other with a strong, fine wire that allowed us to turn and shape their formation. Celia had arranged the colors from purple to warm pink, then to softer shades of mustard, oatmeal and mint.

"That color transition works," Charlie concluded. "Good job, Miss C!"

He high-fived the girl and we stepped back to examine the installation from a distance. Matthew and Harry appeared, circling it, making appreciative comments. A few minutes later, the rest of the ladies arrived, setting up their finished sculptures and paintings around the studio.

Leonie clapped her hands at the front. "Welcome to our final

Rubie Ridge Showcase! I'm so excited. Let's pop the champagne. We also have some grape juice for those who are not drinking or"—she glanced at Celia—"who are a little too young."

As the cork hit the ceiling and fizzing flutes were passed around the room, I stepped closer to Charlie, feeling inexplicably proud and happy. It was only a silly art show for a silly art class, but I felt elated. Energized.

"Is this what work feels like to you?" I whispered. "I mean—"

"On a good day," he answered, somehow understanding my vague question. "It feels like I'm channeling something, watching it all come together." He pinned me with an intense look. "You're part of it. You're always there. You finesse and tweak and fix it. When you're there, I know it's good. I know we didn't overlook something. You're my secret weapon. But..."

"But what?"

He lowered his voice. "But you're more than that. You're a creative. And it should feel like this, for you."

A few days ago, I would have dismissed his comment. I would have argued back, convincing myself and everyone around me that I was just a Production Assistant. A cog in the machine. But now I wasn't so sure. Something in me wanted to fly a little higher. I wanted to feel like this again. I'd never be Charlie, but maybe I could find my own path. Maybe I could do it safely, on the side of my job. Take on a more creative challenge as a freelancer or something.

We raised glasses, listening to Leonie's elaborate speech about creativity and imagination. I took a little sip, trying to swirl the bubbles in my mouth so it was safe to swallow. Nope. There was too much air that would get trapped in my stomach and cause pain. I tried to stop Celia, my fellow non-burper, from drinking her fizzy grape juice, but she kept dipping her tongue in it, too curious to stay away.

"I have three prizes," Leonie announced, lifting three envelopes. "The first prize is a week's paid art retreat, much like this one, here at Rubie Ridge. And then I have two-hundred-dollar vouchers, sponsored by the wonderful Rockies Art Connection, your art material supplier. Let's vote!"

Butterflies erupted in my stomach as she handed out voting cards and pens and the participants started circling the room, scribbling down their top three choices.

"Let's vote for us!" Celia bounced on her heels.

We couldn't vote for ourselves, obviously, but managed to agree on our top three choices after careful deliberation. Harry's landscape painting of vibrant red and yellow fall foliage was impressive, as was Miranda's Pinterest-worthy color splash, but it was Matthew's line drawing of falling leaves that took my breath away. Unbeknownst to us, he'd drawn Celia, dancing among the leaves. She looked so happy and carefree, arms outstretched and eyes sparkling. He obviously had incredible talent, unmatched by anyone in the room.

"It's me! It's me!" Celia could hardly get over her shock and excitement.

"You can have it," Matthew whispered to the girl as we stepped closer. "Take it home with you."

I shook my head in shock. "We couldn't."

"She means we're delighted and honored and will cherish this gift," Charlie countered, shaking Matthew's hand. "Thank you."

Matthew smiled back a little cautiously, his eyes flicking between the two of us, quite possibly wondering about our relationship dynamic. Welcome to the club, I thought, my cheeks warming.

We returned to our own artworks, sneaking chocolates from a tray on the middle table as Leonie counted the votes. After I banned Celia from approaching the chocolates for the third time, she sent Charlie in her place, securing two more treats.

"Matthew's going to win," I said as Leonie looked up from her papers, beaming.

"He is good," Charlie agreed. "But we're great. We have the best story. And the cutest kid."

I frowned. "It shouldn't be about that."

"Awards are never about true skill or achievement. Especially if it's an audience choice. That's a popularity contest, and you're on the winning team."

I huffed at the thought. Bess the Buzzkill. I'd never been popular. Not at school, on social media or at work. Appreciated, maybe. Depended on. And I'd always thought that was enough.

Clutching a little card, Leonie stood up and I held my breath. "Okay. In the third place, with eleven points, we have Angie Hutton with her delightful clay birds.

I swiveled to locate Angie's beaming face. Her birds were cute, but not nearly as cute as her smile and her blond ringlets. Maybe

Charlie had a point. Angie was chatty and seemed to be friends with everyone. We clapped as Angie received her gift card.

"In the second place, with fifteen votes, is Matthew Kendrick with his drawing, titled 'Falling Slowly'."

Multiple emotions rushed through me. I loved the title as much as the subject. But second place? How could it not be the winner? I was still processing as Leonie waved the last envelope. "And the grand prize goes to... you guessed it, our little family of artists, Charlie, Bess and Celia Wilde, for the pinecone sculpture titled 'Spinny Rainbow Hurricane Unicorn'." She stifled a laugh, turning to Celia. "Are you, by any chance, responsible for this title?"

She nodded in earnest, and the entire room erupted in laughter and applause.

"Here you go, Miss Wilde." Leonie handed Celia the envelope.

I opened my mouth to correct her on our last name, but Charlie pre-empted my urge, squeezing my hand. "Let it go."

Celia didn't seem to mind the last name. Granted, she couldn't yet spell her actual one, either. I swallowed my corrections and smiled, listening to the cacophony of applause and congratulations. Tears rose to my eyes, despite everything. If this was a popularity contest, it was the first one I'd ever won. And it was all because of Charlie.

"What is it, Mommy? What did we win?" Celia tried to open the envelope, and I grabbed it from her.

"It's a trip. For one person, I think."

Leonie stepped closer, lowering her voice. "It says for one

adult, and we don't really host families or kids here, but your daughter is welcome to join you, free of charge. I'll make a note of it."

"We can come back here? Another time?" Celia's eyes widened to saucers as she whipped her head from side to side, trying to stay on top of the conversation.

"Yes dear, we'd love to have you back." Leonie smiled, then stepped back to the front of the class and raised her voice. "Thank you, everyone. This concludes our official program here at Rubie Ridge. Enjoy yourselves until tomorrow. Kick back and relax. Consider visiting the Cozy Creek Fall Festival. It'll be on until nine o'clock tonight."

"Bunnies and cotton candy," Charlie whispered to Celia, elevating her excitement to floating-off-the-ground levels.

Again, my throat clogged up, tears burning somewhere behind my eyes. I'd prided myself on being independent, keeping my heart and my daughter safe. But in one week, Charlie had pulled the foundation from under me. I was falling. Slowly at first, but now I was gathering speed, hurling down faster and faster. How much would it hurt when I hit the ground?

CHAPTER 40

Charlie

Cozy Creek was dressed in its festival best, with cute little stalls lining Main Street, bunting hanging between trees and lamp-posts, pumpkins galore arranged on tables. Clearly, the mountain town knew I was trying to impress a girl, and needed all the help I could get. Like cheerful harmonica music and the smell of pumpkin spice.

We turned off Main Street before reaching the area that was cordoned off for foot traffic and parked on a side street. It looked familiar. As we got out, I recognized the thrift store. "Want to grab a pre-loved treasure while we're here?" I asked Bess, nodding at the sandwich board sign where someone had penned the phrase 'Come in and see our "pre-loved" treasures' in shaky old-school calligraphy.

"No, thank you." She smiled. "But it's good to know where you can get an asthma attack if you need one."

We returned to Main Street and approached the main hubbub of action, Celia running ahead of us. Bess's mom walked a few steps behind us. How she moved slower than Bess in her moon boot, I had no idea, but Kathy took her time, studying every detail of the decorative buildings around us.

Celia spotted the bunnies before I did, squealing and jumping by the cages, clearly frustrated with her mom's slow walking pace. The foot injury had dramatically decreased Bess's usual speed, and I could tell she was equally frustrated with the change.

The bunny cages were open from the top, but too high for Celia to reach in.

"Would you like to pet one?" The older man behind the stall asked. He was wearing overalls and a tattered baseball cap, an image of old-time farmer. The smell of hay permeated everything.

I made a donation in the jar, and he handed Celia a fluffy white one.

"Willy is very chilled out. He won't wriggle."

Celia held reverently still, stroking the bunny's pelt with trembling fingers.

"Is this your first time?" The farmer asked, and she nodded.

"I haven't been able to offer her that many experiences," Bess whispered, her cheeks red. "Not since…"

I squeezed her hand. "She's only five. She won't remember much from her earlier years, anyway."

She could end up remembering me, I thought with a pang. If

Bess let me in her life, I could be the only father this little girl remembered. Shit, that was terrifying. Yet, I couldn't stop myself from wanting it. Wanting Bess. I knew she had doubts, but I could also see her softening. It was in her eyes and the way she let me closer, no longer tensing when I touched her.

I'd confirmed the meeting with the client, first thing on Monday. I couldn't bring Bess there without telling her what was going on in the office. She'd find out. No doubt her mouthy friend Teresa was currently trying to reach her to spill the beans. According to Trevor, the whole agency was in shambles, the stress levels so high that someone was crying or throwing up in the bathroom every time he went to take a leak. This was what my father had achieved, casually dropping a bomb and walking away.

Not that I was there, either, as I should have been, I thought. Guilt reared its ugly head again, making it hard to breathe. I'd been busy wooing a woman I didn't deserve. A woman my family business had already discarded. My last name would be on her severance package. And it wouldn't even be a good package, I knew that now. After finding out about Bess's health insurance, or rather the lack of it, I'd contacted Gran to get her personnel files. When I'd seen her actual part-time salary, I'd felt like throwing up. She'd been busting her ass and saving mine for that?

No wonder she'd seemed so stressed out. She didn't seem that way anymore, though. Despite the moon boot, there was a lightness to her step and a smile on her face. Bess was more beautiful than ever before, and the thought of telling the truth and wiping that carefree smile off her face, made me sick.

Gran had warned me about meddling. "Talk to her. Be honest, Charlie. Lay it all down and swallow your own ego. Swallow it like melon."

Setting aside her belief that my ego was the size of a melon, I insisted, "I'm trying to help her. I'm trying to fix things."

She'd let out a mighty groan, mumbled something about the men in this family, and hung up. But Gran didn't understand. Time was running out. I had to give her the bad news, but I needed good news to balance it out. I had to offer her more than condolences or apologies. What the hell were those good for when your life crumbled before your eyes? She'd already experienced that once and was clawing her way back up.

Earlier, I'd excused myself and called my father again, trying to reason with him. It was no use. He'd agreed for Bess to join the client meeting—to represent the end user, mind you, not the creative team—but he didn't want to reconsider the restructure. The production team was as good as gone. Which left me with plan B.

I returned to the parallel world of pumpkins and bunnies, searching for the Killian women, trying to wipe the look of desperation off my face.

Bunnies sufficiently petted, we wandered along Main Street, perusing the stalls. With Bess's permission, I bought Celia her cotton candy, then collected bags of things Bess admired, sniffed or touched. I tried to be discreet, watching her and then making my purchase a moment later, as if due to an unrelated impulse.

"For Gran," I said, bagging the handmade soap bars and hand cream, then two stuffed bunnies.

"Rhonda likes stuffed toys?" She raised an eyebrow.

"Collects them." Gives them to employees' children, more accurately.

They'd find their way to Celia for sure. Thankfully, the little girl was too focused on overdosing on sugar to notice.

"I can take Celia to the merry-go-round," Kathy suggested, giving me a meaningful look. "You two can talk business... campaigns... if you'd like."

She nodded at the small amusement park that had been erected in the middle of the town square. Celia didn't need to be told twice. She sprinted across the road, forcing Kathy to run after her.

"Thank you!" I yelled, then turned to Bess. "I have some ideas I'd love to run past you."

"Sure. Of course."

I steered us to a van selling hot drinks. "Pumpkin spice latte? Before we talk business."

She tried to look nonchalant, but I caught the spark of desire in her eyes. Bess never went out for coffees with the crew at work. I'd always thought she didn't enjoy their company or didn't care for coffee. Now I knew better, and it broke my heart she'd lived on such a tight budget for so long. I desperately wanted to make it up to her. Right every wrong my father had caused, and even the ones my family had nothing to do with. I just wanted to see that smile. That spark.

She inhaled the aroma from the tall takeaway cup, and the look on her face evoked a flashback of us together on her sofa bed. I'd barely seen her face in the darkness, but I'd sensed the pure delight that melted away every worry and doubt, if only for a moment. Pumpkin spice obviously had magical qualities, ones I'd happily exploit in the future. She could sip one as I tasted her.

I had plans. So many plans and so little time.

"I mocked up some slides, based on your ideas," I said, pulling out my phone.

It had been a pain to work in the treehouse, crouched over my laptop in the tiny space. But I'd made a start, something good enough to hand over to Bess maybe. With her help, we could win this client and take them with us.

"We can go to the car to look at them on the bigger screen if you want?" I suggested.

I wanted us somewhere private. Maybe we could go for a drive.

"It's okay. I can zoom in," she said, handing me her drink to work the touch screen with two fingers. "These are great. They just need a little tidying up. Maybe spread these formats over two or three pages, so there's not too much there. One thing at a time."

"Yeah, you're right." I slid my hand around her waist, steering us towards the car anyway, hoping for the best. "I think they'll love it. It's so compelling. The tone of voice, everything. It's perfect. That's why I don't want to put in anything that distracts from it. Keep it simple."

"I agree," she said, limping along.

And that's when I saw Teresa. Tall and dark, her face like a storm warning, she'd already spotted us and was powering across the street, her handbag swinging on her shoulder.

Was there any way to avoid this? Bess could barely walk. We were sitting ducks, waiting for impact.

"You!" Teresa bee-lined to me, her finger held up high. "You bastard! This is where you're hiding when the whole agency is a fucking shitshow and people are losing their jobs!"

"Who's losing their jobs?" Bess looked up at me, eyes filled with liquid fear.

"You don't know?" Teresa cast her an alarmed look. "I keep texting you. Your phone's been off."

"I lost it in the mountains. What's happening?"

Teresa turned to me, lifting a perfectly shaped, angry eyebrow. "Why don't you fill her in?"

CHAPTER 41

Bess

I could barely stand, my head spinning like I was the one on the merry-go-round. But I couldn't lean on Charlie for support. I couldn't lean on anyone.

"What's going on, Charlie?" I asked him again, my voice cracking.

He glanced at his car. "I... I was going to tell you, I swear. They're doing some restructuring at the agency. Some layoffs. I've tried to talk my dad out of it but he won't budge." He cast a dark look at Teresa. "Trust me, it's not my idea."

"But you knew about it, Charlie," my friend shot back. "Why doesn't she know she's losing her job?"

"I'm losing my job?" I couldn't breathe. "When?"

"In two weeks." Teresa stared at Charlie like she was challenging him to a duel. "I bought a condo, Charlie. I signed on the dotted line a week ago. No one warned me about this. No one."

"Wait." Charlie frowned. "*You've* been fired? Dad said it was just the production team."

"Then I must be special," Teresa bit out. "I'm not stupid, though. Everyone kept asking where you were, and nobody seemed to know. Except me.... And it turns out, Trevor. And when I couldn't get hold of Bess....Fuck, I thought you'd made a pelt out of her." She glanced at my leg. "What happened to you? Did he hurt you?"

"No! I tripped and fell. That's probably when I lost my phone." I looked pleadingly into my friend's eyes. "I appreciate you coming all the way here. I hate that you had to worry about me."

She looked a little ashamed. "Well, I was worried about you, but I also wanted to find this guy and hear it from him." She turned to Charlie, her gaze fire and ice. "Your dad's a sociopath, so I expect this from him. But how do you sleep at night?"

Charlie swallowed. "Poorly. I hate this. You must believe me."

"Come on, girl, I'll drive you home." Teresa offered me her arm, along with a compassionate look.

I glanced over my shoulder. "My daughter is here with my mom. They're on the carousel."

"Well, let's go find them," Teresa looked at the town square where colorful lights blinked, and carnival music played. It had sounded so cheerful earlier but now made me think of a horror film soundtrack.

"Please, Bess." Charlie's voice cracked. "Let's go for a drive. I have a plan. I'll tell you everything—"

"It's been a week, Charlie. You've had plenty of time to tell her everything." Teresa stared at him blankly, and Charlie visibly squirmed.

She was right. He could have told me at any point. Before we slept together. Before I fell for him. That hurt. It hurt so much that my insides ached, sending signals of pain all the way to my fingertips. "I can't, Charlie."

"But, I'm trying to fix this. I was going to—"

Just like Jack. Desperately fixing things behind my back, never letting me know how deep a hole he'd dug for himself. I couldn't live like this. Not anymore. My vision blurred, and I stumbled off the sidewalk, along the cobblestones. As one aimless group, we moved towards the town square until Teresa spotted my mother and Celia emerging from behind a hotdog stand.

Charlie ran ahead of us and reached my mom. I couldn't hear what he said, but I saw Mom's posture straighten. What was Charlie saying to her and why couldn't I walk any faster? I'd left the crutches in the car, happy to lean on Charlie. Teresa offered me her arm again and this time I accepted, taking the weight off my aching foot, waiting for Mom to reach me.

She touched my arm, her eyes glossy with tears. "I'm so sorry, Bessie. You don't deserve this. But we'll figure it out. You'll find another job."

Teresa huffed. "There'll be a lot of people looking for that other job now."

"But you have great references. Right, Charlie?" Mom eyeballed him.

"The best! But she won't need them. I'll—"

"I promised Celia a hotdog and an ice cream and there's supposed to be a hayride. Why don't you take Bess for a little drive?"

"She doesn't want to drive anywhere with him," Teresa announced.

"Why don't we let Bess decide," Mom countered softly.

I stared at them, my heart in tatters. My only work friend who'd always had my back, and the man who'd lied to me all week. The man I loved, against my better judgement, just like I'd loved Jack. I'd survived one blow. Would I survive another? Mom seemed to think so, taking Celia's hand, pointing at the hotdog stand.

"I don't know," I said, fighting tears. "I can't make this choice."

"I can," Charlie said, scooping me up and throwing me over his shoulder. "We'll be back in an hour."

"That's kidnapping, you fucking ogre!" Teresa screeched as I wriggled in Charlie's firm grip. "I'm recording you on my phone. She'll sue you! We have evidence."

"She can clean me up any time," Charlie muttered, too quietly for Teresa to hear.

From the clicking of heels, I knew she was right behind us. Charlie didn't care, marching across the square and down the road. I directed my anger at his backside, hammering it with my fists. He didn't react or even slow down, but clutched me so tightly I couldn't have escaped. Not that I wanted to. There was no strength or conviction behind my thrashing arms, only despair. I didn't want to get away from him. I wanted him to hold me tightly to his chest until I woke up from this nightmare. I wanted him to tell me none of it was true.

We'd had something good. So good. And he'd taken it away. Destroyed it. How was it possible to love and hate someone at the same time?

When we reached the side street and his car, Charlie shoved me into the passenger seat, slid behind the wheel and locked the doors before Teresa caught up with us, leaving her standing in the middle of the street, her phone held high.

"You're kidnapping me?" I asked Charlie, my heart pounding in my chest.

He sped down the street, not looking at me. "I only need to imprison you for forty-eight hours for the Stockholm syndrome to kick in."

"What?"

"Just kidding."

Was he kidding? I fastened my seatbelt, scanning the road ahead. Could I throw myself out of the car next time he had to stop? I couldn't run. He'd catch me in seconds.

"Don't even think about it, Bess. I know this isn't right, but I have no choice. I need you to hear me out."

"Is it not true? Have I not lost my job? Did you not know about it and choose not to tell me?"

"No, that's all true. But it's not the whole truth."

"You seduced me. You made sure that when I found out, it would hurt so much more." I fought for a breath, tears gushing out.

"No! I never meant to sedu... I never planned for anything to happen between us. I mean, I liked you. I admired you. I thought you were hot. But I just wanted to help. I wanted to find a way to save your job. Get you to help me with the campaign and get you a new job in the creative team."

"So, that was your grand plan? For me to jump teams to save my skin when everyone else gets fired?"

"Well, yeah."

Everyone I worked with, gone. And me, hooking up with the Creative Director, securely employed by his side. I shuddered at the image.

"That's not who I am, Charlie. I know I'm screwed financially, but I wouldn't do that. I don't want to win like that."

"Well, it was the best I could think of, at the time. I can't save everyone."

"So, you decided to just save me?" A terrifying thought bubbled up. "Is that why I'm here? The retreat at Rubie Ridge... it was you, wasn't it?"

"Yeah, it was me. But I think you deserved it. I think your work is outstanding. And you have so much more to offer. You're smart and strategic... you have great ideas. I wanted you to see that. I wanted everyone to see that."

I sighed, thoroughly exasperated. "You can't fix me or my life, Charlie. I'm not your project! If you want to be with me, you have to be honest with me. I want a partnership. I want open communication. Not this." I shook my head, tears streaming down.

"I know I messed up. Trust me. But by then it was too late. I couldn't go back in time. I couldn't change anything. And I was going to tell you."

"When? You had all week."

"I know! I was going to tell you now. That's why I asked you to go for a drive."

I took a deep breath, adjusting to the new reality. I had to face it. "Well, we're driving now. What else is there? What else have you kept from me?"

He slowed down, turning onto a gravel road until we came to a mailbox. Charlie parked in the driveway, helping me out of the car. "Let's start with this."

He led me around an old wooden villa, on to an overgrown backyard. He gestured at a shoddy-looking treehouse with a hanging ladder. "This is my motel room. I couldn't find anything else."

"Seriously?" I limped closer, examining the worn-out rope ladder moving in the breeze.

"You might have trouble getting up there with your leg, but I wanted to show you, anyway. So that I don't leave anything out."

Feeling more than a little stubborn, I positioned my healthy leg on the first rung, using every ounce of my strength to pull myself up. Charlie didn't try to stop me, but stood underneath, spotting me as I slowly climbed up—foot, knee, foot, knee—until I reached the small doorway. As I crawled in, I felt him behind me, trapping me inside.

Maybe it wasn't the best idea to come up here. I couldn't storm out. I had no exit strategy. But Charlie had been good to me. I'd had the best and worst week of my life, and he was inseparably wrapped up in all of it. There was still a chance I was carrying Charlie's baby. I had to hear him out.

I perched myself on the edge of the mattress and I waited for him to look at me. "What did you say to my mom? Why was she pushing me to go for a drive with you?"

He sat back, looking away. "I talked to her a bit earlier. I told her I'm in love with you and…"

"And what?"

He drew a sharp breath and met my gaze. The afternoon light pouring through the window reflected off his eyes, turning them into liquid pools. "I told her about your job, and how I was trying to fix it. What I was going to do."

I blinked twice, as if to dispel the image. "What? You told her before you told me?"

"I needed her help."

A flash of fury rose to my chest. "So this is all some elaborate kidnapping plan you cooked up with my mother? That's why I'm here?" I sat up on the bed, hitting my head on the low ceiling. "Ouch!"

How had Charlie spent a night in this tiny space?

His voice brimmed with desperation. "I'm not trying to manipulate you or make you feel anything. If you want to go, go. I won't stop you. I'll drive you back. I only brought you here because I needed you to hear the whole story. I couldn't let you walk away thinking the worst."

"Thinking what? That you brought me here on false pretenses, that you've been playing with my feelings all week, trying to win me over, get me to help you with a campaign that you're failing at by appealing to my sense of duty over a job I've already lost. Then sleeping with me and asking me not to worry about a broken condom because you might want a baby... I still haven't taken that pill, by the way." I filled my lungs, my whole body shaking. "Is that the worst, or am I leaving something out?"

He reached for his pocket and pulled out my phone, handing it over with hands that shook as much as mine. "I also took this so you wouldn't hear about the job stuff before I could tell you."

"Seriously? You stole my phone?" I stared at it, still as dead as it had been in the forest.

"I don't have a charger for it, sorry."

"What else, Charlie? Did you drug me and harvest my kidney? Is that why my back hurts?"

He winced. "That'd be the hammock. Mine's killing me." He leaned against the wall, grimacing from the pain. "Gran warned me about this, and she doesn't know the half of it. But she knows me, I guess. She told me to come clean and beg for mercy. My plan was terrible. It was so stupid. But it got us closer. I got to know you. And that's the part I don't regret. That's the best part. I always liked you. I had a crush on you... but I didn't plan to fall in love."

My chest squeezed, and I spent a moment fighting tears. I stared at the dust particles that floated in the air between us, illuminated by the light streaming from the small window. "Why are we here, Charlie? Why Rubie Ridge? You could have asked me to help you with that campaign anywhere."

Charlie chewed on his bottom lip. "My dad sent me to Rubie Ridge, to think about the campaign. But I knew I needed help. I needed someone who understood the target audience."

"And that's where I came in?"

"Sort of." His voice sounded a little choked up, eyes searching around the room like he couldn't bear to look at me. "You have to understand... I've had this crush on you for a long time. There's something about you. This strength and determination. Purpose. This passion you try to hide... You're one in a billion, Bess. And I'm the luckiest guy to spend any time in your presence."

His voice cracked, and he looked out the window, clearing his throat. "I know it looks like I have it all, but I don't. I'm quite lost. I feel useless. Undeserving. I get reminded about that daily. But with you, I feel grounded. Like I have a purpose and a... home. Like I don't have to look for something else or order something. I've always wanted to make a difference, not just sell shit. With you, I feel like maybe I could."

He was quiet for a while. I could barely breathe. I just watched him, my heart aching.

When he spoke again, he was finally looking at me, eyes burning with conviction. "I want to break free, Bess. I've been planning... I want to start my own business and run it differently. Pick meaningful jobs. I don't have that much capital. It's all tied up with my family. In trusts. And once I tell Dad, those taps will close. But I can sell my stuff. I've already got Trevor sorting it out. He's joining me. Him and Lee."

"You don't want Teresa?"

He glanced up, surprised. "I didn't think she'd be interested. And frankly, I'm scared of her."

"Me too," I admitted. "But she has a good heart."

"Yeah, sure. And she's a great designer. But I don't think she'd ever want to work with me."

"Don't assume. Ask her." I owed my friend that much.

"If you want her, I'll take you both. But I need you, Bess. Will you join me?"

My heart was in danger of hammering right out of my chest. "You want to start a new company and want me to work for you?"

"Not as an employee. As a shareholder."

My breath hitched. "But I have nothing. Nothing but debt."

"Your debt is my debt, Bess. We'll handle it together. I spoke to your mom. You're paying crazy high interest. I want to pay off your loan. You can pay it back to me instead, whatever you want. I don't care. But we shouldn't put any more money into the loan sharks' pockets."

"We? It's my loan. Jack's loan."

"Whatever it is, it stands in the way of you living life. So, it needs to go."

"But how can you afford that? Even if you sold everything—"

"Gran is investing in the business. She'll do the accounts."

I took a deep breath, my head still spinning. "You've been busy, Charlie."

He nodded. "I'm sorry I kept things from you. You're allowed to hate me for that, but please don't run away. Please don't leave me. I'm terrified of all this. I can't do this without you."

I'd never seen a grown man cry. Jack must have, in the end, but he hid it from us. He hid everything, whereas Charlie sat there in the dim little doll's house, weeping his guts out.

"Charlie," I said, my heart pulling me to him, fueled by some unstoppable force. "I'm not running away. I've only got one leg." I edged closer until he was sobbing against my shoulder. "Also, I think Stockholm syndrome is kicking in."

"Is it?" He lifted his chin, blue eyes red rimmed, yet filled with hope.

"Yeah, it must be. Because I think I'm in love with you, Charlie."

His tear-stained face broke into a huge grin, and he wrapped his arms around me, squeezing me so tightly I had to fight to fill my lungs. "Finally."

He hugged me for a long time until his breathing settled, and tears dried. "I love you, Bess. Am I allowed to say it now? I love you so much. I love Celia. I didn't even want to think about losing you. It hurts too much."

"So, you kidnapped me?"

"It felt like the sensible thing to do." He laughed, wiping his eyes on his sleeve.

Then he kissed me with such purpose, I would have fallen had I not been sitting. Charlie half-dragged, half-carried me onto the mattress, trapping me under his weight. I was truly kidnapped now, with no hope of escape. Did I want to run?

"Is there anything else, Charlie?" I asked breathlessly.

"Nothing else, I swear. You already know my spending is out of control and my family is… complicated. But—"

"I'm not looking for perfection. I'm not perfect. We'll both make mistakes."

"I've made quite a few this week." He placed a kiss on my collarbone. Warmth spread through my body. This wasn't fair. He'd made mistakes, but it wasn't the whole truth now that we were laying it all on the table.

"Charlie," I said, wiping a wayward tear off his cheek. "You've been so good to me. You've reminded me of what I've been missing, and that's been amazing… and painful. Because I can't go back to my life like it once was. I can't. If it weren't for you, my life would be shattered. What if you hadn't done all this… what if you didn't love me? What if you weren't here to catch me? I'd lose my job and fall off a cliff." The thought of it made my insides clench. "I'd have to move in with Mom. I'd fall behind on my payments and—"

"But I am here. And I will catch you."

"I'm supposed to look after myself and Celia."

"Why? Why can't anyone help?"

I buried my face in my hands, turning away. "Because then I'm relying on them. On you. And it means I've failed."

He lowered himself onto the mattress next to me, leaning his head on his arm so he faced me. "But… what if it was meant to be? What if this whole week and everything we went through was part of some divine plan? People need different things, Bess. It's not all about money. I need you in ways I can't even explain. I don't want to imagine my life without you. If you go, you'll rip my heart out."

My heart squeezed in my chest, echoing his words, and my mind shifted, the light of understanding flooding the darker corners. Charlie needed me. Could I accept that and give myself up to this thing that vibrated in the air between us, this scary force that would once again inseparably tie me to another being, risking all the pain down the road? I searched for courage, letting that feeling travel like warm liquid spilled from my heart into every part of me.

"I have to take my chances with you," I swallowed against the stickiness in my throat. "I have to take the risk."

He held my face between his hands and kissed my cheekbones, then my nose, finally my mouth. "Yes. It's the only way. Take the leap, Bess."

I released a deep sigh. "Okay. But I don't want you for your money, Charlie. I want you for you."

It was true; I realized. Even if I had a million dollars, I didn't want to be without Charlie.

"I know." He squeezed my hand, smiled, and rolled onto his back.

We lay in bed for a long time, staring at the ceiling, breathing the same air. Getting used to the new reality. Or maybe he was giving me the time to do that, since he was already there.

"Do we still have time?" I finally asked, turning to face him. "Because I've never had sex in a treehouse before."

"Me neither." His gaze ignited with hunger, infused with joy, and he kissed me, long and slow.

As my body woke up to his touch, nerves waking with need, a nagging thought emerged.

"Do you have another condom? There's only so much risk I can handle all at once."

He emptied his pockets. A stick of gum, a five-dollar bill and two condoms. "This one's a different brand."

"Great."

He helped my jeans off and pulled up my shirt. The cool air caressed my skin, making it pebble. His warm hand landed on my stomach, sliding down. "It's a bit cold in here. Should we risk the heater?"

I nodded, and Charlie flicked it on. It felt like a hairdryer on my bare skin, relaxing me into the mattress.

For a moment, he teased me through my underwear, building anticipation, making my breath seize. I felt myself getting wet; the liquid seeping through the thin fabric, meeting his gentle tongue. "Just rip them off," I grumbled.

He took his time, making me writhe under his light touch. How could he make me burn like this?

Finally, he pushed my legs against the mattress and slid the underwear all the way down. The warm breeze caught my lady parts, making me shiver. In an instant, Charlie's mouth was on me, hot, slow and teasing. Feather-light. With his tongue, he drove every other thought out of my mind. I could only feel the fire, my breath coming in erratic bursts.

"Good girl," he whispered. "Stay there. Don't come yet."

"Why... not?" I panted as the sheer, condensed pleasure built to a sensation I'd never felt before—like something I'd only ever experience as a whiff, airborne, had suddenly become condensed. Liquid. I wanted to give myself over to it. Over to him. I bucked my hips.

"Wait. Don't rush it," he whispered again. "I want this moment to last."

But I couldn't last. Not with the way he kept teasing me. My hips moved on their own, meeting with his tongue, until that liquid pleasure spilled over. My spine arched against the bed and my fingers grasped at the air. For a moment, nothing else existed. Only pleasure.

I lay still for a moment, waiting to return to Earth.

"I want you inside me, Charlie," I finally rasped.

I reached for him, and he climbed on top of me, pulling on the condom and filling me in seconds. I watched his lips part and eyes glaze over. Charlie, rendered speechless as he drove into me, again and again, pushing me over the edge I was still hovering on.

I loved him. I loved him so much. All that he was and wasn't. All his faults and mistakes and his good heart.

Afterwards, we held still, both catching our breaths, staring into each other's eyes with a sense of wonder.

"From now on, I'll tell you everything," he said. "Good and bad. We're in this together."

I breathed in so deeply I must have exceeded my lung capacity. As I let the air out, words followed. "Oh, Charlie."

And this time, I said it with love.

Bess

"Two minutes, ladies," Charlie announced, glancing at the map on the car screen as he took another tight turn on the narrow mountain road.

We were almost there. Back in Cozy Creek. It had been two long months. Two months of business planning, viewing office spaces and dreaming more than I'd dared to dream in years. Everything was still in progress, with many things undecided, but Charlie had been resolute that we take a break over Christmas and escape the city. Cozy Creek felt like the obvious choice since we still had the voucher for a week's free lodging at Rubie Ridge.

Celia was beside herself with excitement, bouncing against the backseat, spilling her juice box down the front of her thermal jacket as she tried to see through the windshield. The fresh snow made driving a challenge, but the scenery was worth all the trouble.

"It's Christmas!" Celia yelled as the view of the opulently decorated Main Street opened in front of us.

The fall festival bunting and pumpkins had been replaced by Christmas garlands and fairy lights, which were already burning bright against the darkening evening sky, along with the streetlamps. Big, fat snowflakes floated down, smacking wet kisses on the windscreen. The faint glow of the day hung behind the dark silhouette of the mountains, the sky a gradient of blues.

"Why don't we live somewhere like this?" I sighed, thinking of the grim scene I'd witnessed in my old street: A broken shop window, police tape flapping in the cold wind. Charlie's street was tidier, but nothing like Cozy Creek.

"Probably because we can't run a business here," Charlie mused.

"Not a big business," I agreed. "But what if it was small?"

"How small? Small like you designing a logo on your laptop, sitting on the floor?" He grinned.

Charlie had visited our tiny apartment once and had witnessed my freelancing setup, among other depressing things. He'd immediately marched home to rearrange his top-floor apartment (which was three times the size) so that we could move in. I kept saying it was too soon, but in the end, not paying rent allowed me to take a pay cut until the business was up and running, which was vital. And I had to admit it was nice to work at a dedicated desk, not right next to my child eating cereal. Or cross-legged on the floor.

Before the move, he'd taken me out on a date, wearing his flannel and baseball cap. I'd ordered the least expensive item on the ridiculously expensive menu, and he'd ordered more behind my back, making sure we had one very fancy, very delicious meal, before I left my old life behind.

Charlie's apartment was owned by his family trust. It was a bachelor pad of sorts, in a fully serviced apartment building featuring a swimming pool and a games room. Celia was fascinated by all of it, including Yuki the robot she'd adopted as her sister.

She would have to settle for Japanese technology for now. I wasn't pregnant. It had been a huge relief, even if I was happy I'd allowed for that risk with Charlie. Starting a new business was more than enough to keep us busy—and max out my tolerance for risk.

Charlie still wanted a baby, but agreed to wait until we had some steady income. He'd make an amazing father one day. I knew that because he was already that to Celia, giving my girl the attention, stability and hope she needed. Living under the same roof was an adjustment. We were learning new things about each other every day, but they were mostly good surprises—like discovering Charlie could make delicious lasagne and had a collection of poetry books. Sure, he also sucked at recycling and paid someone to do his laundry, but he was open to changing and learning. I'd been worried about disrupting his perfectly comfortable routine, but Charlie didn't want his life to stay the same. He wanted to build something new, and that willingness made all the difference. I didn't want my old life, either. I didn't miss the loneliness or the struggle.

So far, Charlie had kept his departure from the family business on the down low, with a few private arguments with George and an agreement to not go after their clients. If they followed him of their own accord, we wouldn't turn them away. And that's where conflict awaited. Although I had a feeling George was waiting for our 'little side hustle' to die an ugly death, like he'd predicted. But if we succeeded, he'd most likely retaliate and kick Charlie out of the apartment. Knowing this, we'd agreed to find something more family friendly, with fewer rooftop parties and maybe a park nearby.

One day.

But the business planning had quickly overtaken other plans, such as our living arrangements. I had to trust it would work out. If nothing else, I was now an official shareholder in a brand-new company and I'd already received a hefty end-of-year bonus that covered my debts. I was free. Whatever happened, Charlie had changed the course of mine and Celia's life. We had options now, and it felt like such a luxury.

Charlie parked on the side of the road, right under a streetlamp. It painted his face in its yellow glow, picking up the sparkle in his eyes. "I bet we could find a small and reasonably priced office right up there." He pointed at the Victorian building with an ice cream parlor. The light was still on inside and I saw someone cleaning the tables. The second-story windows above looked dark, with a faded 'FOR LEASE' sign on one of them.

"You think it's an office?"

"Whatever it is, I think it's small and cozy. We can put Trevor in the closet. Teresa in the bathroom."

I had to laugh at that idea. I was pretty sure those two had hooked up at an office party before. My first thought had been to place them as far away from each other as possible. It didn't matter, since neither of them would ever move to Cozy Creek. But every office space we'd checked out in downtown Denver so far had been scary expensive. Charlie had shortlisted three, but my risk meter was in the red, screaming. We'd need to grow our turnover so fast I'd have to grow two more arms to do everything.

"We decided we won't compete with your dad on the AI services, right?"

"Right." Charlie was still looking up at the window. "I'm glad he's doing it, though. If he only works with AI, he's far less likely to cause human suffering."

I stifled a wayward laugh. I still found it hard to laugh about George. The big boss. He was to be feared, not laughed at. Except he wasn't my boss anymore.

"If we rent an office in the city and try to grow that fast, we'll have to use AI. Maybe more than we planned. But if we keep it small and specialized with low running costs, we could do the human thing. Human services—"

"Human to human." Charlie's eyes flashed. I'd began to recognize the lightbulb moment. An idea was loading behind his eyes. "That's brilliant. Human to human is the new business to business. AI is fine, but we'll always need H2H on the side. We can offer that."

"It might fail."

He caught my gaze and held it. "Totally."

I took a deep breath, waiting for that ill feeling to lessen. I was getting used to it. "Then we'll have to risk it."

"But we're in this together. I'm not keeping anything from you."

It was true. He'd showed me his investment portfolio. Everything he had, everything we could use as collateral. I knew what he was doing—showing me that he wasn't too proud. That he wasn't Jack. The far more painful part had been matching that openness and sharing my own dreadful finances. But we'd made it through, laying everything on the table. We needed every resource to succeed. Me with nothing but debt and him without his family's backing. Well, other than Rhonda. She'd walked out on George, telling him off for the dreadful restructure she called a 'heartless firing spree'. Rhonda was ready to invest, but I didn't feel comfortable with that. Charlie teased me about my 'fierce independence', which he thought was more of a hindrance than help with getting a new business off the ground.

"Can I get cotton candy?" Celia called from the backseat.

"There's no Fall Festival. Nobody is selling cotton candy here, sweetie."

"But is there a Christmas festival?"

In her mind, Cozy Creek was all festivals, nothing else. I had to admit, I felt the same, even if it made no sense.

"Maybe there's something going on tomorrow," Charlie suggested. "It's only a week until Christmas. But we'll drive up to Rubie Ridge first and stay the night, okay?"

"Can I sleep upstairs?"

"In the loft?" I shook my head at Charlie, hoping he wouldn't promise something I'd later have to retract. It had been hard enough to keep my child off those floating stairs last time.

"Don't worry. I booked a cabin with two rooms. No loft. I thought it'd be the safest."

I released a sigh, regarding him with a mix of gratitude and surprise. Charlie had gradually advanced from being the fun uncle to being a real parent.

Last week, we'd collected the rest of Charlie's gadgets and other impulse buys and listed them on eBay. Trevor had already helped him sell the big-ticket items. Charlie had seemed oddly okay with it, to the point of disinterest. It must have been the act of supporting those Kickstarter campaigns that had excited him. The actual owning of things didn't matter to Charlie. He was all about making people happy.

He'd made me happy. It was a risk to let someone else make you happy. To become reliant on them. But how could I not? My desperate quest for independence had been just that. Desperate.

We drove down Main Street and turned onto the road leading up to the mountain. With snow on the ground, everything looked different. Fresh and untouched, like a blank canvas. Something I was getting ready to face at the retreat.

"Is there a program like last time?" I asked.

Charlie hadn't given me much information beyond the dates.

"No. Apparently, this is one of the chill weeks. Christmas catering, hot tub, massages… and the studio is open for everyone to work on whatever they want, but no art teachers. I don't think they've hired anyone since Ilme."

We'd received a Facebook message from the Estonian artist inviting us to her gallery opening in Tallinn. Considering the event was on another continent, the invitation was probably more of a life update. But I was happy for her. She'd returned to her home country but was showing her work.

Rubie Ridge hadn't changed, but I had. The polished luxury of the castle-like building no longer intimidated me. It filled my soul. The place had been built for the utmost beauty and enjoyment. Why not enjoy it?

Celia ran ahead of us, charging down the path toward the Cerulean cabin she remembered, until we called her back and dragged her to the main building to visit the reception.

"It's the Wilde family!" Leonie called from behind the reception desk and insisted on meeting us on the other side for hugs. "Welcome! I hope you have an amazing week. We've been planning some holiday activities and there's a Christmas market in town. The tree will be officially lit in our yard tonight." The fairy lights hanging from the ceiling reflected off her eyes, adding extra sparkle.

We got our keys and found our cabin. A huge evergreen wreath hung on the door. The interior was decorated with deep red and brass accents and felt warm and cozy. Celia ran ahead to examine her room.

"Hot tub?" Charlie winked at me.

"You can go if you want. I'll have to stay with her," I nodded toward Celia's excited squeal. "That tub won't be relaxing with her in it."

"It doesn't matter," he insisted. "But I organized babysitting. That girl Harley."

"The rainbow haired one?"

"Yeah. Leonie said she babysits for locals in Cozy Creek."

"Okay. But you don't have to—"

"No." Charlie stopped me in the middle of the room and lifted my chin, ensuring eye contact. "I see what you're doing, but she's not just your problem, you know."

"She's my child. It's only fair."

"Maybe it's fair, but it's not what I want."

"What do you want?"

He caught his bottom lip between his teeth and paused. The intensity in his eyes made me pause, too. "I want everything to be *our* problem."

A bit back my laughter. "Why does everything have to be a problem?"

"No, I mean..."

"I'm just messing with you, Charlie." I smiled to soften my words, which were pouring out from my core. "When you're a parent, everything is *your* problem. It's exhausting. There's no break, ever. Why would you choose that? Why would you give up your freedom?"

I couldn't imagine it.

Charlie picked up my hands and interlaced his fingers with my own. "Because I want a real partnership and that's the price."

I stared at those fingers, tightly wound, blending into a pattern.

"I don't want to enjoy my freedom when you don't have any. I don't want to be that guy. I don't want to choose convenience over love. And I love you. Both of you. I know you said we don't need to hurry... But I've been thinking..."

My stomach turned into a bag of potatoes, rolling down the stairs. I knew that look. The way he'd looked at me in the treehouse.

The nervous part of me wanted to fill the silence, but I held my breath. I waited.

"Would you—"

"Charlie! I love this house!" Celia crashed into his legs like a hurricane of purple pom-poms. "Thank you, thank you, thank you!"

Charlie erupted in nervous laughter, lifting the girl in his arms. "You're very welcome. In fact... I better include both of you because I have a feeling we will be interrupted."

I gave him a slight nod, emitting a silent apology.

He cast Celia a serious look, and she stilled for a moment. "Would you like to be a flower girl at a wedding?"

The girl nodded wildly, her eyes enormous. "What's a flower girl?"

"She walks ahead of the bride and groom and throws flowers."

"On the floor?"

Charlie lifted a shoulder. "Yeah."

"Then who picks them up?"

Charlie and I exchanged a look, both of us holding back laughter, although my amusement was mixed with nerves. Was he proposing? What was I going to say? I couldn't imagine myself throwing another wedding. It felt wrong somehow. Wasteful and self-indulgent. There were a lot of things I wanted to do and achieve in life, but organizing a huge, expensive party wasn't one of them.

"Charlie," I said. "Please, I—"

"Don't reject me before I ask the question, Bess." His eyes went dark as thunder as he turned back to me. "If you think you're saving me the embarrassment, I don't care. I'm going to take it on the chin. In front of a witness." He glanced at Celia, then jutted out his chin like he was expecting a punch. "Bess, will you marry me?"

I could see him steeling himself, every muscle activated. My sweet Charlie.

"If you agree to do it on a budget," I said, my mouth twitching.

Tension melted from his body so completely he nearly dropped my child, catching himself last minute. "Phew. Sorry, CeCe. Your mom drives a hard bargain." A smile split his face, radiating relief as he continued in a mock-offended tone. "What the hell kind of answer is that to a proposal? You can't stop me from spending money on you. On us." He huffed. "Maybe Celia wants to be a flower girl?"

"I won't stop you from spending money on us. But I don't want to spend on a wedding, okay?"

"Can we spend on the honeymoon? I've always wanted to go to Estonia."

"You want to see Ilme's exhibition?"

"That'd be a bonus. But also, Tallinn has this medieval old town and some exciting start-ups and innovation. Including this incredible new compostable bubble wrap alternative—"

"You've already pledged some money, haven't you?"

"A tiny bit. And I'd love to meet with the team before I invest more."

"You're investing in eco-friendly packaging?" Old pain squeezed my chest, like an echo from the past. "Why?"

"Because... I investigated Jack's case, and I hate that there's no legal action that makes sense. They wormed their way in. He shared everything, hoping to get an investor and they wiped their asses with his NDA. Right?"

I winced, but nodded. "They never actually signed the NDA. They said they would, and Jack was too trusting. He kept kicking himself about it."

"And while we can't fight them in court, we can invest in a better innovation and take over the market. Jack's idea was good, but it's not the best. This Estonian stuff is easier and cheaper to produce, weighs less and composts faster."

"Wow. Okay. And you want to invest?"

"Not money, necessarily. But we could do some pro bono work. We could help them enter the US market."

That was Charlie to a T. Thinking big. Betting on the underdog. Believing in the impossible.

"I love that! Maybe we can elope to Estonia?"

"Let's!"

"What's Estonia?" Celia asked.

"A magical place, far, far away," I told her.

"Does that mean 'yes'? You haven't said yes." Charlie regarded me with an unsure smile.

I took a breath. "Yes, Charlie. I will marry you."

What else could I say?

He pulled me into his arms and held me so tight my feet lifted off the floor. I felt like I was falling, falling slowly through vast galaxies. But I was with him, and I was safe. I was ready for the next adventure.

Want more Bess and Charlie? Check out a bonus scene for Falling Slowly *when you sign up for Enni's newsletter!*

Scan the QR code to get your bonus scene:

BookHip.com/MJKZDJX

THE COZY CREEK COLLECTION

Fall I Want by Lyra Parish
Fall at Once by Nora Everly
Falling Slowly by Enni Amanda
Fall Too Well by Erin Branscom
Fall Shook Up by Piper Sheldon
Fall Me Maybe by Laney Hatcher

www.cozycreekbooks.com

REFERENCES

Poverty isn't a lack of character; it's a lack of cash
(TED Talk by Rutger Bregman, 2017)

Watch the video:

ACKNOWLEDGMENTS

I want to thank the wonderful Erin Branscom for inviting me to write for the Cozy Creek Collection. I grew up in Finland and live in New Zealand, so I had my doubts about writing a US-based story. But it turned out to be so much fun! I'm grateful to all the ladies in this collaboration, including Lyra, Nora, Piper and Laney. You've all been lovely to work with. I've learned so much for each of you and I'm incredibly proud of what we've achieved.

Before this, I'd only ever written books based in existing locations, mostly in New Zealand. But now, Cozy Creek feels real to me. In my mind, I can walk down Main Street and see it as clearly as any town I've ever visited for 'book research'.

A special thanks to my beta readers Tammy, Linda, Charlotte, and Jenny. Your comments were invaluable! And a very special thanks to the brilliant author Evie Alexander, who hugely encouraged me and picked up mistakes others had missed. Love you to bits!

I'm also grateful to my husband Sami and my sons, who continue to tolerate my writing obsession.

ABOUT THE AUTHOR

Enni Amanda is a graphic designer moonlighting as a rom-com author, or maybe it's the other way around. In 2006, she and her husband moved from Finland to New Zealand and fell in love with the gorgeous islands and their laid-back people. They spent eight years traveling between the two rather inconveniently located countries, studying filmmaking and running a film festival.

Through all the filmmaking, Enni discovered a passion for screenwriting, which eventually led to writing books (a slippery slope). Her heart-warming, funny stories explore real-life issues like identity, found family, and the housing crisis. These days, she lives in the Waikato, close to the rolling hills of the Shire, raising two cute, rambunctious boys while writing away and ignoring housework.

Sign up for her newsletter here:

sendfox.com/enni.author

ALSO BY ENNI AMANDA

A Tiny House on Wheels
Coffee on Waihi Beach
Christmas in July (novella)

LOVE NEW ZEALAND SERIES

Nest or Invest
Hidden Gem
Night and Day

LOVE ISTANBUL SERIES

My Lucky Star
My Turkish Fling

You can find all of Enni's books and more information on her website: **enniamanda.com**

Printed in Great Britain
by Amazon